Praise for

The Central Park Five

A Film by Ken Burns & David McMahon & Sarah Burns

"*Central Park* is at first discomforting, then enraging, then illuminating."
                                                    —*The New Yorker*

"As grim a portrait of the criminal justice system as can be imagined."
                                                    —*Detroit News*

"Timeless. . . . It encapsulates an era."
                                                    —*San Francisco Chronicle*

"Watching *The Central Park Five* is a deeply affecting experience."
                                                    —*The Wall Street Journal*

"Measured in tone and outraged in its argument, it is an emotionally stirring, at times crushingly depressing cinematic call to witness."
                                                    —*The New York Times*

"A patient, righteous documentary."
                                                    —*Entertainment Weekly*

SARAH BURNS

The Central Park Five

Sarah Burns graduated from Yale University in 2004 with a degree in American studies and went on to work for Moore & Goodman, a small civil rights law firm based in New York. She has produced a documentary film with Ken Burns based on this book. She lives in Brooklyn, New York.

The
Central Park
Five

The Untold Story Behind One of
New York City's Most Infamous Crimes

Sarah Burns

VINTAGE BOOKS

A DIVISION OF RANDOM HOUSE, INC.

NEW YORK

FIRST VINTAGE BOOKS EDITION, APRIL 2012

Copyright © 2011 by Sarah Burns

All rights reserved. Published in the United Stated by Vintage Books, a division of Random House, Inc., New York, and in Canada by Random House of Canada Limited, Toronto. Originally published in hardcover as *The Central Park Five: The Chronicle of a City Wilding* in the United States by Alfred A. Knopf, a division of Random House, Inc., New York, in 2011.

Vintage and colophon are registered trademarks of Random House, Inc.

Due to limitations of space, permission acknowledgments appear on page 243.

The Library of Congress has cataloged the Knopf edition as follows:
Burns, Sarah.
The Central Park Five / Sarah Burns. —1st ed.
p. cm.
Includes bibliographical references and index.
1. Rape victims—New York (State)—New York.
2. Violent crimes—New York (State)—New York.
3. Judicial error—New York (State)—New York.
4. Criminal justice, Administration of—New York (State)—New York.
I. Title.
HV6568.N5B87 2011
364.15'3209227471—dc22
20100396661

Vintage ISBN : 978-0-307-38798-1

Author photograph © Michael Lionstar
Book design by M. Kristen Bearse
Map by Mapping Specialists Fitchburg, Wisconsin

www.vintagebooks.com

Printed in the United States of America
14 16 18 20 19 17 15 13

For Antron, Kevin, Korey, Raymond, and Yusef

I think that everybody here—maybe across the nation—will look at this case to see how the criminal justice system works. . . . This is, I think, putting the criminal justice system on trial.

—MAYOR ED KOCH, *April 21, 1989*

PREFACE

On December 19, 2002, Justice Charles J. Tejada of the Supreme Court of the State of New York granted a motion to vacate the thirteen-year-old convictions in the infamous Central Park Jogger case. He did so based on new evidence: a shocking confession from a serial rapist and a positive DNA match to back it up. In 1990, Antron McCray, Kevin Richardson, Korey Wise, Yusef Salaam, and Raymond Santana, Jr., had been convicted and sent to prison for a combination of rape, sexual assault, and attempted murder of a female jogger named Trisha Meili in Central Park on April 19, 1989. The young men had already completed their sentences, having served between almost seven and thirteen years—but now they finally had the weight of felony convictions and sexual offender status lifted from their shoulders.

That the victim had been a twenty-eight-year-old successful white investment banker and that the five young men who were convicted were black and Latino teenagers from Harlem was not lost on the public or the media in 1989. In the weeks and months after the brutal rape, a media frenzy erupted, steeped in the emotions and fears that circulated throughout a city paralyzed by crime and a country struggling with its own complicated racial history. The media coverage of the crime exposed a racism, rarely acknowledged or examined, rife in American society, and the language used to describe the supposed perpetrators was filled with imagery of savage, wild animals, the same racist language that had been used to justify lynchings earlier in the century. The vicious rape exposed the deepest fears of New Yorkers in the 1980s, and also in the country at large—fears lurking just beneath the surface for over a century: reckless, violent, dark-skinned youths rampaging unchecked, raping and beating a helpless white woman. The outraged response to the crime helped usher in the return of the death penalty in New York State and an era of aggressive law enforcement in New York City.

But even with the convictions vacated, based on a compelling confession and clear forensic evidence and supported by the same district attorney on whose watch the case had been vigorously prosecuted in 1989, many of those who participated in the original prosecutions, including many within the NYPD and one of the ADAs who oversaw the prosecution, still insist on the teenagers' guilt. They agree that another man raped the Central Park Jogger, but they argue that his culpability does nothing to contradict the guilty verdicts of the five young men, despite the overwhelming forensic evidence and the teenagers' confused and contradictory confessions.

These arguments, coming from individuals and organizations with powerful voices and a wide audience, have been effective in preventing the true story of the Central Park Five from reaching those who had followed the coverage of the convictions back in 1989. Many people have heard of this case, but most do not know the facts, and that the convictions were vacated. If they do, they believe that a "legal loophole" was responsible for the exoneration, or that because the teenagers gave confessions, they must be guilty.

During the summer of 2003, before my last year of college, I worked as a researcher for civil rights lawyers involved in a civil suit on behalf of Antron, Kevin, Korey, Yusef, and Raymond. The convictions had only recently been vacated, and I was drawn into the stories of the young men who had been wrongly convicted, who had their lives stolen from them. I wanted to know how something like this could have happened. I went on to write my undergraduate thesis about the racism I saw in the media coverage of the case, but the story continued to haunt me, to demand my attention. I wrestled with the many explanations for this miscarriage of justice, and none was simple or satisfying.

The media coverage was certainly not the only reason these teenagers were wrongly convicted. The police, the prosecutors, and the defense lawyers all played a role. But this was not a case of rogue detectives beating confessions out of suspects, or of the police and prosecutors conspiring to frame individuals they knew to be innocent. If that were so, we could blame it all on those bad seeds and move on. Instead, this case exposes the deeply ingrained racism that still exists in our society. It shows us who and what we fear, and how easy it is for us to believe the sensational stories we hear from the media, who often fail to apply the skepticism their profession demands when competition drives them to sell newspapers or attract more viewers.

The false narrative, disseminated by the police and the media, was swallowed whole by the public because it conformed to the assumptions and fears of the city and the country. *Everyone* bought the story. But the fact that so many continue to promote this narrative tells us that even though we live, as some like to say, in a "postracial" society, the racism that fueled the original rush to judgment persists, and that we have not evolved enough from the days when even the suggestion that a black man had raped a white woman could lead to a lynching.

My goal in reexamining this case is not just to tell the story and explain the facts, to prove wrong those who refuse to admit that a miscarriage of justice occurred, but also to try to understand the broader forces that shaped the outcome of this case, to figure out a simple, but for me a persistent and nagging, question: How did this happen?

The
Central Park Five

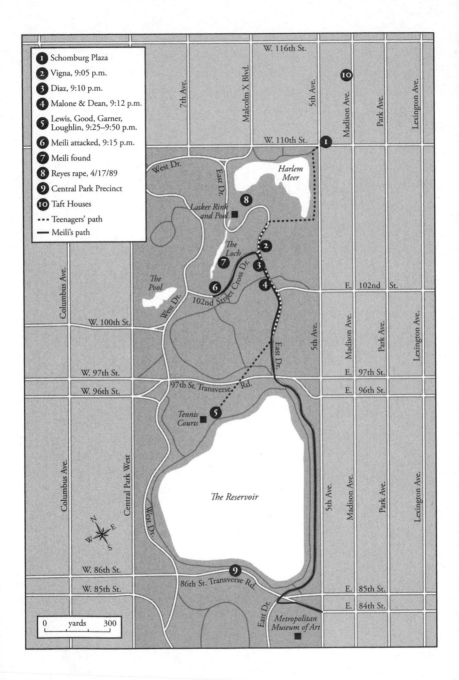

1 Schomburg Plaza
2 Vigna, 9:05 p.m.
3 Diaz, 9:10 p.m.
4 Malone & Dean, 9:12 p.m.
5 Lewis, Good, Garner,
  Loughlin, 9:25–9:50 p.m.
6 Meili attacked, 9:15 p.m.
7 Meili found
8 Reyes rape, 4/17/89
9 Central Park Precinct
10 Taft Houses
- - - Teenagers' path
——— Meili's path

W. 116th St.
W. 110th St.
7th Ave.
Malcolm X Blvd.
5th Ave.
Madison Ave.
Park Ave.
Lexington Ave.

Harlem Meer

West Dr.
East Dr.

Lasker Rink and Pool

The Loch

The Pool

West Dr.

102nd Street Cross Dr.

E. 102nd St.
W. 100th St.

5th Ave.
Madison Ave.
Park Ave.
Lexington Ave.

W. 97th St.
97th St. Transverse Rd.
E. 97th St.
W. 96th St.
E. 96th St.

Columbus Ave.
Central Park West
West Dr.

Tennis Courts

The Reservoir

5th Ave.
Madison Ave.
Park Ave.
Lexington Ave.

Columbus Ave.

W. 86th St.
86th St. Transverse Rd.
W. 85th St.
E. 85th St.
E. 84th St.

East Dr.

Metropolitan Museum of Art

N W E S

0   yards   300

CHAPTER ONE

The day it happened, Wednesday, April 19, 1989, Raymond Santana, Jr., walked over to the Taft Houses in East Harlem to visit a friend. Raymond, whose family had moved to New York from Puerto Rico before he was born, lived with his father and grandmother in an apartment building on 119th Street, a few blocks north of the project, but he often hung out in the courtyard of the Taft Houses, where some of his friends lived. At fourteen, he was of average size—about five six and 130 pounds—with curly hair and small features. He was well liked at school, where his good sense of humor made him popular with girls. Even though there were always kids playing sports around the neighborhood, especially basketball and football in local school yards and the decrepit project courtyards, Raymond was more interested in drawing. He took art classes and spent a lot of his free time sketching.

As Raymond sat with his friend in the Taft courtyard that warm afternoon, a bunch of kids who lived there and in the surrounding buildings arrived. One of the boys in the group was Antron McCray, an exceptionally shy fifteen-year-old African-American from Harlem. Antron lived with his mother, Linda, and his stepfather, Bobby McCray, on 111th Street. He had adopted his stepfather's name at an early age and always considered Bobby his real father. The McCrays were devoted to their only son and were involved in his activities. Though he was a tiny five three and weighed only ninety-eight pounds, Antron was a good athlete and played shortstop on a neighborhood baseball team that his stepfather coached. They had gone to Puerto Rico together for an all-star tournament, a highlight of his Little League career. Antron was enrolled in a small public school program called Career Academy, where he enjoyed his social studies classes and got pretty good grades. Antron and Raymond had seen each other before, since they went to different schools housed within the same building, but didn't know each other well.

Over the next hour, the group in the Taft courtyard grew to about fifteen teenagers. Raymond and Antron joined them as they all began to wander south along Madison Avenue, then turned west onto 110th Street, heading toward Central Park. A block ahead, at the corner of the park, was an apartment complex called the Schomburg Plaza. The Schomburg is made up of two narrow thirty-five-story octagonal towers and, behind them, a large, squat, rectangular building. The two towers sit facing the northeast entrance to Central Park on a traffic circle centered at the intersection of Fifth Avenue and 110th Street. They are by far the tallest buildings in the vicinity and dominate, like sentinels, that corner of the park. Built in 1975 as a city development for middle- and low-income families, all three of the unsightly structures are constructed of beige concrete, with deep grooves running vertically like scars up and down the walls.

Yusef Salaam and Korey Wise, both African-Americans, lived in the northwest tower of the Schomburg Plaza complex. Yusef and Korey were good friends but could not have been more different. Yusef was skinny and tall, nearly six three, even at age fifteen. Korey, at sixteen, was only five five, and stockier. Yusef was a talented kid. He had been accepted at LaGuardia High School of Music and Art, a highly selective public school that requires the submission of an art portfolio for admission. Yusef, like Raymond Santana, had been drawing since he was five and was interested in jewelry making and wood sculpture. He also liked to take electronics apart to see how they worked and to try to put them back together. Korey, on the other hand, had had hearing problems from an early age and a learning disability that limited his achievement in school. He was in the ninth grade in April 1989, but his reading skills were nowhere near that level.

Yusef came from a strong family. His mother, a freelance fashion designer and part-time teacher at Parsons School of Design, raised three children on her own, and pushed them to succeed. Yusef was a practicing Muslim and followed the tenets of his religion closely. But he had been kicked out of LaGuardia when a knife was found in his locker. After his expulsion, Yusef switched schools several times; by April of 1989, his mother had placed him at Rice, a private Christian school in Harlem. She had also signed him up for the Big Brothers Big Sisters program, which paired him up with David Nocenti, an assistant U.S. attorney with whom he'd been spending time for the past four years. Yusef, who was gregarious and laid-back, prided himself on having friends from all over the neighborhood.

Korey Wise was also raised by a single mother, Deloris, who was pregnant in April 1989, and he had three older brothers. Korey was a good friend to Yusef, fiercely loyal, and well liked. At that time, he was dating a girl named Lisa Williams, who lived with a foster family in the same Schomburg tower. But his childhood had been especially difficult. Korey had only recently moved back in with his mother in the Schomburg Plaza; before that, he'd been living in foster care, at a group home in the Bronx. He moved there, he said, because his brothers were "coming and going," and he needed a more stable environment, but Aminah Carroll, a director at the Catholic foster agency that monitored Korey's case, remembered a much more troubled household. Carroll suspected that Korey's hearing problems had resulted from physical abuse, and when she tried to get him treatment, his mother refused to sign the necessary paperwork. A few years earlier, Korey had been on a trip to an amusement park, where he was molested by a group leader.

At sixteen, Korey was a gentle, emotionally stunted boy, his problems amplified by his hearing loss. Korey's development was severely delayed and his ability to comprehend his complicated and sometimes dangerous surroundings was woefully inadequate.

That afternoon, Yusef Salaam, Korey Wise, Korey's girlfriend, Lisa, and their friend Eddie were sitting on a bench near the entrance to

Central Park. They were watching out for an older boy and his friends, who, they feared, were coming to start a fight. The young man wanted to date Eddie's sister, and Yusef and Korey were prepared to help Eddie fend him off. Korey, true to his loyal personality, had offered to fight the offender on Eddie's behalf. Eddie had taken a metal bar, at least a foot long, from Korey's apartment for protection, and it ended up in the pocket of Yusef's long coat. It was a solid piece of metal wrapped with black tape that was used in the Wise household to brace the apartment door against unwanted intruders.

As they headed back toward the Schomburg towers, Yusef noticed a large group of teenagers approaching along 110th Street from the other direction. He was certain it was the other kid and his gang coming back to fight, until he recognized a friend from his building, Al Morris. The group also included Raymond Santana, Antron McCray, and their friends from the Taft and other nearby housing projects.

Using Yusef's nickname, Al called out to him, "Yo, Kane!" and invited him to come hang out in the park. Yusef saw safety in numbers and joined them. He, in turn, invited Korey, who left Lisa behind and followed Yusef into the park. Still more Schomburg residents joined the crowd that was now headed into Central Park, including a fourteen-year-old African-American named Kevin Richardson.

Kevin lived with his mother, Gracie Cuffee, in the same Schomburg building as Yusef and Korey. Their small apartment was on the thirty-fourth floor of the tower, with a spectacular view of Central Park laid out below the window. Kevin's parents had split up, but his four older sisters often visited. He was the baby of the family, the boy his mother had always wanted, and the women in his family doted on him and taught him to be polite and thoughtful. Kevin attended Jackie Robinson Junior High School on Madison Avenue at 106th Street, where he played the saxophone and participated in a hip-hop dance troupe called Show Stoppers.

Kevin had started playing football while living in Virginia for a few months when he was twelve, and he had dreams of making the team at Syracuse University. He was quiet and respectful at school and his teachers remembered him as having a good moral compass, though his grades showed that he was having trouble keeping up in class. Kevin looked young for his age, with a round baby face and large features. Kevin recognized Yusef and Korey from the building, but didn't know them well.

As the group, including Kevin Richardson, Korey Wise, Yusef Salaam, Antron McCray, and Raymond Santana, congregated at the northeast entrance to Central Park in the darkening twilight, Raymond counted thirty-three boys.

That same day, Patricia Ellen Meili woke up early, as she always did, so she could be at her office by 7:30 a.m. Trisha, as she was known to her family and friends, often worked long days at the office. She was employed at Salomon Brothers, an investment bank in downtown Manhattan, as an associate in the Corporate Finance Division. She had been at Salomon since moving to New York after finishing business school at Yale. At five o'clock, Meili decided that she would have to call off her dinner plans because she still had too much to do at the office that evening. She phoned her friend Michael Allen to cancel.

A few hours later, her colleague and former roommate Pat Garrett popped his head over from the adjacent cubicle. He wanted to know about the stereo system Meili had just gotten for her new apartment.

"Why not come over and take a look at it?" she said.

"Sure," he replied.

"Come around ten. That'll give me time to go for a run before you get there."

They made a plan to meet at 10:00 p.m. and Meili went home to her apartment on East Eighty-third Street, near York Avenue, where she lived alone. At ten minutes to nine, with the sky already dark, Meili left for her run, wearing black leggings, a long-sleeved white T-shirt over her sports bra, Saucony running shoes, and an AM/FM radio headset. Her keys were in a small Velcro pouch attached to one of her sneakers. She also wore a delicate gold ring in the shape of a bow.

On her way down the stairs from her apartment, she bumped into her neighbor James Lansing, who was on his way back from the gym. They chatted for a few minutes about jogging in the park, and then Meili left the building at five minutes to nine. She headed for Central Park.

The year 1989 had begun with New Yorkers still in shock over the news of a terrorist attack. A bomb smuggled into the luggage hold of Pan Am Flight 103 had detonated as the plane flew over Lockerbie, Scotland, on December 21, 1988. The 747 had been on its way from London Heathrow to New York's JFK Airport, and all 259 people aboard, as well as eleven on the ground, were killed when the plane exploded in midair. It was clear from newspaper articles on January 1, 1989, which included obituaries for some of the victims, that people were still trying to piece together what had happened. Many of the passengers on the flight had been New Yorkers heading home.

The New York they were returning to that winter little resembled the prosperous, vibrant metropolis it had once been. Despite the charms that still made it the place of dreams for many, life in the city had become for others a nightmare that recalled the terrifying, gritty, crime-infested, and corrupt Gotham City of comic books. Over the past decades, New York City had experienced a staggering decline and had reached a low point in its history, with soaring crime rates, which no one had ever seen before or could have imagined just a few decades earlier. It was a place people wished they could leave, and in which today's relative wealth and safety seemed an inconceivable pipe dream.

In Harlem, where Antron, Raymond, Yusef, Kevin, and Korey lived, the streets were filled with thousands of abandoned and burned-out buildings. Bankruptcy for the city had been narrowly averted in the seventies, but funding for many services, especially those most valued by residents of poor neighborhoods, had been severely cut or eliminated.

Fire stations, libraries, and rehab clinics had been shuttered. After-school programs disappeared and park maintenance faltered. Graffiti covered the subways and buildings throughout Harlem and other parts of the city. Empty lots became repositories for debris and garbage. New Yorkers, especially the poorest among them, mostly African-Americans and Latinos, were desperately in need of services and protection, but the city lacked the resources to fight the increasing challenges that its ghettos faced.

Citywide, muggings were regular events, and no one felt immune. Cars were broken into with startling regularity, often for prizes as minor as a shirt fresh from the dry cleaner's hanging inside the window. Falling asleep on the subway could mean waking up and finding that your pants pockets had been slashed with a box cutter and the contents removed by "lush workers," master pickpockets who preyed especially on drunks. Apartment doors were double-, triple-, and quadruple-bolted, and the "police lock," a piece of steel several feet long that was wedged diagonally between a lock on the inside of the door and a brace on the floor, was a standard protective measure.

Residents had become desensitized to the indignities of city life. When commuters in the Times Square subway station walked down to wait for their train one day, they found a man, stark naked, passed out on the platform. Most simply stepped over him and on to the express train. One woman covered him up with a shopping bag from Saks Fifth Avenue. When a TV producer sitting on the subway realized that a woman near her on the train was relieving herself, the woman could only shrug hopelessly at another passenger across the aisle.

The subways could also be terrifying. One Brooklyn woman was approached on the train by a brazen group of young men who spit into their palms for lubrication before trying to pull the rings from her fingers.

Women especially feared the subways during the winter of 1989, where, among other dangers, a man was on the loose, attacking and dragging women into the endless miles of tunnels beneath the city and then raping, sodomizing, and robbing them. A flyer handed out by the transit police advised women to travel with others and remain close to the token booths while in the stations.

On average, thirty-six people were murdered every week in New York that year. Gruesome stories of homicides, burglaries, and rapes dominated the headlines and evening news, making it impossible for many New Yorkers to believe that their city could ever recover. In the first months of 1989 alone, the tabloids of New York City displayed on their covers headlines that included: DEATHTRAP: ROOMING-HOUSE BLAZE KILLS 7; HUMAN SHIELD: BOY, 3, SHOT AFTER BEING SNATCHED FROM HIS MOTHER'S ARMS BY YOUTH FLEEING GUNFIGHT; OPEN SEASON ON COPS; PISTOL-PACKIN' PRE-SCHOOLER; DOCTOR SLAIN: PREGNANT 33-YEAR-OLD BEATEN IN HER OFFICE; and simply, VIOLENCE.

The police seemed unable to combat the growing crime rates. They were understaffed after cuts in the late 1970s, measures that had been needed to keep the city from going bankrupt. Newspapers regularly reported on police officers who had been shot or killed. *The New York Times* ran articles on at least a dozen incidents that year in which a police officer was stabbed, shot, or killed. When a woman approached a transit officer in a subway station and pointed out to him that a man in front of them was jamming the turnstile and stealing tokens, the officer replied, "Lady, leave me alone. Do you want me to get hurt?"

A new drug epidemic had hastened the decline, as crack cocaine laid waste to inner cities across the country. Crack had shown up in New York around 1984, and it quickly took hold as a scourge more virulent than heroin. Crack, the free-base form of cocaine, was cheaper to produce than its powdered relative, and more addictive. The drug, a rock crystal that makes a cracking sound when heated, is smoked in pipes, allowing the drug to reach the bloodstream faster and creating a more euphoric—but also a shorter—high, one that can lead to twitchiness, anxiety, paranoia, and violent behavior in those who use the drug. Crack addicts desperate for a fix committed robberies to fuel their habit, and dealers, who were often very young men, carried and used automatic weapons as they battled over turf. That January, a sixteen-year-old from the Bronx had stabbed his mother to death with a steak knife after she refused to give him money for crack.

As the drug trade exploded, more women were arrested and charged with felonies than ever before. By April 1989, the number of women in city jails had increased by 33 percent from only a year earlier. In 1985, Rikers Island, the city's sprawling jail complex, had added a nursery. As the police developed new tactics to target drug dealers, jails became overcrowded, and the justice system as a whole was overburdened. The city couldn't come up with enough funding for the district attorneys, corrections and probation officers, and Legal Aid lawyers needed to prosecute and administrate all the new cases. Instead, many accused drug dealers were released or sentenced to shorter terms because the system simply didn't have the means to keep them any longer.

The dealers who plied crack and heroin around the city were centered, for the most part, in the poorest areas. Those neighborhoods—Harlem in Manhattan, Bedford-Stuyvesant and Bushwick in Brooklyn, and the South Bronx, among others—had become crowded ghettos over the last decades.

Housing projects dotted their landscapes. Billed as "urban renewal" and constructed throughout the middle of the century, the tall, spare, ugly buildings clustered on massive plots of land taking up several city blocks had instead created "worse centers of delinquency, vandalism and general social hopelessness than the slums they were supposed to replace," according to writer and activist Jane Jacobs. They had weakened the sense of community and neighborhood that these areas had once had, pushing out businesses that had encouraged street traffic and destroying the once-vibrant stoop culture of smaller buildings. Children no longer played on the street while their parents watched from the front steps, simultaneously keeping an eye on the whole neighborhood. Instead, ensconced in tall buildings, families were kept separate, and the playgrounds and courtyards of the projects remained abandoned and dangerous.

Drug dealers found safe haven in housing projects; with their often unlocked hallways and vestibules, and courtyards hidden from the street, they provided many routes in and out when the police arrived.

Another new and terrifying epidemic, AIDS, had also hit New York City especially hard. Though only discovered and named in the early 1980s, by 1989 an estimated 200,000 or more people in New York were infected with the virus that causes AIDS. Hospitals, like the city jails, were desperately overcrowded, and many poor AIDS patients found themselves without homes or hospital beds.

More than 25,000 homeless individuals checked in to city shelters that year, but untold thousands of others lived on the streets and in the seven hundred miles of subway tunnels belowground, where they could find shelter and privacy but also risked being hit by trains or being electrocuted by the live third rail. Many were drug addicts or mentally ill, having been deinstitutionalized from state hospitals in the 1970s.

It was common to see the homeless on the streets of midtown Manhattan or in the subways, begging for change, talking to themselves, or passed out in a stupor. Some beggars, known as "squeegee men," would rush up to cars stopped at traffic lights, quickly wash the windshield with a filthy tool, and then demand payment from the driver, sometimes snapping off a windshield wiper if it was refused.

Schools, especially in poor neighborhoods, were failing. The school buildings themselves were crumbling, with unrepaired broken windows and overly crowded classrooms. At one Brooklyn high school, only one-fifth of those students who had entered as freshmen graduated within four years. A budget proposed by Governor Cuomo for 1989 included between $80 and $90 million in cuts for New York City schools. Students sometimes threatened teachers with knives, and violent fights could erupt between youths. In early 1989, a new program placed metal detectors in five high schools to try to keep knives and guns out of the hallways. After the metal detectors were installed, a security task force found hundreds of weapons stashed outside the five schools, left there by students unwilling to walk to school without protection.

People were giving up on New York City. Governor Mario Cuomo was demoralized: "I don't see how we can manage this problem with our resources in New York," he lamented. "It's possible you won't be able to solve the problem. That's how horrible it is." Pete Hamill, the celebrated columnist and a lifelong New Yorker, wrote that the city was dying, and described his frustration and anger: "In the barbarized city of New York, there is no horror these days. We no longer seem capable of that basic human emotion, which is why so many of us have begun to lose all hope for a more decent future. The cause of this municipal numbness is simple: We have seen too many atrocities."

Most of those atrocities were happening in the poor and minority ghettos of the city, neighborhoods filled with vacant lots, abandoned buildings, and failing schools, the evidence of years of discrimination, neglect, and hardship. Over the past decades, millions of blacks and Latinos had moved from the South as well as the Caribbean, especially Puerto Rico, to New York City, chasing jobs and opportunity. Despite this influx, the city's population overall remained fairly stable, as nearly three million mostly middle-class whites fled. They had left the city for the suburbs, which had better schools and lower crime rates, and businesses had followed suit, leaving a shortage of decent jobs for the new African-American and Latino arrivals. The whites who remained, now barely the majority, felt under siege from the twin plagues of drugs and crime they saw as emanating from the ghettos. Many wealthy whites, those who were making fortunes on Wall Street, spent their riches protecting themselves, living in doorman buildings in Manhattan, sequestered from the dangers of the streets. Meanwhile, working-class whites established enclaves along the shores of the outer boroughs, in places like Howard Beach and Bensonhurst, and prepared to defend their neighborhoods from the encroachment of minorities.

The fear and suspicion of blacks as criminals was so powerful that the newly inaugurated president had taken advantage of it in order to get elected. George H. W. Bush, in his campaign for the presidency, had repeatedly bashed his opponent, Massachusetts governor Michael

Dukakis, as soft on crime. During Dukakis's tenure as governor, Willie Horton, a black man and a murderer sentenced to life without parole, had been given a weekend pass to leave prison as part of a furlough program. Horton failed to return, and he went on to rape a white woman in Maryland and stab her fiancé before being caught again. Bush raised the story repeatedly on the campaign trail, and supporters of the president's campaign ran a television ad showing images of Willie Horton with his large Afro and describing his crimes, while words like *kidnapping, stabbing,* and *raping* appeared on the screen. Bush eventually distanced himself from the ad, but not before its message had been broadcast for nearly a month. The fear instilled by the image of Willie Horton and the associations the ad conjured—violent, black, rapist, and murderer—helped destroy Dukakis's candidacy.

The New York news media also reinforced the stereotype of the minority criminal, projecting images of black and Latino men in perp walks or mug shots, confirming the wise decision of those who had left for the suburbs and enflaming the fears of those who remained.

Frustration with crime and violence and the tendency to blame it on African-Americans led to a series of iconic violent encounters that became part of the collective memory of the city's residents. These famous incidents came to define the city and its problems for New Yorkers in the 1980s.

In several cases, working-class ethnic whites, pushed to enclaves along the outer edges of the city by the growing minority population, lashed out at "trespassing" blacks. In 1982, Willie Turks and two fellow New York City Transit Authority workers, all black men, stopped in the Gravesend section of Brooklyn on their way home from work to buy bagels. They were accosted by a group of Italian-American teenagers, who attacked the three men with sticks and bottles when their car stalled as they were trying to drive away. Turks was beaten to death by the mob.

In 1986, four black men from Brooklyn were driving along the Belt Parkway when their car experienced engine trouble. They exited the highway and managed to drive for a few miles before their car broke down completely, leaving them stranded along Cross Bay Boulevard in Queens, on a small and isolated island called Broad Channel in Jamaica Bay. While Curtis Sylvester stayed with the car, the other three men, Michael Griffith, Cedric Sandiford, and Timothy Grimes, went looking for help. They walked nearly four miles along the boulevard back into Howard Beach, a mostly white, Italian neighborhood near JFK airport. When a group of white teenagers saw them buying slices of pizza, they called some other friends and returned with baseball bats to beat them up. The three black men, now outnumbered more than four to one, ran, but the gang chased down Griffith and Sandiford and severely beat them. Eventually, Griffith managed to escape through a hole in a chain-link fence that led back to the Belt Parkway. He was almost all the way across the busy highway when he was struck by a car and killed.

Three days before Christmas in 1984, Bernhard Goetz, a thirty-seven-year-old white engineer, stepped on to a downtown number 2 express train at Fourteenth Street. He sat near a group of four African-American teenagers, who approached him and demanded five dollars. He pulled an unregistered .38 caliber Smith & Wesson from his pocket and fired four shots, one at each of the teenagers who surrounded him. When one teenager appeared unhurt, he said, "You seem to be [doing] all right. Here's another," and fired a fifth bullet, severing Darrell Cabey's spinal cord and permanently paralyzing him from the waist down.

Goetz fled the scene and remained nameless for more than a week, but in the meanwhile, he became something of a hero to many New Yorkers frustrated with increasing crime and fearful especially of black teenagers. When the NYPD set up a hot line for callers to provide information about the whereabouts of the still-at-large gunman, dubbed the "subway vigilante" by the press, they were deluged with calls from supporters. Untold thousands celebrated his actions, columnists praised his bravery, and many suggested that the police abandon their search. Others offered to help pay for his defense. A few even recommended that he run for mayor. A national poll conducted after the shootings showed that 47 percent of Americans approved of Goetz's actions and that only 17 percent believed he was wrong.

After he turned himself in, Goetz advocates outside the courtroom during his trial held banners that read BERNIE GOETZ WINS ONE FOR THE GOOD GUYS, and CRIMINALS WATCH OUT. WE'LL GET YOU! An editorial in *The Wall Street Journal* a few days after the shooting admitted that vigilante justice could not be tolerated, but it raised questions about the effectiveness of the city's legal system if its citizens felt the need to protect themselves. "If the 'state of nature' has returned to some big cities, can people fairly be blamed for modern vigilantism?" the editorial asked, making a coded reference to the race of those seen as to blame for the city's decline. The assumption was that the teenagers were violent, dangerous criminals. Articles reported that the young men concealed sharpened screwdrivers in their pockets and that each had an arrest record. It was true that two of the boys carried screwdrivers, but the implication that they were weapons was exaggerated by a press eager to paint these teenagers as a violent menace. The screwdrivers were actually unsharpened, probably tools for breaking into arcade games to steal quarters. Goetz, later acquitted of charges of attempted murder and assault, was convicted only for illegal possession of a gun.

The tendency to see African-Americans as violent criminals often extended to the police, who used excessive force against blacks in two separate well-known incidents in the 1980s. In 1983, a twenty-five-year-old black graffiti artist named Michael Stewart died after falling into a coma while in police custody after his arrest for spraying graffiti in a subway station. Experts disagreed about exactly what had caused his death, and though the police officers were charged with criminally negligent homicide, assault, and perjury, an all-white jury found them not guilty.

A few months before Bernhard Goetz opened fire in that subway car, Eleanor Bumpurs was fatally shot by the police while being evicted from her Bronx housing project. The sixty-six-year-old African-American woman had a history of mental illness, and when housing authority officers arrived to remove her from her home, she refused to let them in, allegedly yelling threats through the door. An Emergency Services Unit, not unlike a SWAT team, was brought in. They battered down the door and entered her apartment in full riot gear. Bumpurs was standing inside, holding a kitchen knife. Although police knew she was mentally unstable and were equipped with pepper spray, they chose not to use it. When Bumpurs lunged toward an officer with her knife, he fired his shotgun twice, first striking her in the hand, then in the chest. She died at the hospital.

These incidents and others provoked impassioned responses from all sides and highlighted the ongoing racial divides facing the city. Though the poorest neighborhoods of the city, and those with the highest crime rates, were inhabited by many Latinos as well as blacks, the fear of crime was directed more than anything at black men, who have for centuries been stereotyped as menacing and criminal. Each new event increased divisions within the city, making black residents even more distrustful of the police, and encouraged growing racism and fear of blacks among whites.

Though minorities were regularly portrayed and feared as criminals, it was the black and Latino residents of the city's poorest neighborhoods who were most at risk of becoming crime victims themselves. In general, crime rates tend to be highest in poverty-stricken ghettos. Because of their desperate circumstances, the poor are most likely to be the perpetrators of street crime, such as assault, burglary, and arson. They are also apt to commit those crimes when opportunity strikes, in their own neighborhoods, making their neighbors the victims.

A study that looked at data from the beginning of the 1980s found that Harlem had the highest mortality rate of any area in the city, and double the rate for whites throughout the country. It determined that men in Harlem were "less likely to reach the age of 65 than men in Bangladesh," one of the poorest and most desperately needy countries in the world. Young black and Latino men were especially at risk. Pete Hamill pointed out that "blacks kill other blacks at a rate that would make the Ku Klux Klan envious. Black youths are killing or being killed over sneakers, jackets, over the choice of songs on boom boxes, over women and attitude and casual quarrels." Walks to and from school could be treacherous. The leading cause of death for a young black male was homicide.

The violence and danger of the drug trade was especially present in the lives of the teenagers who lived in the Schomburg Plaza and the blocks surrounding it. Yusef watched one day from the window of his twenty-first-floor apartment in a Schomburg tower as cop cars screeched up to the front of one of the Taft buildings, just two blocks to the north. As people on the street scattered, he saw a man step out of the building with two guns and open fire on the police cars before running back inside the building. "Violence was a part of everyday life," Yusef recalled.

Many residents of Harlem and other minority neighborhoods saw the police as antagonists rather than protectors. After the deaths of Eleanor Bumpurs and Michael Stewart and countless other harassments and offenses, many blacks and Latinos were fearful and mistrustful of a police force that seemed especially insensitive to their community. Parents would warn their children not to talk back to the police, for fear of them escalating a dangerous situation. Teenagers in Harlem were more likely to be harassed by the police, stopped and patted down or handcuffed in a subway station while the police "checked" on the validity of their transit passes, than to be protected from a gang who wanted to steal their coats or shoes.

Yusef Salaam kept the knife that got him kicked out of LaGuardia for protection. He was afraid of a teenage gang from Brooklyn that called themselves the Decepticons, after the villains in the popular TV cartoon series *Transformers,* and who preyed on the artsy LaGuardia High School students on their way to the subway after school. By the mid-1980s, New York's serious gang problem had largely faded, but teenagers remained fearful of gang members and carried weapons, studied martial arts and other ways to fight, or sought safety in large groups as protection. When Yusef joined the boys heading into Central Park on April 19, 1989, he was hoping that the size of the group would protect him from an older boy he feared. And yet it was this very type of behavior that could get kids in trouble with the police, and which helped to encourage their reputation as a criminal menace.

Episode by episode, the media only amplified the sense that the city's most at-risk population was the source of all crime, that blacks and Latinos, especially male teenagers, were criminals—murderers, thieves, rapists, and arsonists.

It was dark when Kevin Richardson, Korey Wise, Yusef Salaam, Antron McCray, Raymond Santana, and at least twenty-five other young African-American and Latino boys entered Central Park around 9:00 p.m. on April 19, 1989, but the moon was almost full and cast a bright glow on the quiet park. They meandered along a path that ran parallel to Fifth Avenue, heading south, laughing and playing around. Most of the boys were between thirteen and sixteen, and though many didn't know one another, they had the loose connections of their neighborhood, apartment buildings, and schools. Raymond, Antron, Yusef, Korey, and Kevin did not usually visit the park in such large numbers, and none had ever been arrested or been in serious trouble before, but there were some in the group who had more troublesome pursuits in mind.

Central Park, the vast playground at the teenagers' doorsteps, is the most famous urban park in America, an iconic symbol of the city itself, featured in scores of films, plays, and works of literature and art. The park, 843 acres of gardens, ball fields, running paths, meadows, playgrounds, and woods, was conceived by Frederick Law Olmsted and Calvert Vaux in 1858 as a source of pleasure, relaxation, and fascination, a romantic ideal of nature in the city.

But in 1989, Central Park had come to mirror the deterioration of the city around it. Renovated in the 1930s by Robert Moses, the park had fallen into disrepair in the sixties and seventies as the city—in the midst of a financial crisis—could no longer afford its upkeep. Without the money to supervise or repair the park, garbage piled up and graffiti was left unscrubbed on park surfaces. The once-lush green areas of the Great Lawn and Sheep Meadow were now only dirt and dust, and many of the once-elegant structures in the park were crumbling into ruins. A 1980 *New York Times* article described the city park system as "a dirty, unkempt, vandalized shadow of its former self."

Central Park had also come to be known for its scandalous crimes, engendering a feeling that danger lurked there at night, and as a new symbol (along with the subways) of a lawless and out-of-control city. When *The Tonight Show* with Johnny Carson moved from New York to Burbank, California, in 1972, Central Park became the source of many of his jokes and one-liners at the city's expense: "Some Martians landed in Central Park today . . . and were mugged." "It was so quiet in Central Park last night you could have heard a knife drop." Cartoonists regularly used Central Park as the clichéd site of muggings. The poet Ogden Nash wrote in the 1960s about visiting the park after nightfall:

> If you should happen after dark
> To find yourself in Central Park,
> Ignore the paths that beckon you
> And hurry, hurry to the zoo,
> And creep into the tiger's lair.
> Frankly, you'll be safer there.

Any crime in Central Park was highlighted in the media as especially newsworthy, exaggerating the feeling that it was a dangerous place to go, especially at night.

There had been concerns about crime from the very beginning. Even Olmsted himself warned women not to go into the park at night, "and I answer for no man's safety," he said, "from its bullies, garroters, or highway robbers after dusk."

Despite these fears, news of particular crimes and "crime waves" in Central Park, going back a century, have been greatly exaggerated. In reality, Central Park's crime rates have always been lower than in any other part of the city, largely because no one actually lives there. But it has been hard for people to believe that Central Park is safe when incidents in the park are so overrepresented in the news. The park's significance as an oasis, a peaceful garden in the middle of a concrete jungle, has always led to inflated media reports on any violence there; it seems scandalous to hear about anything bad happening in such a romanticized and idyllic place. As the captain of the Central Park police precinct noted in 1959, "Crime in Central Park is usually exaggerated. It shocks people like crime in heaven."

Just after nine o'clock on the evening of April 19, 1989, the series of events that would come to be known, in the following weeks and months, as "wilding" began.

First, the group of teenagers came across a Latino man, but someone indicated that he knew him, so they let him continue on his way. Then a couple walked by and one member of the group suggested that they leave the guy alone because he was with a "lady."

Officer Raymond Alvarez was driving through the park that night on his way to the West Side to deliver mail to another precinct when he spotted the group of boys around 106th Street. He shone his spotlight on them, and they scattered, heading south. Alvarez continued west on his errand.

As the teens began to regroup, a young man named Michael Vigna was riding a racing bike north on the East Drive, headed in their direction. It was 9:05 p.m. When they saw him, some spread out across the East Drive, forcing Vigna to swerve to his left to get around them. As he passed the group, one boy took a swing at him, narrowly missing his head as he sped by.

As the group of teenagers continued south along the East Drive, they came upon a middle-aged Latino man, Antonio Diaz, who was rumpled and dirty. They assumed he was homeless. Diaz was carrying a container of food and four bottles of beer. He was already drunk and still drinking from an open beer bottle as he stumbled through the park. Someone knocked him to the ground and a few of the boys started hitting and kicking him in the head and back. Many of the other teens were scattered around the same area but did not participate. Yusef Salaam stood nearby on a rocky outcropping across the road and saw another teenager eating. He asked him where he'd gotten the food. "From the bum," he said. After hitting and kicking and robbing him of his food, several boys dragged Diaz into the grass on the side of the road and left him there, bleeding from the head.

A few hundred feet farther south, the loose confederation of boys saw a couple on a tandem bike heading toward them along the East Drive. The group was in a grassy area just east of the road. At 9:12 p.m., as the cyclists, Gerry Malone and Patricia Dean, approached, several boys moved out onto the road, their backs to the bikers. The couple angled to their left, trying to avoid hitting anyone in the road, but as they got within one hundred feet, some of the teenagers scattered across the road, then turned around and faced the couple with their knees bent and their arms outstretched; some had hoods or hats pulled low over their faces.

With their arms spread, they spanned the entire roadway, and there was nowhere left for the riders to go. Malone and Dean started pedaling faster, heading to the far left. At the last moment, they swerved toward the group, heading straight for a taller boy in the middle. Just before they collided, the boys in the bike's immediate path jumped aside, and the couple flew past at nearly thirty-five miles per hour. One or two of the boys grabbed at them, but Malone and Dean managed to get away without being harmed.

The group of teenagers continued their southerly course. A few of them threw rocks at passing cars, including at a taxicab, whose driver got out and yelled at them. When they continued pelting him with rocks, he drove off. But now some worried that he would call the cops, so they moved off the road and walked through the North Meadow, south toward the Ninety-seventh Street Transverse. Another police car appeared to the north and shone a light on them. The group scattered again. Korey and some others left the park and went home, while some of the kids ran farther south, into the park. Yusef and several others climbed down the wall to the transverse, crossed the road, and climbed back up to the area just north of the reservoir. There, Yusef reconvened with some of the original group, who had also found their way to the reservoir. He recognized another boy who lived in his building, Steve Lopez.

At 9:25 p.m., Officer Alvarez was driving back through the park to the East Side. When he reached the East Drive, Antonio Diaz, the "bum," approached his car. Diaz explained that a few minutes earlier he had been assaulted by about five or so black and Hispanic youths. Diaz got into Officer Alvarez's radio car and they began driving around, looking for the group. A few minutes later, Michael Vigna, the bike racer, approached Alvarez and gave a similar description of the group that had harassed him on his previous lap. Alvarez then radioed other cars in the area with a description of the roving gang. Officers in and around Central Park now began looking for the boys.

Meanwhile, the smaller group of teenagers who had crossed the transverse reconvened just off the jogging path north of the reservoir. The Central Park Reservoir is a 106-acre pool encircled by a jogging track a little over a mile and a half long. Between the track and the water was a chain-link fence, built in the 1930s to keep people from committing suicide by jumping into the water during the Depression. It was still there in 1989.

At 9:25 p.m., David Lewis, a young man with blond hair, jogged by on a lap around the reservoir. By then, some of the boys had gathered near the tennis courts next to the running path. As Lewis approached, several boys assembled just off the path. One said, "Ready?" They were crouched, each with one arm to the ground, in the three-point stance of a football lineman. One threw a rock, which narrowly missed Lewis, bouncing off the fence just beyond him.

"Do you want to race?" Lewis asked.

"Yeah, we'll race all right," one of the boys replied.

Lewis then picked up his pace, unaware that up ahead about five more teens were coming out of the woods onto the path. Two stood in the middle of the path, blocking him. Lewis tried to run past, moving to the left, between one attacker and the chain-link fence along the reservoir. As he sprinted past, the boy hit him in the right arm. A couple of the other boys tried to run after him, but Lewis was too fast for them and was soon out of sight. He ran all the way to the Central Park Precinct along the Eighty-sixth Street Transverse, where he reported what had happened.

Over the next fifteen minutes, three more solitary male joggers ran by that same spot. About eight or ten boys were milling around on the path when a runner named David Good approached. As he neared the group, one said, "You better run faster than that." Seconds later, other teenagers in the group started throwing rocks and sticks at him. Good broke into a sprint, and as he ran past the last two boys in the group, one threw a heavy branch at him, hitting him squarely on the back of the leg. It hurt, but Good was able to continue running. Like David Lewis, he immediately headed for the Central Park Precinct to report the assault.

Just after 9:30 p.m., Robert Garner approached the group along the reservoir path. This time, fifteen or more boys ran out onto the track and surrounded him. They forced him off the path to the right and one boy started punching him. Garner asked what they wanted. The boy who had punched him replied, "Money, of course," and some of the others laughed. Garner told them he didn't have any money, then explained that the rattling sound of metal was coming from keys tied around his waist, not change in his pocket. One of the boys told him to leave, and he sprinted back to the edge of the park and then walked home.

As Garner was being surrounded, another runner approached the group. John Loughlin was wearing a green army jacket, camouflage pants, and a portable radio with headphones. He, too, was jogging around the reservoir when he saw from a distance what looked like a group of teenagers attacking someone on the ground. When the gang first saw him, some of the youths thought Loughlin was a cop, because of his army jacket and athletic build, and because he was running slowly and seemed to be watching them. At first, some were reluctant to harass him. But as Loughlin slowed to see what was going on, one of the boys, Jermain Robinson, got closer and asked, "What are you looking at? Are you some kind of vigilante?" Robinson then called out to some others who were nearer to Loughlin, telling them that this was "one of those vigilantes." Others picked up the mantra, referencing Bernhard Goetz.

Robinson ran up to Loughlin and threw him to the ground, where he and others started kicking and hitting him. At some point, the metal bar from Korey's house that Yusef had carried into the park was used to beat Loughlin. Jermain Robinson was the most aggressive assailant and some of the boys had to pull him off the battered jogger. He ran back for a few more punches, angry because his jacket had been ripped in the course of the attack. Eventually, they left Loughlin lying on the jogging path, bleeding.

He had been beaten badly and had cuts on his forehead and the back of his head. He had also been hit on his back and legs and had scrapes on his shins. A police officer who took Loughlin to the hospital said that he looked like he had been "dunked in a bucket of blood." His injuries were so serious that he spent two nights in the hospital.

After this attack, the teens still remaining in the park left, walking out in small groups onto Central Park West.

Just after 9:00 p.m., as the group of teenagers was winding its way south along paths in the park, Trisha Meili jogged into Central Park at the Eighty-fourth Street entrance. It was a clear, moonlit night, and warm for April. She followed her typical route, turning north onto the East Drive. Though friends and family had expressed concern about her running alone in the park at night, Meili took pleasure in defying their warnings. This was her city, her park, and running was the one activity that was all her own. Her only compromise was to jog the northern part of her loop first, so that she would pass the area of the park that seemed more dangerous earlier in the night. She turned onto the 102nd Street Cross Drive, planning to head south again on the West Drive and run a loop back to Eighty-fourth Street south of the reservoir.

The 102nd Street Cross Drive, which connects the two main roads on the east and west sides of the park, is frequented by joggers and bicyclists, but is not open to regular traffic. The Cross Drive curves as it heads west, and much of the road is lined with trees. There are streetlamps along it, but they are far enough apart for much of the road to be dark and secluded. Trees and brush run along much of the north side of the path, and to the south the ground rises up over large boulders, so that the playing fields just on the other side are obscured. As one moves west, approaching the curve in the road, the trees are taller and grow on both sides, creating a canopy and making the road feel quieter and more isolated.

At approximately 9:15 p.m., about halfway between the East and West drives, Trisha Meili was attacked. The music coming from her headphones probably prevented any awareness of the imminent assault. She was hit on the back of the head with a large branch and fell forward. Her headphones skittered across the pavement. Bleeding from the head, she was then dragged off the road to the north, through a grassy area, and then into the woods that began forty feet from the road. She came to and began to fight back. Meili broke away and ran, but she fell and was beaten again. She was then raped and battered over and over about the face and head with a rock near an unpaved pathway north of the Cross Drive that meanders along a small body of water known as the Loch. Finally, Trisha Meili was tied up with her own shirt and abandoned, left there to die in one of the most secluded areas of the park.

Officers Eric Reynolds and Robert Powers were among those who had heard the radioed description of a gang of rowdy youths and were out looking for them in the park that night, patrolling in a Parks Department van. They saw the headlights of other police cars canvassing the area, and around 10:00 p.m., they decided to search for the gang around the outer edges of the park. As they drove north along Central Park West, they saw a small group of African-American and Latino teenagers slowly walking up the street across from the park. Officer Powers turned the van west onto 102nd Street, pulling directly into the path of the group. He and Reynolds jumped out of the van and yelled, "Stop! Police!" All but two of the boys scattered, some running back into Central Park. The two who remained, Raymond Santana and Steve Lopez, were arrested.

Officer Reynolds stayed with the two boys while Officer Powers followed the others, chasing them over the stone wall bordering the park and across some baseball fields. Powers, a stocky white officer, caught up to Kevin Richardson and tackled him, leaving a scratch on Kevin's left cheek.

Meanwhile, Lopez and Santana were taken to the Central Park Precinct. They were held there with Kevin Richardson and two other boys the police had arrested in the park, Lamont McCall and Clarence Thomas.

One of the detectives who arrived in the park that night, responding to calls about the unruly group of teenagers, was from the 23rd Precinct, on East 102nd Street. He was working undercover, driving a yellow taxicab; another detective sat in the passenger seat. As they entered the park at 102nd Street, they stopped a teenager they knew from the neighborhood who was walking out of the park. The young man, Matias Reyes, who had not been with the group, worked at the bodega across the street from the precinct, so he was familiar to many of the officers there. The detectives in the cab asked him about the group in the park, but when he said he hadn't seen them, they sent him on his way. He was listening to a radio headset.

CHAPTER TWO

The Central Park Precinct sits facing the Eighty-sixth Street Transverse, near the middle of the park. The U-shaped building is the oldest standing police precinct in the city, put up in 1871 and originally designed as a stable for the horses that helped to maintain the park. It is constructed of brick and brownstone, a small building with front-facing gabled dormer windows with green frames. The entrance is a low, dark, imposing doorway with arched glass double doors. New York's 22nd Precinct has been housed in the former stable ever since the mid-1930s, when it was moved there from the Arsenal Building, an even older stone behemoth on the east side of Central Park. Few renovations had occurred since then, so in 1989 the precinct sat in a state of perpetual disrepair, with sagging beams, a leaky roof, and boarded-up windows to keep out the park's inquisitive squirrels.

When officers took Kevin Richardson, Raymond Santana, Steve Lopez, Lamont McCall, and Clarence Thomas to the Central Park Precinct around 11:00 p.m. on April 19, 1989, Trisha Meili was still hidden off the path in an isolated area of Central Park, bleeding and barely alive.

Officers made phone calls to the boys' parents, who soon began to trickle in to the decrepit precinct building. A second structure, the smaller Community Affairs building, had only two rooms, a clerical area, and, behind it, the Community Affairs office, which doubled as the precinct's designated "youth room," where the young men were held that night. Gracie Cuffee, Kevin's mother, was the first to arrive, around midnight. She waited in the office area just outside the youth room, and after half an hour without any information, she asked about the delay. Officer Eric Reynolds, who had arrested several of the teenagers just outside the park, told her that they were just waiting for all of the parents to arrive. Clarence Thomas's mother showed up with Antron McCray and his mother, Linda. Officer Robert Powers asked Antron if he'd been involved in the assaults in the park. Antron admitted that he'd been in the park but said that he hadn't touched anyone. Believing him, Officer Powers sent him home.

Vinicio Moore, an unemployed construction worker, and Carlos Colon, a welder, were drinking a few Budweisers that night on 101st Street just west of Central Park. It was after 1:00 a.m. when they decided to head back to their apartments on the East Side, but rather than take the bus, Vinicio suggested that they walk instead. They entered the park at 100th Street and followed a footpath that runs down below the paved road and jogging path, along the thin waterways that weave through the park. In the daytime these paths are idyllic, but at night they take on a quiet eeriness. Though there were no lights on the path, the moon was nearly full and because the night sky was clear, the path was illuminated by its glow.

Around 1:30 a.m., as they strolled along the Loch, Carlos, who was a few feet ahead of his friend, heard a muffled moaning sound coming from the side of the path. He looked to his right and saw a body so bloodied, he could barely tell what it was. He called to his friend, "Look, Vinny." The sight was so horrific, a blood-drenched body jerking and twitching, that they barely paused before breaking into a run. They darted through a grassy area up to the 102nd Street Cross Drive, where they found two police officers sitting in a parked car at the corner of the East Drive. The two men breathlessly told the officers that there was a man, badly beaten, down by the path.

Moore and Colon led the officers in their car down to where the body lay, the headlights illuminating the scene for the first time. Officer

Joseph Walsh got out and approached. He quickly realized that it was, in fact, a woman, naked except for her jogging bra, which had been pushed up around her armpits. She lay in a muddy puddle, with her hands bound, palms facing each other, in front of her face. Her legs were violently but involuntarily kicking at the air. He quickly turned back to his partner and yelled for him to call a "bus," police lingo for an ambulance. When he turned back, he noticed that one of her eyes was puffed shut and it appeared that there were cracks in her head. Walsh tried to talk to her, to reassure her, but he got no response. Then he noticed that behind her hands she was gagged. He gently pulled a wad of cloth out of her mouth, letting it fall around her throat. This loosened the restraints on her hands and her arms began thrashing, as well.

Walsh tried again to talk to her, hoping that with the gag gone she could respond. At first he thought she might, as her open eye seemed to be looking at him, but he soon realized that there was no recognition there. She was looking right through him, completely unaware of his presence. He tried putting a blanket over her, but the involuntary jerking of her body kept throwing it off.

At 2:08 a.m., an ambulance arrived at the 102nd Street Cross Drive. EMS technicians quickly checked the vital signs of the injured woman. Trisha Meili's open eye did not respond to a flashlight, indicating that she'd suffered some type of brain damage. Estelle Paris, one of the EMTs, felt a soft spot in her skull that suggested a fracture, but the bones in her lower extremities seemed to be intact. Most of her torso was lying in an inch or two of water, and her body felt cold to the touch. Her pulse was so weak that they were unable to take a reading from her wrist and only got a faint pulse from her carotid artery. Paris carefully untied the cloth that was binding Meili's hands. It was her long-sleeved T-shirt. The sleeves had been twisted into a rope and were wrapped tightly enough to reach around her head to gag her. The shirt was so soaked with her blood that no trace of white remained.

There was no identification on the jogger, and even her keys were missing, so the EMTs and police had no clues as to her identity. The

EMTs put Meili on a stretcher and took her back up to their ambulance, which was still idling on the Cross Drive. By then, two other ambulances had arrived and more paramedics attended to Meili. One of the EMTs cut off her jogging bra and intubated her to help her breathe. They put MAST trousers on her, inflatable rubber pants that add pressure to the lower extremities to increase the blood flow away from the legs and toward the brain. They also took a blood sample and gave her IV fluids before racing to the hospital.

Metropolitan Hospital, on First Avenue between Ninety-seventh and Ninety-ninth streets, on the border of East Harlem, is a complex of light gray brick boxes with little sense of architectural style. Metropolitan is one of the city's public hospitals, designed in the 1930s but not built until the late 1950s, when things began to return to normalcy after World War II. Dr. Isaac Sapozhnikov, the attending physician on duty there that night, was the first to treat Trisha Meili when she arrived by ambulance at 2:29 a.m.

Her situation was grave. "Functionally exsanguinated," the doctors called it; Meili had essentially bled out, losing between 75 and 80 percent of the blood in her body. She rated a 4 on the Glasgow Coma Scale, the common measure of neurological function used by doctors. The lowest possible score on that scale is 3, for someone in a deep coma or dead. Her blood pressure was 70 over zero, and she was hypothermic, with a body temperature close to eighty-five degrees. She was pronounced "likely to die."

Gracie Cuffee, Kevin's mother, still suffered from the lingering effects of a stroke she'd had seven years earlier. At the Central Park Precinct around 2:30 a.m., weak and tired, she asked again about when she could take her son home. By then, parents of three of the other young men had arrived; only Raymond Santana did not have a guardian present at the precinct. The police had tried to reach his father, but when he hadn't arrived within a few hours, they'd begun calling Raymond's older sister and grandmother, as well. Officer Reynolds explained to the waiting parents that as soon as all the family members had arrived, they would hand out tickets to appear in family court and then send them home. The parents continued to sit, believing that they would soon be able to leave with their sons.

The officers at the Central Park Precinct had actually intended to send the teenagers home with summonses, as they had told their parents. But at 3:00 a.m., Detective José Rosario, who had been dispatched to Metropolitan Hospital to check on the jogger, called the Central Park Precinct. He ordered the desk officer to continue holding the teenagers. A woman had been brutally raped and beaten in Central Park and she would probably die.

Detective Robert Honeyman, from the Crime Scene Unit, arrived at Central Park around 4:00 a.m. on the twentieth of April. Detectives from the Nightwatch squad were there, too, as well as Patrolman Joseph Walsh, who'd been first on the scene with his partner. It was still dark as Honeyman examined the area with a flashlight. He started on the Cross Drive, where he noted two spots of blood on the road. He saw a narrow path, where the grass had been flattened, clearly visible in the dewy ground, leading north away from the road. He measured its width to be between sixteen and eighteen inches across. He followed the drag marks to a large tree more than seventy feet away. Next to the tree was more blood. He looked north again into the woods, where he saw the headlights of a patrol car through the trees. Droplets of blood led from the tree down to the area where the car waited. The lights were shining on the bloodiest part of the tableau, the exact spot where the victim had been discovered. The ground cover there was damp and stained with blood in a pool five feet in diameter. Honeyman's shoes were covered in mud by the time he was finished.

The detective took blood and soil samples from each location and collected hairs from the crime scene. He found a rock with blood and hair near the large tree, then discovered the victim's sneakers, pants, and socks scattered into the woods, sometimes dozens of feet from where Trisha Meili had been found. One sneaker had been untied and the insole was found discarded near the pool of blood.

By the time fourteen-year-old Raymond Santana's father and grandmother finally arrived at the Central Park Precinct around 5:00 a.m., the police officers knew that a woman had been raped in Central Park, and what had before been a relatively simple matter destined for family court had suddenly become a major case.

When a serious crime is committed between the hours of 1:00 a.m. and 8:00 a.m., the first detectives to respond are those in the Nightwatch squad, who begin the investigation and then turn it over when the regular precinct detectives arrive for their shifts at 8:00 a.m. Detectives Farrell and Whelpley of the Nightwatch squad were at the Central Park Precinct early that morning and began their investigation by interviewing Lamont McCall, one of the teenagers arrested in the park the night before, at 5:00 a.m. Since Lamont was only thirteen years old, police could not speak to him without a guardian, as is the law with anyone under the age of sixteen. When McCall's mother was called in to the youth room, where the teenagers had been waiting throughout the night, the four other youths were sent out to sit with their families in the waiting area.

Lamont McCall described his evening in the park to the detectives, including chasing a male jogger by the reservoir and witnessing another male jogger being hit with a pipe by one of the other kids. The interview lasted less than an hour and McCall was sent home with a court appearance ticket. At 6:00 a.m., the detectives called Clarence Thomas and his mother into the juvenile room. His statement was similar, though somewhat more detailed. He listed many of the others who'd been in the park that night and described them beating "the bum," throwing rocks at cars, and chasing and assaulting male joggers along the reservoir path. Soon Thomas, too, was sent home with a court date. It seemed to the remaining parents that their sons would also soon be released.

Back at Metropolitan Hospital, doctors and nurses were desperately trying to resuscitate Meili. Intravenous fluids were given, then blood. A CAT scan was conducted to look for internal injuries; given her state, it seemed likely that she must be bleeding internally. Because of her jerking movements, the CAT scan was somewhat inconclusive, but it didn't seem to show any internal bleeding. The doctors were surprised but unconvinced.

Trisha Meili's unconscious but still-flailing body was taken to the surgical intensive care unit after the CAT scan. Though the doctors believed that the most important task was keeping the woman alive, they also knew that a crime had occurred, and they needed to preserve any evidence they could. Dr. Junith Thompson, a fourth-year OB-GYN resident, was called in at 6:00 a.m. to perform what is called "a rape kit." Meili was strapped to the bed to control her involuntary movements. Dr. Thompson and a nurse used Q-tips to collect swabs from Meili's cervix and rectum, and combed for pubic hair samples. The nurse scraped under Meili's fingernails, looking for other valuable evidence. Though they suspected that the victim, still unidentified at that point, had been raped, because of the way she'd been found nearly naked at the scene, Dr. Thompson did not note any trauma to the genital area or uterus. This did not rule out rape, as victims do not always show bruising or tearing, and bits of leaves and other debris found in the genital area seemed to confirm their suspicions.

Around 8:00 a.m., Dr. Robert Kurtz, the director of the surgical intensive care unit, arrived to take over the treatment of the woman, whose identity was still a mystery. Another CAT scan was done, which confirmed that she had no internal bleeding, meaning that she'd lost nearly all of the blood in her body just through the lacerations on her scalp.

Further examination revealed that her skull was fractured above the left eye and that there was also a "blowout fracture" around that eye, which occurs when blunt force is applied to an eyeball, transmitting that force through the eye in all directions and shattering the bones of the socket.

A neurosurgeon set up an intracranial pressure-monitoring device, and when it showed swelling in the brain, doctors administered a drug to subdue the inflammation.

The initial efforts of the EMTs and emergency room doctors had worked; Trisha Meili was now stable, though she remained in a deep coma. Her doctors marveled that she had even survived the first few hours.

Just as Dr. Kurtz was first seeing the unidentified patient, whose survival and recovery would occupy him for weeks, Pat Garrett arrived at the Salomon Brothers office on Broad Street in downtown Manhattan. A friend and colleague of Trisha Meili, he'd made plans to meet her at her apartment to see her new stereo at ten o'clock the previous evening. When he'd arrived there, he'd rung the buzzer but gotten no answer: then he'd called from a pay phone and left a message on her answering machine. Garrett had been worried, but he decided against calling the police and eventually went home.

When Garrett arrived at work around 8:00 a.m. and Meili wasn't in yet, he became alarmed. She was usually at her desk by then. Her secretary hadn't heard from her, either, and they knew she wasn't traveling. Meanwhile, another of Meili's colleagues, Peter Vermylen, had heard a report on the radio on his way to work that morning about a woman who had been attacked in Central Park. He knew that Meili ran in the park, and concerned that it might be her, he checked in at her office as he got to work. When she wasn't there, he spoke to her secretary and then immediately called the police. He reached a detective, who asked if she wore any "distinctive piece of jewelry." Vermylen asked Meili's secretary, who described to him the small gold ring in the shape of a bow. He passed this detail back to the police. "It's her," the detective said, and asked if someone could come to the hospital to make an identification.

Linda Fairstein, the chief of the Sex Crimes Prosecution Unit of the district attorney's office, learned of the horrific rape at 9:00 a.m. and immediately sprang to action. Fairstein was already famous, having prosecuted Robert Chambers, the so-called Preppie Murderer, but she rarely tried cases anymore. As head of the Sex Crimes Unit, she assigned cases to the ADAs who reported to her.

A seventeen-year veteran of the Manhattan DA's office, Fairstein had been hired right out of the University of Virginia School of Law. By 1976, she was in charge of the Sex Crimes Prosecution Unit, and she made a career out of advocating for victims. She wore designer clothes and was well connected in New York social circles, and she would later be considered for attorney general under President Clinton. Fairstein was part of District Attorney Robert Morgenthau's inner circle, but she had a history of contentious relationships with the other high-ranking women within his office, including Nancy Ryan, the deputy chief of the Trial Division and another of Morgenthau's protégées. Ryan also heard about the rape that morning, and she began her day by assigning the case to homicide prosecutor Peter Casolaro. Fairstein was soon in Ryan's office, ready to do battle for the case. She argued that since the victim was still alive, the case should not be assigned to a homicide prosecutor, saying that her team was well up to the task. Ryan backed down and let Fairstein take the case.

Fairstein called on Assistant District Attorney Elizabeth Lederer, whom she trusted to handle the inevitable media frenzy calmly while working the case. Lederer, thirty-six, was a petite woman with short, tight curls in her brown hair and a curt and professional manner. She was newly married and lived on the Upper West Side, not far from Central Park, where she sometimes ran along the same paths as Trisha Meili.

She had joined the DA's office right out of Suffolk Law School in 1979 and had been working in the Sex Crimes Prosecution Unit for five years. She had taken a year off from the district attorney's office to work at a law firm for a larger paycheck, but she found that she preferred criminal work for the "sense of justice" she felt in putting criminals behind bars. Lederer was known as a competent but unforgiving prosecutor who was always thoroughly prepared and who rarely lost a case. This new challenge, however, would define her career.

Waiting in the clerical area of the Community Affairs office at the Central Park Precinct, Gracie Cuffee was exhausted and weak from staying awake all night, hoping that her son, Kevin Richardson, would be released. She'd seen Lamont McCall and Clarence Thomas sent home after interviews with the detectives in the youth room, so she pleaded that Kevin be allowed to go next. By then, members of the Central Park Precinct's own detective squad were beginning their shifts, taking over from the Nightwatch detectives. At 9:40 a.m., eleven hours after his arrest, fourteen-year-old Kevin and his mother followed Detectives Carlos Gonzalez and John O'Sullivan of the Central Park Precinct into the juvenile room. The room was fairly small, with four desks and a few filing cabinets. Kevin and his mother were seated behind a desk in the back of the room. The detectives started by reading Kevin his Miranda rights and then began asking questions.

Because the rape had occurred in Central Park, Detective Humberto "Bert" Arroyo of the Central Park Detective Squad was placed in charge of the investigation. But soon, as word of the crime reached the upper echelons of the NYPD, elite detectives from the Manhattan North Homicide Squad began arriving at the Central Park Precinct. The Manhattan North unit is made up of the most experienced and effective detectives on the force, who are often called in on important cases to assist the local precincts in investigations. There was no homicide yet in this case, so typically Sex Crimes Unit detectives would have handled the case, but the jogger's condition was so grave that she was not expected to survive.

Twenty minutes after Kevin Richardson's interview began with the Central Park detectives, Detectives John Hartigan and Scott Jaffer, both of the Manhattan North Homicide Squad, entered the juvenile room, joining Detectives Gonzalez and O'Sullivan. Detective Hartigan was one of the NYPD's very best, a veteran with twenty-five years on the force, twenty of them with a detective's shield. He excelled at interrogations, at convincing suspects to open up to him, and at getting them to confess under any circumstance.

The goal of any interrogation, by definition, is to elicit a confession from a guilty party, not to investigate the truth of a denial. The common tactics used to gain confessions are based on the idea that only guilty people are interrogated in the first place. In theory, when a suspect is brought in for questioning, detectives begin with an "interview," in which information is gathered and the police make an assessment as to the guilt or innocence of the party. In this step, a nonaccusatory question-and-answer period is meant to allow the detective an opportunity to gather more information and to make observations about the suspect that might indicate that he is lying. Once they decide that they are speaking with a guilty party, the interrogation begins. Detectives often believe that they are experts at separating truth from lies, but studies have shown that this is a false confidence.

In this case, scientific evidence was not yet available to the detectives, so their decision to aggressively interrogate Kevin Richardson and others who were in the park that night was entirely based on their own instinctive assumptions about the young men.

Around 10:00 a.m., Pat Garrett, Trisha Meili's friend and colleague, arrived at Metropolitan Hospital to try to identify the woman still known to the police and the hospital staff as Jane Doe. An officer there showed him photographs, but the body they depicted was so battered that he couldn't recognize his friend. He was then led to her room, where he saw a face so swollen, cut, and bruised that he was still not sure if it was Meili. Then he saw the gold ring.

Doctors and police now knew that her name was Patricia Ellen Meili, but most newspapers, which were just beginning to piece together the story of the brutal crime, followed an unwritten rule not to publish the names of rape victims. Instead, they called her the "Central Park Jogger."

Just before noon, a group of detectives were dispatched to pick up Antron McCray and Clarence Thomas and take them, along with their families, back to the precinct. Though Thomas had already been interviewed, detectives decided they had more questions to ask. In his apartment in the Martin Luther King, Jr., housing project in Harlem, Clarence told the detectives that a metal pipe he'd seen in the park had been passed between his friend Antron McCray and "the tall guy," probably a reference to Yusef Salaam, who was six three, but he said that neither of them had wielded the pipe in the beating of a male jogger that he'd witnessed. He also told police that Lamont McCall and three others had beaten "the bum" before dragging him off the road, leaving him there bleeding.

Thomas and his mother, Gloria, went with the detectives back to the precinct. On the way, they picked up Antron and his parents, Bobby and Linda McCray, from their apartment on 111th Street. At the Central Park Precinct, the media had begun to gather outside, forcing the detectives, the suspects, and their families to pass through a throng of reporters and cameras just to move between the two separate buildings of the precinct. Antron and Clarence and their families were soon taken to the 20th Precinct, a more traditional and spacious building on West Eighty-second Street, where the investigation would continue.

Back at the Central Park Precinct, Kevin's interrogation was still going on and becoming increasingly intimidating and aggressive, especially when his mother was called outside the room to speak with other detectives. At times, as many as five detectives were standing around him in the youth room. After a long night, Gracie Cuffee was not feeling well enough to stay there any longer. At 11:40 a.m., she signed a consent form that allowed her twenty-four-year-old daughter, Angela, to sit in with Kevin as the detectives continued their barrage of questions. Angela arrived having no idea of the kind of trouble her little brother was in.

At one point during the interrogation, the detectives noticed a scratch on Kevin's left cheek. Kevin explained that he'd gotten a bruise from the police officer who'd tackled him the night before, but the detectives didn't believe him. Detective Gonzalez said that he would call that officer, and he threatened that if the officer didn't back up Kevin's story, Kevin would have a problem.

Over the course of nearly three hours, the detectives convinced Kevin to provide a statement, admitting that he'd witnessed and even taken part in the rape of the female jogger. At 1:00 p.m., Kevin signed a statement that he'd handwritten. By then, his father, Paul Richardson, had arrived, so he and Angela signed the statement, as well. The statement described the night in the park, including the assault on an "old man," throwing rocks at a taxi, reaching for a couple on a two-person bicycle, and beating up a male jogger. Then he wrote about the rape:

> . . . she was knocked out thats when Antron, Raymond, and Steve took her close off. Before that happened when Mike hit her down I tried to grab her. I got scratch on my face, so I moved back and everybody started feeling on her I saw somebody (Raymond) pulling her pantys off, I saw somebody holden her arms and legs. Raymond had her arms and Steve had her legs and Antron had sex with her. Before, thats when she was yelling stop and help. She was unconscious when they had her on the floor. Before this happen they had dragged her into the bushes. Everybody left and she was still their. The cops stoped five of us and arrested us and I was the one that didn't rape her.

Though Kevin had not admitted to raping the jogger, the fact that he had placed himself at the scene, saying he had touched the jogger and witnessed others rape her, was legally just as significant. The law does not require someone to have committed a rape to be convicted of it, only to be "acting in concert" with those who did, though of course Kevin didn't understand that. The detectives had what they needed, though Kevin had gotten many of the details wrong, most notably inventing shorts that the jogger had not been wearing, describing a tank top rather than a long-sleeved shirt, and mentioning that someone had ripped her "blouse."

Despite his statement, Kevin and his family still believed the officers when they said that he would soon be going home. After his statement was signed, officers moved Kevin and his family to the 20th Precinct, where the investigation was continuing.

Still at the Central Park Precinct, Raymond Santana had waited fifteen hours since his arrest the evening before. His interview finally began at 1:40 p.m. on Thursday. Detectives Hartigan and Jaffer from the Manhattan North Homicide Squad worked with Detective Arroyo, who was leading the investigation for the Central Park Precinct. Though Raymond's father and grandmother had arrived at the precinct around 5:00 a.m., his father had left for work soon after that, not yet understanding the seriousness of the situation. When the interview began, only Raymond's grandmother, Natividad Colon, was there to serve as his guardian, and she spoke limited English. Detective Arroyo, a Puerto Rican, translated the Miranda rights into Spanish for Mrs. Colon's benefit. But once they began asking questions, the interview shifted entirely into English.

The detectives yelled and swore at Raymond. They asked him the same questions over and over, and various detectives kept coming in and out of the room, sometimes pulling Raymond's grandmother out with them, so that he could be more vigorously interrogated.

Three hours later, Raymond's interrogation had produced a detailed written statement, in which he admitted having witnessed the attack on Antonio Diaz, the "bum," from afar, as well as the assaults on several male joggers near the reservoir. It mentioned nothing about the rape. Raymond and Detective Hartigan signed the statement, but Raymond's grandmother refused to because she didn't understand it, so Hartigan wrote that she had been present during the interrogation. Then Raymond Santana, Sr., Raymond's father, returned to the precinct after his shift as a nurse's aide at the Terence Cardinal Cooke Health Care Center, located on Fifth Avenue, across from Central Park. When he saw that Raymond had already given a statement, he and his mother left to get something to eat and bring food back for Raymond. Hartigan and Arroyo remained with Raymond, who still believed that he would be released now that he had signed the statement.

Meanwhile, as Raymond's interrogation was being conducted, Antron McCray and his parents were taken into room 215 at the 20th Precinct. At 3:15 p.m., Detectives Hildebrandt and McCabe of the Manhattan North Homicide Squad and Detective Carlos Gonzalez from the Central Park Precinct began their questioning.

With intense pressure from the detectives on Antron to admit that he had participated in the rape, Linda McCray was crying and yelling, insisting that Antron was telling them everything he knew. The detectives asked Mrs. McCray to leave the room, under the pretense that Antron might be shy about making admissions in front of his mother, but it effectively separated Antron from his greatest supporter and protector. Bobby McCray, Antron's stepfather, remained in the room. Detective Hildebrandt pulled Bobby outside and encouraged him to help the detectives get Antron to confess. Though Bobby believed that his son was telling the truth and had not participated in the rape they were accusing him of, he was also afraid that they were not going to let Antron go unless they got what they wanted. He, too, still believed that Antron would go home if he provided a statement. Bobby spoke to Antron alone, telling him that he believed him but that he had to tell the police what they wanted to hear, or else they were going to put him in jail. At first, Antron responded that he wasn't going to lie, and in his frustration and anger at the situation, Bobby McCray threw a chair across the room.

By 5:00 p.m., Antron had signed an incriminating statement. In it, he admitted to participating in the attack on the "bum," seeing the duo on the tandem bike, assaulting a male jogger with a pipe, and holding the arm of a female jogger while others "jumped on." Antron placed the rape of the female jogger before the assault at the reservoir, unlike Kevin, who'd said it was the last event of the night. And Antron described the rape as having happened near the reservoir, rather than by the Loch, almost half a mile away, where the victim was actually found, and he incorrectly described what the jogger had been wearing. He implicated Clarence Thomas, Kevin Richardson, and the "tall black kid" in the rape. Antron and his parents signed the statement. Detective Hildebrandt told the McCray family that they would be there for a while and that the district attorney would probably want to videotape Antron's statement. The McCrays went out and brought pizza and soda back, and then they sat, stunned, eating in the juvenile room.

Back at the Central Park Precinct, while Raymond's father and grandmother were out getting food, Detective Hartigan spoke to Raymond alone, despite the standard practice of not interrogating suspects under sixteen without a parent or guardian present. After that conversation, Raymond made an addition to his original statement. The new part said that after they had beaten the male jogger, Raymond had seen Kevin Richardson, with a scratch on his face, "struggling" with a female jogger. "Steve [Lopez] came over and was holding her arms with his legs, Antron came and started ripping her clothes off, Antron pulled her pants off and she was screaming, Steve covered her mouth with his right hand and Kevin pulled down his pants and had sex with her. When she was on the floor, I grabbed her tits." Raymond's father and grandmother had left the precinct, so only Raymond and the detectives signed the addendum at 5:40 p.m.

Afterward, Detectives Michael Sheehan, Rudy Hall, and August

"Augie" Jonza, all from the Manhattan North Homicide Squad, drove Raymond over to the 20th Precinct. On the way, they went looking for the pipe that had been used in the assault on John Loughlin, which Raymond thought might have been dropped outside the park after Antron had used it to break lightbulbs at a construction site on Columbus Avenue. During their ride, Raymond admitted again to having been present at the rape but tried to diminish his own culpability. "I didn't have anything to do with the rape of that lady. All I did was touch her tits," he said.

When Raymond Santana, Sr., and Natividad Colon returned to the Central Park Precinct with burgers from a fast-food joint, Raymond had already been moved. They finally caught up with him at the 20th Precinct, where he had a chance to eat his first meal, twenty hours after his arrest.

At the Central Park Precinct, Detectives Hartigan and Arroyo began to interrogate Steve Lopez, who had been arrested alongside Raymond just outside Central Park the evening before. It was now 6:00 p.m., nearly twenty hours after his arrest. His parents, Eldomiro, a postal worker, and Magdalena, a homemaker, both from Puerto Rico, joined him at the precinct. They, too, lived in the north tower of the Schomburg complex, downstairs from Kevin Richardson, Korey Wise, and Yusef Salaam.

His statement was signed three hours later. In it, Lopez described the events of the evening, including the incidents with the tandem bikers, Antonio Diaz, and four male joggers near the reservoir. He didn't admit any participation in those assaults, claiming only to have witnessed them. Lopez and his parents signed the statement, but the detectives weren't satisfied; Kevin, Antron, and Raymond had already implicated Lopez in the rape, and the detectives still hoped to get a confession out of him. They continued pressing about the jogger, asking more questions, but Lopez would not admit to anything related to the female jogger, even as a witness. Finally, Lopez's father, Eldomiro, told the detectives to stop, ending the interrogation, though Lopez would later repeat a similar story in a videotaped statement.

Although Detective Hartigan had been able to get an incriminating statement out of Raymond Santana earlier in the evening, it had not been made in the presence of a guardian, making its admissibility shaky. When Raymond Santana, Sr., returned again to the precinct at 10:00 p.m., Detectives Sheehan and Jonza showed him Raymond's earlier statement and told him they needed to go over it with his son again. With his father now present, Sheehan told Raymond to tell him just what he had said to Detective Hartigan, without leaving anything out. This session produced a second written statement, elaborating on the admissions he'd made earlier, including his participation in the rape, his claim that Kevin, Antron, and Steve had been present, and that he had "felt her tits." This time, Raymond and his father both signed.

The Manhattan North Homicide team working at the 20th Precinct continued their investigation by picking up other teenagers who'd been named by those already in custody. On the evening of April 20, twenty-four hours after those first arrests, four detectives from Manhattan North arrived at the Schomburg towers with a list of names.

At 10:45 p.m., Detectives Taglioni, Hall, Freck, and Bier got off the elevator on the twenty-first floor of the north Schomburg tower, looking for Yusef Salaam. Unlike most of the other kids who'd been in the park the night before, Yusef Salaam had gone to school that day, a Thursday. He went to Rice, a Christian school, which didn't have the day off for Passover, which the city's public schools did. When he got home that afternoon, Yusef went over to Korey's girlfriend Lisa's apartment, where he learned about the rape in the park from the news.

When the detectives arrived at Yusef's apartment, Yusef's sister Aisha answered the door and told them that Yusef wasn't home. Just then,

Yusef, Korey Wise, and their friend Eddie de la Paz stepped out of the elevator. Detective Taglioni asked for their names and ages, aware that anyone under sixteen had to be interviewed with a parent present. Yusef had on him a student transit card that had his handwritten birth date listed as 2/27/73, making him sixteen. But Yusef had written the wrong date on the card, pretending to be older to impress girls. His actual date of birth was February 27, *1974*, and he was really only fifteen. Though they had come looking for Yusef in particular, they asked all three boys to accompany them to the 20th Precinct.

Yusef's interview began just after 11:00 p.m. on Thursday in the Sex Crimes office of the 20th Precinct. It was located on the third floor, its cinder-block walls enclosing a clutter of police desks and file cabinets. Yusef sat alone in the room with Detectives McKenna, Taglioni, and Hall.

Downstairs, Yusef's family and friends began arriving at the precinct. Yusef's cousin and her fiancé, as well as David Nocenti, the assistant U.S. attorney who acted as Yusef's mentor, were told that they could not see him. Linda Fairstein, chief of the Sex Crimes Prosecution Unit of the district attorney's office, came out and took issue with Nocenti's presence, pointing out that as a U.S. attorney, he had no business interfering. She lectured him about legal ethics and threatened to call his supervisor. When Nocenti suggested that she try to put herself in his shoes, and explained that he was Yusef's Big Brother, Fairstein replied, "You did a real shit job at it."

Upstairs in the interrogation room, Detective Thomas McKenna lied to Yusef, telling him that they'd found fingerprints on the jogger's satin pants and that Yusef would be going down for rape if he didn't tell them what had happened. Detectives often believe that a bluff of this sort is a perfect tactic, because they are not going so far as to tell the suspect that evidence they fabricated points to him specifically, only that there might very soon be evidence against him. In theory, only a guilty person would worry; an innocent person would remain confident that any tests would exonerate him. But herein lies a problem; innocent people have been known to confess especially *because* they believe that a scientific test will soon exonerate them, invalidating their confession. When the promise of DNA tests or fingerprint comparisons is only a bluff, there is often no evidence to contradict the confession, or juries may believe a confession even when scientific evidence proves otherwise. McKenna's ploy worked on Yusef.

Around 11:45 p.m., Yusef's mother, Sharonne Salaam, arrived at the precinct and asked to see Yusef. Linda Fairstein explained that detectives upstairs were questioning him and that she could see him as soon as they were finished. Mrs. Salaam then demanded several times to see her son immediately, saying he was a minor, but it was not until she specifically stated that he was fifteen that Fairstein and the detectives took notice. Fairstein said that they believed him to be sixteen, but Mrs. Salaam persisted. Fairstein demanded documentation, which Mrs. Salaam did not have with her. Eventually, Fairstein and the detectives relented and decided to take her word for it, only then halting the questioning.

Yusef never signed the statement that Detective McKenna had been writing, but he did sign the back of a Miranda card when the interview was interrupted at 12:30 a.m. It was now Friday. That statement, though unsigned, was still damning. Like the other boys who "confessed," Yusef described a group of kids entering the park, beating up a "bum," seeing a couple on a tandem bike, and later beating up a male jogger in army gear near the reservoir. The statement also described a rape that took place before the assault at the reservoir. Yusef's statement implicated himself, Kevin, and Korey as participating in the attack, though Yusef denied raping the woman. Yusef, like the others before him, described the rape as having happened near the reservoir, where the male joggers had also been harassed and assaulted, nearly seven hundred yards from where Trisha Meili had actually been attacked. Now that his mother had succeeded in halting the interrogation, the detectives and prosecutors would not have another chance to question him.

———

Around the same time, at 12:30 a.m. Friday morning, Detectives Robert Nugent and John Hartigan of the Manhattan North Homicide Squad began an interview with Korey Wise in the Sex Crimes office of the 20th Precinct. Unlike Yusef, Korey actually was sixteen years old, and he did not ask for a lawyer or guardian to be present, so his interrogation was conducted alone, with only the detectives in the room.

Korey signed a written statement after a two-and-a-half-hour interrogation with Detective Hartigan. In his confession, Korey admitted to having been in the park, having witnessed the attack on "the bum," and having chased a few other joggers and bicyclists. He said that he ran from the park when a police car came with its spotlight on, and that he had heard the next day from Yusef Salaam about the beating of a male jogger near the reservoir and about the attack and rape of a female jogger by Kevin Richardson and Steve Lopez. He also explained that Yusef had told him that Kevin and Steve Lopez later beat up a guy in a van and then were arrested, possibly a distortion of what he'd heard about Kevin and Steve having been arrested by officers in a Parks Department van.

After the statement was signed, Hartigan left and Korey remained sitting with Detective Nugent. They had a brief conversation, after which Nugent reported that Korey suddenly mentioned for the first time having witnessed the rape, admitting that he'd watched the attack on the female jogger from behind a tree.

By that time, Antron McCray and his family had been moved from the 20th Precinct to the 24th, located on 100th Street between Amsterdam and Columbus, to make a videotaped statement. The 24th Precinct is another large, traditional-looking police station. It is a drab, gray 1960s building, with the space and technical capabilities to videotape confessions. The recordings took place in room 101, a crowded space with a small table in the center and filing cabinets lining the walls. Room 101 was separated from the rest of the area by metal partitions with windows. Elizabeth Lederer, the assistant district attorney who would prosecute the case, conducted the videotaped statements.

Now, at 1:00 a.m. on Friday morning, Antron sat behind a desk, facing Lederer and a video camera. His parents and Detectives Hildebrandt and McCabe sat in the room, as well. Lederer advised the family of their Miranda rights and proceeded to ask Antron about the events of April 19. In a quiet, almost feminine voice, Antron delivered the answers he thought they wanted to hear, while rocking slightly back and forth, as if in a trance. He described the attack on Antonio Diaz, the boys chasing a couple on a tandem bike, and throwing rocks at cars. According to Antron's story, they'd seen the female jogger near the tennis courts just north of the reservoir and attacked her there. Again, Antron got the location of the attack and the description of the victim's clothing completely wrong. He said they'd hidden in bushes until she came by and then pounced, hitting and kicking her, including the "tall black kid," who had hit her with a pipe.

Then Antron listed many people who "got on top of her": first the "tall black kid," then the "Puerto Rican kid with the hoodie," then Antron, then Clarence Thomas, then Kevin Richardson. Though Antron said that he "got on top of her," he denied that any penetration occurred; he said that he just wanted the other boys to think that he was having sex with her. He said that they had left her near the reservoir, just off the path. Antron then described the attack on jogger John Loughlin as having taken place after the rape. They finished the videotaping around 2:00 a.m.

At 2:30 a.m., ADA Lederer taped Raymond, who gave his statement after more than twenty-seven hours in custody, having had little sleep. His father and Detectives Hartigan and Arroyo sat in. In room 101 of the 24th Precinct, Raymond sat in a desk chair that swiveled. He nervously turned the chair back and forth as he spoke in a soft monotone. He sat, slouching, with his arms crossed.

The content of Raymond's statement was similar to his most recent written statement, where he had described having come upon Kevin Richardson and Steve Lopez struggling with the female jogger. His version asserted that Kevin, Antron, and Lopez had all participated in some way in the attack and rape of the female jogger. According to the statement, the other boys had been hitting her, and while Kevin raped her, Raymond had felt her breasts. But he said that he'd left before anything else happened.

Like Kevin and Antron, Raymond described the location of the attack as just off a path not far from the reservoir—nowhere near the spot where Trisha Meili had actually been assaulted. When Lederer asked him if she'd been "bleeding a lot," Raymond said no, though earlier in his statement, Raymond had described Steve Lopez hitting Meili in the face with a brick. During the questioning, Raymond was still wearing the clothes he had had on the night before, which bore no traces of blood.

Steve Lopez gave the next videotaped statement to ADA Lederer around 3:30 a.m., repeating essentially the same narrative he'd provided in his written statement the evening before, still mentioning nothing about a female jogger.

Just before five that morning, Kevin Richardson gave a videotaped statement to ADA Elizabeth Lederer. By then, Kevin's sister had left, and his father sat in as the guardian for the session.

On the videotape, Lederer repeatedly had to ask Kevin to speak up, as the obviously frightened boy often whispered his answers or merely shook his head. She methodically retraced his steps that evening, eliciting even greater detail about the events in the park than Kevin had previously related in his written statement to the detectives. By the end of the questioning, Kevin had described the attacks on Antonio Diaz, the couple on the tandem bike, John Loughlin, and lastly the female jogger. He denied actually having participated in any of the attacks, implicating instead some of the other kids, including Antron McCray, Raymond Santana, and Steve Lopez. Kevin said that he'd only grabbed the female jogger's arm in an attempt to stop the rape.

As with the other statements, there were obvious problems and inconsistencies in the video that should have jumped out at an experienced prosecutor like Lederer. Kevin described the site of the attack on Meili as being on the same road where they'd attacked John Loughlin, along the northern side of the reservoir, and at Lederer's prompting, he said that the jogger had been moved just slightly off the road. In fact, Meili had been found almost half a mile to the north, above the 102nd Street Cross Drive, and she had been dragged nearly a hundred feet away from the road, into a secluded area near the Loch. Kevin had also incorrectly described her attire. In his statement, he said that she had been wearing gray shorts, black biking pants, and a white tank top, whereas Meili had actually been wearing black pants, not shorts, and a long-sleeved white shirt. Kevin said that he hadn't seen anyone tie up the jogger, even though she had been found gagged and bound, with her hands tied together in front of her face. Lederer asked Kevin multiple times whether the jogger was bleeding when they left her, and both times he said that he hadn't really been able to see. In fact, Meili was so covered in her own blood that the men who found her hadn't been able to tell whether she was male or female. Yet no one seemed to doubt the authenticity of Kevin's or any of the other teenagers' statements.

At 7:00 a.m. on Friday, ADA Linda Fairstein and Detectives Michael Sheehan and Augie Jonza of the Manhattan North Homicide Squad took Kevin and Korey to the crime scene. There, they followed an officer down a muddy incline to near where Meili had been found. Then

Fairstein and Sheehan walked Kevin back up the slope to a large tree, where the leaves and branches on the ground were clearly covered in dried blood. Sheehan asked Kevin if anything looked familiar. Kevin pointed toward the blood and said, "This is where it happened."

"What happened?" Sheehan prompted.

"The raping," Kevin said.

Kevin returned to the car and then Korey was led up the hill to the bloody scene. Before Sheehan could ask Korey anything, he began muttering to himself, "Damn, damn, that's a lot of blood," over and over. Sheehan asked why the blood surprised him, and Korey said that it had been dark, so he hadn't been able to see how much blood there was. When Sheehan then asked him if the site looked familiar, Korey said, "This is where they raped her." Detective Sheehan, knowing that Korey had claimed to have witnessed the rape from behind a tree, asked him to point out his hiding spot, but Korey was unable to identify a tree that could plausibly fit his statement.

They also went up to the 102nd Street Cross Drive, where Trisha Meili had first been attacked. According to Sheehan, Kevin and Korey were taken out of the car one at a time and each was asked, "Does any of this look familiar to you?" Kevin replied, "This is where we got her," and Korey said, "This is where they snatched her." But the boys each pointed to slightly different spots, neither of which was near the area where some blood had been left on the roadway and where Meili had actually first been hit on the head from behind.

Back at the 24th Precinct, Detective Hartigan took another pass at interrogating Korey, since he had mentioned witnessing the rape to Detective Nugent only after his statement had been signed. A second written statement was produced, with many of the same details as the first, but this time Korey placed himself at the scene as a witness. His statement implicated Kevin, Raymond, Antron, and Steve Lopez. Korey said that Steve had cut the woman's legs with a knife and that Steve and Raymond had "jerked off on her." He said that after Steve and Raymond left, he and Eddie de la Paz went closer to look at the victim, whom he described as "black and blue." In fact, Meili had not been cut with a knife, nor had enough semen been found on her body and clothes to account for Korey's dramatic description. Had Korey actually approached the victim after the attack was over, he would have seen a woman covered in blood and, only minutes after the beating, not yet black-and-blue. Both Korey and Detective Hartigan signed the new statement.

Then Detective Hartigan went to check out Korey's story about hiding behind a tree by visiting Eddie de la Paz and asking him if he had been with Korey. Eddie denied it, saying that he had not been in the park at all but that he'd seen Korey running out of the park, "looking scared."

At one point, Korey's mother arrived at the 24th Precinct, looking for him. Five months pregnant, she'd already been to the Central Park Precinct and central booking in her search for her son. When she asked to see Korey, a detective said, "Why would you want to see a scumbag like him?"

At 12:35 p.m. on Friday, April 21, Elizabeth Lederer began a videotaped interview with Korey. He repeated many of the same details from his second written statement, including his assertions that the jogger had been cut on the legs with a knife, that Steve and Raymond had ejaculated onto her body, and that the other boys had raped her while Korey and Eddie watched from behind a tree. When Korey again claimed that he'd been with Eddie, Lederer interrupted him, saying that Eddie had denied his story. Korey tried to cover his tracks by claiming that he'd been fibbing for Eddie, who had asked him to lie, but then Korey went right back to describing the crime scene. He said that there had been blood all over, but he also said that the jogger's arms had been spread out to the side, though Meili's hands had actually been tied in front of her face.

Korey described the location of the attack better than the others had, but he had been to the crime scene earlier that morning and had been shown where in the park the rape had occurred. Lederer also held up photographs of the crime scene during the interview to refresh his recollection. She even showed him photos of Meili's injuries.

"Do you see the side of her head? How did those marks get on her head?" Lederer asked.

"Mark knife . . ."

"Those aren't the injuries of a knife. The doctor says she has a fractured skull," she said, correcting him.

Lederer went on to ask Korey, "Did you see anybody with a stone or brick or any kind of object?" Korey said that someone had told him about a brick or rock the next day. First, he said it was Al Morris, but Lederer pointed out that Korey had earlier said that Al wasn't even there. Korey then said it was Yusef who had told him. He continued to dig himself deeper and deeper into a hole, desperately trying to give Lederer what he thought she wanted, creating more inconsistencies with every answer. Toward the end of the taping session, Lederer again asked him about the injuries to Meili's face, and he said that the other boys had punched her.

Lederer responded, "You get a punch, you see a fighter, you get, you get a punch, you get a bruise."

"Yeah, that's true," Korey replied.

"You don't get bleeding, you don't get these lines, you don't get a fractured skull from it."

"The more it look, the more it look, like it's, it's for, like a rock, rock wound," Korey stuttered.

"Did you see anybody hit her with, with anything but their hands?"

"I seen . . ."

"I don't want you to think that you have to say that, but I want to know what you saw that explains how she got so badly hurt."

"I did see Kevin pick up a, a hand rock, a small hand rock, hit her across the face with it."

Korey's videotaped statement hadn't resolved anything, except to make Lederer and the detectives even more skeptical about his version of events. His descriptions were detailed, sometimes bizarrely so, as when he answered Lederer's question about what drew him to the scene of the crime: "See, I knew it was no rabbit because rabbits don't make noise coming towards trees and stuff, but I heard a lot of giggling and a lot of running coming down the hill . . ." Often his explanations didn't make sense, and given the variations between all three of his statements, the detectives and prosecutors were worried about the doubts a good defense attorney could raise in the minds of jurors.

After the session, Detective Hartigan pulled Korey aside and told him that it looked very bad for him, that no jury would believe him because of these three different statements. Hartigan offered Korey the chance to change his story one more time, and Korey agreed to sit down for another videotaped statement. Korey was under the impression that he would be allowed to go home once he provided the statement the detectives wanted.

The second video began at 3:15 p.m. Korey had been up all night, and his body language demonstrated his tiredness and his difficulty understanding and communicating. He sat leaning forward, as if craning to hear and understand; he constantly raised his eyebrows and nodded, as if to prove that he understood and agreed with what was being said. This time, Korey admitted to a greater participation in the various attacks that evening. He said that he had kicked the "bum" and the jogger by the reservoir during those attacks. When he described the rape, he put himself closer, with Kevin, Raymond, Steve, and Yusef at the scene, rather than watching from afar. Korey said that he had just been "playing with her legs" and that his friend Yusef had only touched her breasts, but Steve, Raymond, and Kevin had all raped her.

In another strange account, Korey described the object that was used to beat the jogger, but from her point of view: "Kevin hit her in the face with a rock, that's what knocked her out. She thought it was a punch, but it was a rock that hit her."

Korey also expressed some remorse, promising never to do it again. "So we were looking at her and I felt kind of bad and I kind of, this is my first extreme I did to any type of female in the street. This is my first rape. I never did this before and this is going to be my last time doing it."

Though this fourth and final interview would prove most damning, it still did not resolve the many inconsistencies in his story, and indeed those of all of the teenagers. Each of the boys had implicated others and tried to minimize his own culpability, but all of them had nonetheless placed themselves as accomplices and even participants in the gruesome crime.

Within thirty-six hours from the time Detective José Ramón Rosario called the Central Park Precinct from Metropolitan Hospital to tell the desk sergeant not to release any of the teenagers arrested in the park that night, detectives had extracted incriminating statements about the rape and beating of a female jogger from Kevin Richardson, Antron McCray, Raymond Santana, Yusef Salaam, and Korey Wise.

The detectives and prosecutors hoped that DNA and other forensic evidence gathered at the scene and from the suspects would confirm what they already believed, but the confessions, even if they would have to stand alone, were powerful evidence. Legal scholar C. T. McCormick wrote that a confession "makes the other aspects of a trial in court superfluous, and the real trial, for all practical purposes, occurs when the confession is obtained."

The very persuasive techniques that the experienced detectives of the Manhattan North Homicide Squad used to elicit confessions from five of the teenagers in the Central Park case are, for the most part, accepted and commonplace in interrogation rooms in this country.

Ideally, interrogation subjects are isolated in a stark room, with as few distractions as possible, separated from the support of family and friends, and prevented from having any control over the environment, such as raising or lowering the heat, having something to eat or drink, or simply getting up and moving around.

Though the particular psychological strategies for gaining confessions vary, the basic process is almost always the same two-step approach. Known as "maximization" and "minimization" to those who train police officers to be effective interrogators, this strategy is a version of the familiar "good cop/bad cop" routine so often seen on television and in films. First, the bad cop comes on strong, aiming to convince a suspect that his situation is hopeless. He describes the terrible fate that awaits the suspect in prison or on death row. A detective might refer to prison rapes, or how badly rapists in particular are treated, or what being executed feels like. Interrogators also frighten a suspect by making him believe that his guilt is already proven. Detectives describe, exaggerate, and invent an insurmountable pile of evidence that often doesn't exist. It is a perfectly accepted and legal practice to lie about evidence. Detectives routinely falsely tell suspects that their fingerprints, blood type, or DNA matched samples from the crime scene, or that an eyewitness or accomplice identified them as perpetrating a crime, or that they failed a lie-detector test, just as when Detective McKenna told Yusef that his fingerprints would be found on the jogger's pants. Many of the teenagers were told that others had implicated them as participating in the rape of the female jogger.

In another aspect of maximization, detectives interrupt any attempts at denial or offers of an alibi, hoping to demonstrate that these protestations are falling on deaf ears, are not credible, and will not be investigated. Indeed, to the teenagers interrogated in the Central Park case, it became clear sometime during their interrogations that repeated denials were getting them nowhere and would be disbelieved or ignored. This tactic worked brilliantly on Kevin Richardson, when Detective Gonzalez refused to believe Kevin when he explained that the scratch on his cheek had come from a police officer who had tackled him.

At the desperate and hopeless moment that these maximization tactics induce, detectives move on to the second step, minimization, appealing to the fear that grew out of the first part of the interrogation and providing an apparent way out of that terrifying situation. The person playing the role of good cop offers positive incentives for confessing, trying to convince the suspect that this is in his best interest. He might appeal to a suspect's sense of morality or religion, suggesting that he will feel better if he gets it off his chest. Or the detective might give the suspect an opportunity to minimize his involvement or the significance of the crime by suggesting that it was an accident, or self-defense, or that coconspirators forced him into it.

Detectives told the Central Park defendants that they believed them but that others had implicated them and that they should just tell the police what had happened, either as a witness or as a less culpable participant in the crime. The teenagers believed that they would soon be able to go home if they helped the detectives by giving statements and agreeing to go to the crime scene. They had been tempted by the common offer of being a "witness." Each young man tried to minimize his own involvement and place the blame for the rape on the other boys. Antron McCray listed four others who had raped the jogger, and said that he "got on top of her" but only pretended to rape her, because he felt pressure from his peers. He tried to convince the police that he was not a rapist, and he believed that by implicating others, and explaining his involvement as different from theirs, that he would not receive the same harsh punishment.

Korey Wise first claimed that he'd witnessed the attack from behind a tree and had not even been with the group. Later, during his first videotaped statement, he referred to "the accident." When Lederer asked him what he meant, he said he was talking about "the lady." Lederer pressed the subject.

"An accident is when somebody slips and falls down," she pointed out.

"Oh, my mistake. The incident," Korey said, correcting himself.

"What you saw, you saw people drag her down there?"

"Yes."

"You saw people beating her up?"

"Yes."

"You saw her so beaten up that she looks the way she looks in pictures, you call that an accident?"

Korey shook his head no. Korey's reference to an accident seemed callous to Lederer, and she reprimanded him for it. However, he might have picked up the language from one of the detectives. The suggestion that a crime was actually an accident is a common minimization technique among detectives and may well have been used in this case.

Certain detectives play to their strengths as either intimidating or friendly in the interrogation room. After Detective McKenna implied that Yusef's fingerprints would be found on the jogger's leggings, Detective Rudy Hall, the only black detective on the squad, acted sympathetically toward Yusef, trying to make him more comfortable. Similarly, Detective Hartigan played the role of the understanding good cop to both Kevin and Raymond, after the frightening presence of Detectives Gonzalez and Arroyo in their respective interrogations. The teenagers described being yelled and cursed at by detectives, and feeling intimidated. The teenagers came to believe that others were implicating them and that these kindly detectives, the good cops, could help them out of their situation if only they would help them out with a statement. Broken down by the pressure, they did.

Most of these techniques, including lying to a suspect about evidence against him or others who have implicated him, are perfectly legal and accepted. In fact, detectives are specifically trained in these methods, and there are few rules limiting what they can do in interrogations. In 1936, the Supreme Court decided in *Brown v. Mississippi* that evidence obtained through physical torture, in this case being hung from trees and whipped, was not admissible in a trial. In 1940, the Supreme Court overturned the convictions of three men in *Chambers v. Florida* because they had been held for nearly a week and subjected to continuous and intimidating interrogations in the presence of up to ten police officers at once before confessing. The court found that these extreme conditions, though not physical torture, still constituted circumstances that invalidated those confessions. Despite that second ruling, there is still no absolute definition of when this type of psychological pressure crosses the line and constitutes coercion or, worse, torture.

In the Central Park case, the teenagers were in custody for many hours, often without being offered food or the chance to sleep. Korey gave four different statements in four separate sessions, the last one ending more than seventeen hours after he was arrested. Elizabeth Lederer recorded Raymond's videotaped statement twenty-seven and a half hours after he first arrived at the precinct. The young men were often without their parents, though four of them were juveniles and Korey Wise, at sixteen, was hardly capable of protecting his own best interests in the interrogation room. Young people are especially susceptible to the pressures that can lead to false confessions. One study found that one-third of those who gave false confessions were juveniles, and half were under the age of twenty-five.

The best-known development in the rights of interrogation subjects was the 1966 ruling in *Miranda v. Arizona*. The Fifth Amendment to the Constitution states that no person "shall be compelled in any criminal case to be a witness against himself," and the Sixth Amendment guarantees the right to defense counsel. The decision in *Miranda v. Arizona* codified these rights. Now known simply as Miranda rights, and familiar to viewers of scores of films and television programs over the past decades, they state: "You have the right to remain silent. Anything you say can and will be used against you in a court of law. You have the right to an attorney. If you cannot afford an attorney, one will be appointed for you." A suspect must hear, understand, and waive these rights before being interrogated.

Each of the teenagers in the jogger case waived his rights in order to speak with his interrogators. Though logic would suggest taking advantage of these protections, innocent people or those who have little experience with the justice system are more likely to waive their Miranda rights, believing that their innocence will protect them.

Miranda rights can be further diminished by the way police present them. Detectives try to create a rapport with the suspect, hoping that he will let down his guard and try to please the detective by agreeing to waive his rights. Often when Miranda rights are read, they are portrayed as a formality, a bureaucratic nuisance that must be administered. Or detectives imply what many assume—that taking advantage of those rights will only make the suspect appear guilty.

Each of these Supreme Court decisions was intended to prevent coerced confessions by protecting the rights of interrogation subjects. But after the Miranda rights have been waived, these decisions do nothing to restrict what can be said in an interrogation. Courts have long upheld the rights of interrogators to lie to suspects, with a single exception, which stems from an 1897 Supreme Court decision. In that case, *Bram v. United States,* the court held that a confession was not admissible if it came from threats or "direct or implied promises," such as an assurance that a suspect would be treated more leniently if he confessed, or more harshly if he did not. Despite the restriction on both "direct" and "implied" promises, in the years since 1897, courts have tended only to reject confessions when there was evidence of an explicit threat or promise.

Since then, the practices of interrogators have grown more nuanced, to include threats and promises that are merely and subtly implied, and therefore more often accepted in courtrooms as legitimate. Even when an explicit threat or promise is made, it can be difficult for an interrogation suspect to prove that coercive techniques were used, as most interrogations are not recorded in their entirety, and a detective's word can carry more weight with a jury than that of the accused.

The Central Park defendants each cited the simple desire to go home as a motivating factor in his confession. After the grueling interrogations, the hours without food, the terrifying encounters with those playing bad cops, the bone-weary fatigue they all felt, and, for some, the complicated signals they were getting from their own parents and guardians, these young men wanted a respite, to leave the interrogation room and seek the shelter and protection of their families in a familiar setting. The detectives implied, suggested, or stated that they could be witnesses or that if they "told the truth," then they could go home, despite the restriction on implied promises. Desperate for a way out, the naïve teenagers relented and gave the detectives exactly what they wanted.

This desire to go home was amplified in some cases by the suspect's separation from his parents. Korey, who was sixteen years old, and Yusef, who the detectives claimed they believed to be sixteen, were both interrogated without a guardian. Detectives made sure that Raymond, Kevin, and Antron all had a parent or guardian there, as they were required to do, but at times intentionally called those guardians out of the room, leaving the young men alone with detectives who were now free to be even more threatening and intimidating.

Even when parents were there, they were often kept in the dark about the seriousness of the accusations against their boys, believing that disorderly conduct was the only charge. Officer Eric Reynolds told Kevin's mother that after the interview she would be able to take Kevin home. Once the parents were in the interrogation room with the detectives, little was explained to any of them about what was going on or the seriousness of the crimes their sons were suspected of. Gracie Cuffee was not in the room for every moment of Kevin's interrogation. Mrs. Cuffee recalled that in instances when she had briefly left the room, she had returned and heard detectives yelling and cursing at her son and encouraging him to confess, later telling him that they believed he was a good boy and could go home if he just told them what had happened.

The detectives employed this same tactic of separation when they spoke only English in their interrogation of Raymond, when they removed Antron's mother from the room and convinced his stepfather to join them in encouraging Antron to confess, and when they delayed allowing Yusef's family access to him.

Korey Wise, though the least developed emotionally and intellectually of the boys, was the eldest, and as such, the police were not required to invite a parent into the interrogation room, so he experienced the lengthy ordeal on his own. In his first session with detectives, Korey signed a statement about being in the park and witnessing some of the assaults on the East Drive before going home. Afterward, Korey sat alone with Detective Nugent for just a couple of minutes before admitting for the first time that he had witnessed the rape. Though Nugent denied it, Korey later said that Nugent had slapped him in the face in order to convince him to talk about the rape.

Among those other teenagers who refused to admit to anything related to the female jogger, some had parents who were better equipped to defend their interests, as when Steve Lopez's father, Eldomiro, knew how to simply end his interrogation by refusing to let his son answer any more questions when the detectives began badgering him about the female jogger. Hoping to get more evidence against the teenagers they believed were responsible for the rape, detectives had pressured Dennis Commedo, another resident of the Schomburg Plaza, to say that Kevin had told him about the rape that night when he saw him in the park. Dennis later admitted that it was a lie, and his statement was never used against Kevin, but his experience in the interrogation room was not unlike that of the other teenagers, and it led him to incriminate his friend, in the hopes of pleasing the detectives.

The confessions that Kevin Richardson, Raymond Santana, Antron McCray, Yusef Salaam, and Korey Wise gave also reflected the detectives' influence on those interrogations. Kevin's and Raymond's statements contained words they would have been unlikely to use when giving their own versions of the story, such as "unconscious," "additional friends" and "numerous friends," "cyclists," and "eastbound" and "westbound." Several of the teenagers reported being fed those words, as well as details about the rape that they could not have known unless they had been there or the facts were provided to them.

The statements were also not written down from the start of the interviews. The detectives waited until they heard what they wanted about the rape before putting pen to paper, so the statements do not reflect the repeated denials or the complete narratives of the night in the park that the teenagers gave initially but which the detectives disbelieved.

In the statements provided by Antron, Yusef, Korey, Kevin, and Raymond, the descriptions of the rape vary widely, with each teenager listing a different group of perpetrators, disagreeing on the location of the attack, what the victim had been wearing, what her injuries were, and with what instruments they had been inflicted. In contrast, the other incidents in the park that night were described consistently, such as the assault on John Loughlin. Each boy who described that attack knew that it was on the path near the reservoir, that a pipe had been used to beat the man, and that a kid named Jermain Robinson, whom some identified simply by the gold caps he had on his teeth, had instigated and led the attack.

The teenagers in the Central Park case all later explained that they had confessed in the hopes of going home and ending their ordeal. Once they had lawyers and began to understand the situation they were in, they all recanted their confessions. The detectives who interrogated them believed that they were guilty from the start, and the legal—if questionable—tactics used by those detectives to extract the confessions, along with other subterfuges that probably crossed the line, caused a series of reactions in all the young men, and sometimes their families, which eventually led to coerced confessions. This particular type of false confession is known as "coerced-compliant," a situation when someone confesses despite being confident in his innocence because enough pressure is applied during an interrogation that the suspect is willing to implicate himself rather than face any alternative, or irrationally believes that confessing will improve a dreadful situation. Yusef Salaam, Korey Wise, Kevin Richardson, Antron McCray, and Raymond Santana fell prey to the intense psychological pressure exerted by experienced detectives who were already convinced of their guilt, and provided all the evidence that would be needed to prosecute them for a terrible crime they did not commit.

CHAPTER THREE

Trisha Meili grew up in the affluent suburbs of Manhattan and later Pittsburgh, where she took ballet and horseback-riding lessons. During high school, she began running with her older brother, and continued to run regularly when she went away to Wellesley College. Afterward, she studied business and international relations in a graduate program at Yale University. In 1986, she moved to New York City to work for Salomon Brothers. Her life revolved around work; she sometimes spent between twelve and fourteen hours a day at the office and rarely had time for anyone or anything outside of her job. In April 1989, she was dating a coworker, Kevin O'Reilly, but she still found time to jog in Central Park, often later in the evening because of her long hours.

Meili's call to her friend Michael Allen at 5:00 p.m. on April 19, 1989, to cancel their dinner plans was the last thing she would remember for the next five weeks.

The detectives investigating the Central Park Jogger rape, understandably anxious to solve such a horrific crime, had quickly come to a conclusion about what had happened in the park that night, and they soon shared that story with the press. "The Central Park Jogger Rape" was a sensational tale of a senseless crime. It had all the makings of an ideal tabloid story: violence, race, sex, class. The extreme brutality of the attack and the location in Central Park, New York City's "backyard," made it all the more shocking and close to home. Overtly racist coverage exploded onto the pages of many of the city's newspapers, appearing in a frenzy of outraged headlines and op-ed pieces. The victim was depicted as a star with a bright future—smart, young, rich, white. Her alleged attackers (though the word *alleged* was rarely used in the mainstream press) were described as poor, black, and "wild" and were portrayed as having no future and being seemingly prone to random, unprovoked violence. The rape exemplified the type of violence that white New Yorkers feared most.

Yet the rape of the Central Park Jogger was by no means an isolated incident. Twenty-eight other first-degree rapes or attempted rapes were reported in New York City in that same week, and none got anywhere near the attention that this one did. Eight of the victims were under sixteen. One was an eight year-old girl. The victims of those other rapes were overwhelmingly from minority communities, twenty-four of them being black or Latina women. Two were Asian. Trisha Meili was one of three white women raped that week. Two of the other rapes that week also took place in Central Park, and a rape two weeks later proved that an equally violent and horrific crime could go relatively unnoticed. On May 2, 1989, a thirty-eight-year-old African-American woman was accosted on the street in her Brooklyn neighborhood. She was forced up to a rooftop by at least two young men, who raped her and then threw her over the edge of the roof. She fell fifty feet into an air shaft, breaking both her ankles and sustaining numerous other grave injuries, but incredibly, she survived. Her attackers were also African-American. A few small articles appeared in the mainstream press detailing this attack and others, but their number paled in comparison to the coverage of the Central Park Jogger case.

The *Daily News* and the *New York Post* were the two best-selling newspapers in the New York City metropolitan area, followed by *The New York Times* and *New York Newsday*. The *Daily News, Post,* and *Newsday* were all single-fold tabloids, designed to be portable and convenient for commuters, and were hawked from newsstands and in subway stations all over the city. The *Daily News* and the *Post* had been competing with each other for decades; *Daily News* staffers received cash bonuses for coming up with the most dramatic and best-selling headlines. Both newspapers were hemorrhaging money, and with Long Island paper *Newsday*'s entry into city coverage in 1983, the competition had escalated. The rape in Central Park was a perfect story for the shocking headlines the papers craved, and dozens of reporters were assigned to the case.

Even those who didn't buy the newspapers saw the lurid headlines on their daily commute when glancing over the shoulders of fellow passengers on the bus or subway or noticing the papers littering the stations and sidewalks. The language and images of these stories, particularly those on the front page, seeped each day into the collective consciousness of the city.

The fundamental narrative of what had happened—and thus the conventional viewpoint shared by most inhabitants of New York—coalesced before any investigation of the forensics could take place. Once the teenagers' statements had been made, the police were quick to report that they had found the rapists, and local and national media outlets were soon repeating verbatim the story constructed by the police. In the first day of newspaper coverage, the *Post* reported, "A young Wall Street investment banker—on her nightly jog through Central Park—was brutally beaten, raped and left for dead by a wild pack of teens, police said yesterday." Each city paper quoted the same police official, Chief of Detectives Robert Colangelo, on the details of the attack and the arrests of the teenagers from Harlem, who, the police assured the media, had committed the crime.

News outlets competed to see who could be most outraged by the attack and who could make the boys look most guilty. The *Daily News* and *Post* headlines screamed the loudest. In the week following the attack, each paper conspicuously displayed the story on its front page six out of seven days. Frequently, entire sections with several articles each were devoted to the case. Never did those articles question whether the suspects had committed the crime, or use the word *alleged* in reference to them.

WOLFPACK'S PREY, NIGHTMARE IN CENTRAL PARK, and WILDING were all front-page headlines that first week. The story made national headlines as well, with a cover story in *People* magazine and articles in *Newsweek* and *Time*. Television news covered it too, especially in New York City. Once the details of the case emerged and the boys were revealed as suspects, the mainstream news media almost never questioned their guilt, always stating as fact the details of how the rape occurred, even as those details changed when investigators uncovered new information. Their instant judgment of the case, based upon police sources, helped to steer public opinion, and almost everything printed and said in the mainstream media encouraged the public to assume their guilt.

In the weeks after the crime, the suspects were most often seen in classic "perp-walk" photographs, being paraded in and out of police precincts or courthouses handcuffed, covering their faces with hands, hats, or shirts, or ducking away from cameras. Such images, commonly staged by police nearly everywhere, are intended to make a suspect look guilty. These walks can help the police to make their case in the public eye, and newspapers, tabloids especially, love to print them.

Beyond the fact that these mainstream outlets assumed the guilt of the Central Park suspects without any sense of journalistic skepticism, the media coverage also employed blatantly racist language and imagery. Animal references abounded. When referring to the suspects, the words *wolfpack* and *wilding* were used hundreds of times and came to be emblems of the case, a shorthand that nearly everyone used and that still elicits memories of the Central Park Jogger's rape in many minds.

The term *wilding* came to embody the coverage. By April 22, 1989, the New York City papers had grabbed hold of the word. The *Daily News* splashed it across its front page: "Park marauders call it 'WILDING' . . . and it's street slang for going berserk." The *Post*'s headline read: "WILDING"—THE NEWEST TERM FOR TERROR IN CITY THAT LIVES IN FEAR. "We're Going Wilding," *Newsday* quoted the teenagers as saying on its cover. The mainstream media agreed that the word came from the suspects themselves, who had apparently boasted to cops from their holding cells about a favorite pastime. The information, though, had come directly from the police, who frequently passed tips along to the city's reporters.

The true story of the term's origin is more complicated. There are indications that *wilding* or *wilin'* was previously used in inner cities as street slang for acting crazy, though it didn't necessarily have violent connotations. The use of the word as it appeared in the media, however, may actually have had to do with a misunderstanding. While some of the teenagers were in a holding cell, the police reported that they had been laughing and joking and began singing the popular song "Wild Thing," by rapper Tone-Lōc. In the song, doing the "wild thing" refers to sex, but police may have misinterpreted this, thinking the boys were talking about their own activities, and "wild thing" became "wilding."

Wolfpack also appeared often in the media to describe the accused. It linked the boys not just to an animal but to one feared and seen as dangerous, violent, and predatory. Since World War II, the term *wolfpack* had been used from time to time to refer to gangs of teenagers committing robberies or assaults in cities. The idea of a pack of wolves only served to amplify the fear. With the Central Park Jogger case, suddenly everyone was using *wolfpack* to describe the young men.

The New York Times, which typically tended to stay away from using such incendiary language, published an editorial the week after the attack entitled "The Jogger and the Wolf Pack." Back in December of 1987, when a group of white teenagers had attacked two black men, the newspaper called it a "racial assault" and only used the words *wolf pack* when quoting the victims, emphasizing that these were their words and not the newspaper's. "One of two black victims of what the police have termed a racial assault by a group of white youths in the Bath Beach section of Brooklyn on Christmas Day likened their attackers yesterday to 'a wolf pack' intent on hurting or killing them." The title of the article also expressed the newspaper's unwillingness to adopt the term: "Assault

Victims Liken Attackers to 'Wolf Pack.' " Only when the members of the supposed "wolf pack" were minorities did the *Times* embrace the phrase and drop the quotation marks.

The boys—and their alleged actions—were variously called "bestial," "savage," "brutal," "bloodthirsty," "evil," and "mutant." Several columnists and people writing letters to the editor emphasized that they were worse than animals. "I think [calling them a wolf pack] is an insult to animals in general and wolves in particular. . . . Wolves have too much class to do such things," wrote one columnist.

The racism inherent in the type of animal references used to describe the black and Latino teenagers accused of the Central Park rape was not new. For centuries, animal terms have been applied to blacks as a means of separating them from whites and of denigrating their status, and this tradition is especially pronounced when a crime has been committed.

In 1931, nine black teenagers were falsely accused of raping two young white women as they rode the rails through Alabama. They became known as the Scottsboro Boys, and newspapers employed language that would later be echoed in the Central Park coverage. The Scottsboro Boys were referred to as "fiends" and "black brutes." J. Glenn Jordan, writing for the *Huntsville Times,* complained that the boys were in their cells, telling "nasty jokes, unafraid, denying to outsiders that they were guilty, laughing, laughing, joking, joking, unafraid of the consequences." He called them "beasts unfit to be called human."

Newspaper reports indicated similar outrage at the Central Park teens' seemingly callous behavior; it was felt that the boys failed to show enough remorse for the crime nearly everyone believed they had committed. An article in the *Post* quoted one of the boys as saying that "it was fun," and accused them of "laughing and joking" in their cells. A cover of the *Daily News* showed a photograph of Antron McCray, hands cuffed behind him, being led into a police precinct, with the words "she wasn't nothing" attributed to him.

Columns, op-ed pieces, and letters to the editor allowed for even more vituperation in the coverage, and placed on display the most vitriolic reactions to the teenagers. One letter to the *Daily News* asked, "When will people learn not to go into Central Park at night? Don't they know that vicious two-legged animals with sublevel mentalities roam that park just looking for victims? Signs should be posted at each entrance: *Enter at your own risk.*" Another wrote from Rockaway Beach, "If that woman jogging in Central Park had had a gun, she might not be fighting for her life in the hospital. She might be in jail like Bernie Goetz. Some justice!"

In the *Post*, Pete Hamill's first column about the rape fell under the headline A SAVAGE DISEASE CALLED NEW YORK. "This was a savage little pack that came out of the darkness of a spring night, eventually to take what they couldn't get through work or money or love: the body of a woman."

These enraged reactions revealed a desire for swift and harsh punishment. While no one would dispute that rape is a horrific and devastating crime, the same vitriolic response was simply not seen in reaction to the other rapes that occurred in the city that same week. The lack of coverage of the violent rape of the black woman who was thrown from a roof two weeks later underscored not only the fact that black victims received far less attention than whites but that this case had grown into something larger. It provoked an extraordinary level of national indignation, including more and more statements that felt like outright calls for revenge against the alleged perpetrators.

On May 1, less than two weeks after the attack, a full-page advertisement appeared in all four of New York City's daily papers, placed there by real estate mogul Donald Trump. He had spent $85,000 to run the ads. In large capital letters that took up half the page, it screamed BRING BACK THE DEATH PENALTY. BRING BACK OUR POLICE! In the paragraphs below, Trump lamented the deterioration of the city, the increasing crime, and "the complete breakdown of life as we knew it." He blamed excessive respect for civil liberties and "pandering to the criminal population" for having hog-tied the police force. "I want to hate these muggers and murderers. They should be forced to suffer and, when they kill, they should be executed for their crimes." Though the ad never specifically mentioned the suspects in the Central Park Jogger case, the implication was clear when he referred to "roving bands of wild criminals." He wanted revenge.

In the week following the attack, the local Fox station ran a short piece about calls for the death penalty in response to the Central Park rape. The reporter discussed how the attack was "fueling a new battle for the death penalty." She pointed out that any potential new law would not be relevant for the teens accused, since it would only apply to those over eighteen, but the piece quoted two people on the street who wanted the death penalty restored, including one woman who specifically referred to this case. "I'm for the death penalty. If someone were to hurt my family or a loved one, as they did this woman, I would probably want them dead."

On April 26, the *Post* devoted an entire page to an editorial entitled "Channel Your Outrage: Demand the Death Penalty." In part, it read:

> If New Yorkers want to be able to reclaim their city from the murderers and the thugs, they must restore the criminal justice system's capacity to intimidate would-be criminals. And the place to start is the top—with the death penalty.

The editorial explicitly referred to the suspects in the Central Park case: "The thugs who raped, stabbed and bludgeoned a 28-year-old woman jogger gave no thought to the possibility that they might be punished in a manner commensurate with their sadistic crime." The editorial included instructions on how to contact local politicians to demand that the death penalty be reinstated in New York.

Former Nixon speechwriter and conservative commentator Pat Buchanan wrote an op-ed piece for the *Post* that appeared on April 30, "The Barbarians Are Winning."

How does a civilized, self-confident people deal with enemies who gang-rape their women? Armies stand them up against a wall and shoot them; or we hang them, as we did the Japanese and Nazi war criminals. If . . . the eldest of that wolf pack were tried, convicted and hanged in Central Park, by June 1, and the 13- and 14-year-olds were stripped, horsewhipped, and sent to prison, the park might soon be safe again for women.

These calls for the death penalty assume that death would be a punishment "commensurate" to the crime. Yet since the Supreme Court decided *Coker v. Georgia* in 1977, the death penalty had been considered unconstitutional in cases of rape. Even if New York had reinstated the death penalty by that time, the crime that night in the park would not have met the requirements for a capital case. In the Fox piece, the reporter mentioned that the law would not apply to the teens because of their age, but she failed to note that the death penalty did not apply in rape cases, either. The tradition of death as a punishment for rape has historically been reserved for a particular type of affront: the rape of a white woman by a black man. This punishment was frequently carried out not by the justice system but by those extralegal organizations known as lynch mobs.

Lynching, the horrific practice of mob murder that flourished in the southern United States during the decades after the Civil War, was often excused, based on the perverted notion that white society needed to protect white women from the savage and lascivious instincts of black men. Philip Dray, in his account of the history of lynching, *At the Hands of Persons Unknown,* refers to sensational newspaper reports of crimes by blacks in the past. "Stories of sexual assault, insatiable black rapists, tender white virgins, and manhunts led by 'determined men' that culminated in lynchings were the bodice rippers of their day, vying in the South's daily newspapers with exposés about black dives and gambling dens, drunkenness and cocaine addiction. . . . The cumulative impression was of a world made precarious by Negroes." Though the actual reasons for lynching varied widely, an accusation of rape was often used to drum up support from angry white mobs, terrified and incensed at the specter of their women in danger from black men.

Since 1882, when lynching statistics began to be recorded, many thousands of Americans have been murdered by mobs. Calculations vary, but the Tuskegee Institute, which holds the most comprehensive survey of lynching records, recorded 3,437 lynchings of blacks from the 1880s into the 1950s, representing nearly three-fourths of all lynchings. The first incarnation of the Ku Klux Klan, in the years after the Civil War, almost certainly committed lynchings before the 1880s, and some reports suggest that thousands of blacks were lynched before anyone thought to count them officially. These murders did not have to abide by any particular rules; they were, by their very definition, outside the scope of the law and due process. Hanging, shooting, and burning were all common methods, and additional tortures, including castration and other hideous mutilations, often accompanied these killings.

In 1899, Sam Hose was lynched in Georgia for killing his white employer and allegedly raping his wife. Once Hose was captured, hordes arrived by train to witness the lawless execution. As the crowd watched with glee, Hose was tied to a tree, a chain was looped around his naked torso, and wood was piled beneath his feet. Then the torture began. Sam Hose's ears were sliced off, then each of his fingers. Eventually, he was castrated. Finally, a group of men doused Hose and the wood below him with kerosene and set both afire. When Hose, wildly thrashing, momentarily broke free of his bonds, men from the crowd raced forward and used sticks to thrust him back into the fire and then held him there until he was dead. Once the fire had died down, the crowd of thousands pushed forward and helped themselves to souvenirs, including bone fragments, charred flesh, links from the chain that had held him, and chopped-up pieces of the tree. This horrific ritual repeated itself thousands of times in the decades around the turn of the twentieth century.

Ida B. Wells, a black woman born into slavery in 1862, was a pioneering investigative journalist who documented and railed against lynching in her Memphis newspaper, the *Free Speech and Headlight*. In 1892, while she was away in New York, the offices of her newspaper were destroyed, and she learned that some in Memphis had threatened to murder her if she returned to the state. She remained in New York but continued to publish essays and articles throughout the 1890s, describing not only the horrific methods of lynchings but also the underlying excuses and reasoning that whites used to justify them.

She wrote of how Henry Smith, a black man with mental illness, was lynched for killing the young daughter of a white man. Though there was no sign that a rape had occurred, a Methodist bishop helped to summon the anger of a mob by describing the crime: "First outraged with demoniacal cruelty and then taken by her heels and torn asunder in the mad wantonness of gorilla ferocity." Smith was captured and paraded through the streets of Paris, Texas, in front of a crowd of thousands. He was tied up and then tortured with hot irons. Men in the mob first seared his body and then burned his eyes out and stuck hot irons down his throat. Then the crowd set his body ablaze and afterward carried off souvenirs.

Though Smith was likely guilty of the murder of a young girl, Wells found that innocent black men were often lynched, as well. She discovered men who were lynched because of crimes committed by relatives, as in the case of Allen Butler, a respected black businessman in Indiana, who was hanged by a mob because his son had had a consensual relationship with a white servant who worked in their home and who became pregnant as a result of the liaison.

Wells was particularly troubled by the case of a black man who was lynched in Bardwell, Kentucky, in 1893. After two white girls were found mutilated and murdered one morning, "a search was immediately begun for a Negro." When bloodhounds followed a trail from the scene of the crime that led to a fisherman's boat, the angler recounted rowing "a white man, or a very fair mulatto across the river" the previous evening. The bloodhounds followed the trail on the other side of the river to the home of a white farmer.

At the same time, thirty miles to the west, a "strange Negro" was arrested in Sikeston, Missouri. This man, C. J. Miller, was escorted to Kentucky and handed over to "the authorities who accompanied the mob." Though Miller was dark-skinned and insisted that he had never even been to Kentucky, the mob planned his lynching. Miller made a statement to the crowd: "My name is C. J. Miller, I am from Springfield, Illinois. . . . I have committed no crime, and certainly no crime gross enough to deprive me of my life or liberty to walk upon the green earth." He went on to describe his travels, including where he was at the time of the murders. His pleas failed to dampen the mob's enthusiasm, and he was hanged, his fingers and toes severed, and then burned. Wells noted that "since his death, his assertions regarding his movements have been proven true." Wells concluded by saying that "the simple word of any white person against a Negro is sufficient to get a crowd of white men to lynch a Negro. Investigation as to the guilt or innocence of the accused is never made."

Based on these cases and many others, Wells rejected the common claim that lynchings occurred because black men raped white women and were programmed in some way to commit those terrible crimes. She wrote that "nobody in this section of the country believes the old thread bare lie that Negro men rape white women. If Southern white men are not careful, they will over-reach themselves and public sentiment will have a reaction; a conclusion will then be reached which will be very damaging to the moral reputation of their women." Wells was boldly suggesting that many sexual encounters between black men and white women were actually consensual, something that was unimaginable in the eyes of many southerners at that time, and she proved it through her research.

Wells wrote of the lynching of Daniel Edwards, a black man living near Selma, Alabama, who had been in a relationship with a white woman for more than a year. But when his girlfriend became pregnant, a mob hanged him, shot him, and then pinned a warning to his back: "Warning to all Negroes that are too intimate with white girls. This is the work of one hundred best citizens of the South Side." Though it was widely known that the relationship had been consensual, Wells noted that "when the dispatches were sent out, describing the affair, it was claimed that Edwards was lynched for rape."

As Wells discovered that rape was often just an excuse for lynching, she considered the real reasons for these dastardly acts. In 1892, three black store owners whom Wells knew in Memphis had been lynched after an altercation with the white owners of a local business. In this particular case, Wells observed that the lynching was "an excuse to get rid of Negroes who were acquiring wealth and property and thus keep the race terrorized."

Dray describes what Wells had found to be the true goal of lynchings: "Wells was one of the first people in America to perceive that the talk of chivalry and beastlike blacks ravishing white girls was largely fallacious and that such ideas were being used to help maintain a permanent hysteria to legitimize lynching, as it reinforced the notion that the races must be kept separate at all costs." In fact, lynchings served principally as a means of striking fear into blacks and maintaining the oppression that had begun with slavery.

When legalized slavery ended at the close of the Civil War, new methods were needed to enforce control over the former slave population, who were still needed as cheap labor in the South. The economic incentives for white landowners in the South to keep blacks essentially reenslaved were great and required not just legal and extralegal means but a way to justify the continued oppression. During slavery, images of blacks as ignorant and childlike proliferated. This was a practical measure for justifying slavery, an institution seen as a paternalistic means of protecting and controlling these "children." It provided a moral rationalization for slavery. When slavery ended, this fable was no longer useful, but the need for that massive and subservient labor force remained. In place of the myth of blacks as childlike, a new caricature was needed.

White writers began arguing that without the civilizing forces of slavery, free blacks were reverting to a more savage and brutish form. The writer Thomas Nelson Page described this new type of black man as "lazy, thriftless, intemperate, insolent, dishonest, and without the most rudimentary elements of morality."

Frequently animal references were used to describe these traits. One account referred to "the Negro" as "a fiend, a wild beast, seeking whom he may devour." An 1892 article entitled "More Rape, More Lynchings," which appeared in the *Memphis Daily Commercial* on May 17, 1892, exposed the myth's use as a rationalization for lynching: "Southern barbarism . . . preys upon weak and defenseless women. Nothing but the most prompt, speedy, and extreme punishment can hold in check the horrible and bestial propensities of the Negro race."

Ida B. Wells pointed out this baseless shift in stereotype in her writing. "During all the years of slavery, no such charge was ever made. . . . While the master was away fighting to forge the fetters upon the slave, he left his wife and children with no protectors save the Negroes themselves," she wrote. "It must appear strange indeed, to every thoughtful and candid man, that more than a quarter of a century elapsed before the Negro began to show signs of such infamous degeneration."

Yet this myth of the black man as bestial and sexual persisted; it was used as a justification for much of the heinous violence, including lynchings, that was perpetrated on blacks in the wake of emancipation. Though lynchings often occurred in response to a fear of the growing economic progress of blacks, as in the case of Ida B. Wells's three friends, or simply out of the need to keep blacks living in fear and without power, the sensational accusation that black men were raping white women was a far more powerful motivator and symbol. George M. Fredrickson pointed out in his 1971 book, *The Black Image in the White Mind,* that "the only way to meet the criticisms of the unspeakably revolting practice of lynching was to contend that many Negroes were literally wild beasts, with uncontrollable sexual passions and criminal natures stamped by heredity."

——

The image of black men as criminals intent on raping white women continues to the present in only slightly subtler forms. The various descriptions of the teenagers in the Central Park Jogger case as bestial, savage, and "wild," or otherwise animalistic, hearken back to the language used during the era of lynchings. And the particular panic seen in response to the Central Park Jogger rape had to do not only with the viciousness of the crime but also with the inherited fear of the violent and lustful black man. Though by 1989 Latinos were also seen as criminals, coming from the same poverty-stricken neighborhoods as many blacks, the same stereotypes were not always attached. Latinos in the United States have their own complicated history, but one that is more recent and less fraught with the legacy of slavery. Negative stereotypes have been applied to Latinos, such as assumptions about gang participation or illegal immigration status, but the particular image of a violent, bestial sexual predator seems to be specifically reserved for blacks.

The calls for the death penalty in the Central Park Jogger case prove that this fear, planted as a seed in the late nineteenth century, was alive and well in New York City in the spring and summer of 1989.

Everyone had something to say about the Central Park Jogger rape; it was the most covered case of the year, and politicians and public figures used it to campaign, protest, and present their platforms. Ed Koch, looking ahead to a struggle to retain his position as mayor of New York, spoke openly and emotionally about the case, his anger and frustration made clear through his words and tone. Koch described the significance of the incident and its aftermath to New Yorkers when he said at a press conference two days after the attack, "I think that everybody here . . . will look at this case to see how the criminal justice system works." In retrospect, his statement takes on a completely different meaning, but at the time a fearful city hoped that justice as they saw it would be meted out quickly and severely. Unspoken was the pressure on the police and the district attorney's office to solve the case quickly.

A few days later Koch commented, "I don't want to understand what motivates someone to engage in this kind of horror. I want him punished as an example to others." In arguing that the teens be tried as adults, Koch railed against a justice system that might limit their maximum sentences to just a few years. "Anyone who committed this rape is not a child," he said in one of the rare moments when anyone even acknowledged just how young the accused were. Koch also used the word *monsters* to describe the boys, in terms similar to those used in the tabloid media. David Dinkins, the Manhattan borough president, who had ambitions to be the city's first black mayor, publicly referred to the accused teens as "urban terrorists."

Once the narrative about what had happened was laid out within a few days of the rape, there was no turning back. The few stories that were more balanced and less hysterical failed to make any real difference in a city ready to believe the absolute worst about a group of poor black and Latino teenagers.

Weekly papers from the black community took a very different approach. The *Amsterdam News*'s coverage of the case featured Colin Moore, the attorney representing Korey Wise, as their primary, and sometimes only, source. Moore, a forty-nine-year-old lawyer and activist from Guyana, knew how to play up the political dimensions of the case to the media. Moore told the *Amsterdam News* that the police violated the boys' constitutional rights by interrogating them for hours on end without legal counsel, and his comments on the details of the case appeared in the paper throughout the lead-up to the trial. Moore got some points right, such as his complaint about the excessively long and harsh interrogations: "Any attorney worth his salt could prove that these statements given under such conditions by 14 and 15-year olds should be suppressed as being the product of physical and psychological duress."

Yet the *Amsterdam News* also seemed to assume the boys had been the rapists. While the paper occasionally pointed out the importance of using the word *alleged* to describe the suspects, the first front-page article complaining about police brutality still began by describing the teenagers as "the teenage boys involved in last week's rape and beating."

Moore focused more on condemning police brutality and a racist media than on claiming his client's innocence: "How can a system expect to treat African-American people like animals and not expect these so-called animals to strike back against their conditions? As long as this city continues to treat us with contempt, it must be prepared to reap the social consequences." His argument helped to undermine any legitimate claims Moore and the attorneys who would defend the other boys might have had regarding the inadmissibility of the so-called confessions. The continued emphasis on the political elements of the case distracted anyone who might be paying attention from the fact that the confessions were false and had been coerced, not to mention the lack of any evidence linking the boys to the crime scene and the massive inconsistencies embedded in their collective statements.

El Diario/La Prensa, New York's most widely circulated Spanish-language newspaper, relied mostly on AP articles, which reported the same facts and quotes from the police as most mainstream newspapers. In two editorials, the paper challenged readers to understand the social conditions that could lead to such a horrific crime. "They are the product of a pervasive racism that affects every step they take to integrate themselves into society, a society that rejects them," the paper stated. It criticized the lack of options available to the teenagers: "The sad reality is that those boys thought they didn't have anything better to do with their energy than put it to bad uses. So it goes in New York City too often, that the potential for good is perverted by social conditions into a force for evil. Drugs, crime, vandalism and so-called 'wilding' that they engaged in at the park are the void into which young people fall because there are so few positive alternatives for them."

The City Sun, another black-owned paper, used the case as an opportunity to slam politicians, the media, and white society in general. Its first issue after the story broke featured the front-page headline IT'S AN OUTRAGE! and an editorial, which began:

That anyone would set out to stalk, brutally beat and sexually assault a young woman and then leave her for dead is more than an outrage; it is condemnable. That a tragic situation such as this would be used by politicians, the police and the press to accomplish their own base agendas is beneath contempt.

Again, the piece failed to illuminate the actual facts of the arrests, interrogations, and confessions, seeking to score political points rather than debate the merits of the case against the teenagers. The paper did get one thing right: "If the Central Park Boys are innocent, they wouldn't have a fighting chance with the current climate. They will be convicted, even if innocent."

But *The City Sun* also undermined its argument with the hypocrisy it displayed in condemning the "base agendas" of the mainstream media and white society, all the while demeaning the actual crime that took place. "The worst nightmare of New York City's white male-dominated press corps had become unflinchingly real," one article began. "A bunch of horny Black kids had committed one of the gravest taboos. They raped a white woman. This 'wolfpack' of 'uptown project babies,' operating, as they prefer to do, under cover of night, feasted wantonly on The American Ideal—a beautiful body, as white as milk, of ideal smoothness, a tiny body with round hips and pert buttocks, soft wide thighs, slender calves, firm and high breasts." Though trying to make a point about the white press's depiction of the case and its participants, *The City Sun* article crossed a line by referring to the jogger in such sexual terms.

The *Amsterdam News* and *The City Sun* were the only newspapers to print Meili's name. There are no laws barring the use of rape victims' names in the media, only the unwritten ethical rule followed by most newspapers and other media outlets not to use a person's name unless specific permission was given by the victim. In the case of Trisha Meili, no permission was given. In the days after the rape, three local New York news stations, WNBC-TV, WPIX, and WCBS all mentioned her name in their coverage. As the outrage over the attack mounted, the stations agreed to withhold her name in the future and CBS publicly apologized for mistakenly naming her.

An article on May 8, 1989, in the *New York Observer,* a newer and smaller player in the city's newspaper scene, explored the hypocrisy of the media's withholding of the jogger's name while publishing photos, names, and addresses of the young suspects before they had even been indicted. The paper quoted a managing editor from *The New York Times,* who explained that the *Times* generally has a policy to withhold the names of juvenile offenders, but added that in this case they were being charged as adults and were therefore not offered that protection. The *Amsterdam News,* in defending its use of Meili's name, also expressed frustration at the mainstream media's demonizing of the boys and liberally using their names and addresses: "This is hypocritical, clap-trap bull—, and this newspaper mightily resents racist white newspapers for making an effort to impose their phony morality on us, while they continue to do anything they goddamned please."

The New York Times editorial staff had struggled over whether to publish Meili's name; editors there believed that the *Post* was going to do so, and they didn't want to be "scooped." The *Times* finally decided to withhold the name, and the *Post* did not end up publishing it, either.

There were innumerable articles in the mainstream media that posed the question of what had motivated these teenagers to allegedly rape and beat the jogger. The crime, as everyone believed it had occurred, had truly touched a chord in the city and begged a difficult question: How did this happen? The rape in Central Park seemed to be the culmination of a downward spiral into crime and degeneracy. The debate over who was to blame grew to a fever pitch.

Various reasons that might inspire an individual to commit this sort of crime were considered. Race as the motivating factor in the attack was quickly dismissed. On Thursday, April 20, the NYPD held a press conference at the Central Park Precinct. Chief of Detectives Robert

Colangelo told reporters that the rape and beating did not seem to be racially motivated, nor did it appear to be related to money, alcohol, or drugs.

The New York Times ran an editorial that asked, "What caused such savagery? How could so many teenagers lose all sense of morality, even of compassion? The public lunges for explanations." After quickly dismissing drugs and "greed," the editorial explored race and poverty as potential causes.

> Race: Investigators are pursuing reports that a few of the black or Hispanic youths referred to white victims in racial terms. But three of the victims were also black or Hispanic. . . .
>
> Poverty: Cardinal O'Connor asserts that the city must share the blame for conditions that breed crime. Others, similarly, worry about an alienated underclass. But it now appears that this explanation also fails. Reporters find that some of the suspects come from stable, financially secure families. Teachers, neighbors and friends expressed shock and surprise at the arrests. Only one suspect has a criminal record.
>
> Then what is the explanation for this explosion of savagery? . . . The question reverberates.

Once it became clear that none of the typical explanations for crime applied, the questions became all the more disturbing. If neither the desire for money or drugs nor racial animus were motivations, and if it was just for "fun," as newspaper reports about the teens suggested, then how had these kids become monsters? A panoply of arguments and ideas found their way into the press, asking whether society or the individual was to blame. And if society was to blame, what part?

Pete Hamill, the respected columnist for the *Post,* threw his hat in the ring early on:

> Race is part of this demented equation. But as usual when we are talking about race, we are really talking about class. These kids came into Central Park from the north on Wednesday evening, and according to the cops, they had a loose plan of battle: to go "wilding" against the rich. The

details didn't matter because there was no script. But they were coming downtown from a world of crack, welfare, guns, knives, indifference and ignorance. They were coming from a land with no fathers. They were coming from schools where cops must guard the doors. They were coming from the anarchic province of the poor.

Hamill's apocalyptic description of New York City went on:

. . . nothing is a real defense in the sick world in which we now all live. Everybody is vulnerable, the black poor most vulnerable of all. . . . It is no consolation to say that we've seen this coming from the mid-60's and nobody did anything serious to stop it. Now, the fierce and terrible future is here. You reap what you sow.

Hamill had expressed an idea repeated by many—that society's ills had caused these young men to do what they did, and that everyone should have been able to predict this coming cataclysm.

In a later column, Hamill argued that humankind in general is prone to savagery. Pointing to the labeling of the teenagers as a "wolf pack," he defended the honor of wolves: "Only man seems capable of such atrocities. No group of wolves could have planned and executed the Holocaust. No wolf would have done what Pol Pot did to Cambodia. No animal anywhere would bother to invent hydrogen bombs, poison gas or the Uzi. No animal, that is, except man." Hamill's utterly pessimistic take echoed the sense of frustration felt by many over what they saw as the disintegration of society in New York and elsewhere.

On the other side of Hamill's argument were those who would blame society to lessen the blame on the individual teenagers. When Colin Moore suggested that society should "expect these so-called animals to strike back against their conditions," he turned around the racist language that equated the teens with wolves and suggested that their actions were actually a reaction to being treated as such.

Other accounts didn't excuse the crime, but they did explore with fascination the poverty and violence endemic to the Harlem ghetto where these kids grew up. The *Daily News* called it "a place where the young grow up on the edge of violence and where random 'wilding' is therapy for angst that somehow got out of hand." "Though many families do cope and live law-abiding lives, it is a hard place to raise children—and, if the police accounts hold true, a place that produces hard children." These accounts suggest that a particular part of society was to blame, that this "world of Harlem," seemingly another planet from the rest of "us," was the source of the violence and decay of the city.

Bill Perkins, a community leader in Harlem who was the president of the Schomburg Plaza Tenants Association in 1989, was frustrated by it all. He noticed that during the summer following the Central Park rape, Harlem teenagers had a hard time getting jobs, because people assumed the worst about the whole neighborhood, and the whole race. When Robert Chambers, a white teenager who attended private schools, killed Jennifer Levin, a girl he had met at an Upper East Side bar, no one blamed prep school kids in general. It "didn't become a stigma for a community or a class of people," Perkins recalled.

Yet those who would blame the terrible conditions in which the boys were growing up for their apparent behavior were surprised when articles began surfacing that painted a different picture of their backgrounds. Reporters soon found evidence that they were not the high-risk kids from devastated families that many had expected. One lengthy piece in *The New York Times* on April 26 was titled "Park Suspects: Children of Discipline." The article described each teenager and something of his situation. It pointed out that Antron lived with stable parents in a "well-kept" apartment, and that he played on a baseball team his stepfather coached. It mentioned Yusef's relationship with David Nocenti, his mentor from the Big Brother program, and his private Catholic school tuition. A teacher of Raymond's said that "he had a charming, laughing sense of humor . . . he was one of our nicest kids." Most of the profiles quoted someone expressing shock that these boys would have been participants in such a horrific crime. That newspapers featured these articles describing with surprise the fact that the teenagers came from good homes revealed the powerful stereotype that assumed that all kids from Harlem were the children of drug addicts or criminals.

A few other profiles, particularly those in *The Village Voice* and *New York* magazine, which came out later that spring and summer, delved beyond the superficial accounts published in the tabloids or other papers trying to get their stories written by an evening deadline. They found more dysfunction among the young suspects and their families. The articles included accounts of the teens as likable or "good kids," but they also cited examples of past troublemaking behavior and problems at school and at home. Michael Stone's article "What Really Happened in Central Park" in *New York* provided evidence of Korey Wise's sexual abuse as a kid and noted that Kevin Richardson had received a head injury in a car accident when he was nine. These profiles provided more nuanced portraits of the kids. They were not all perfect angels, and though they came from a neighborhood plagued with violence, deteriorating schools, and drugs, they did, to varying degrees, have stable homes and caring parents. These articles painted them as real people, not just scary stereotypes, revealing that they had diverse experiences and were of various backgrounds, something most other reports failed to distinguish.

The debate over who was to blame raged on for weeks in the media. The *Amsterdam News,* the black-owned Harlem paper, published a piece that rejected the idea that society was to blame. It complained that "the apologists . . . are chiming in with excuses for this atrocity." "When whites kill us for no reason, it is racism. When we kill them for no reason, we are socially disadvantaged. . . . Bullshit!" New York's Mayor Ed Koch continued to emphasize that the teenagers were to blame, as much to take the heat off his beleaguered city and the Harlem community as to fully delve into the "cause" of the attacks. Though he called them "monsters," he also cautioned that "one should not brand communities with the individual acts." When asked if there could be an explanation that was societal, the mayor responded, "You name one social reason that would cause 36 people to engage in a wolf-pack operation looking for victims and eight or nine of them to engage in a gang bang."

While Koch contended that there was not a single social explanation for the crime, John Cardinal O'Connor, the prominent leader of the Catholic Church in New York, used his sermon at Sunday mass to claim that the entire city should bear some of the responsibility for ignoring the bad conditions that can lead to crime.

Many argued that the boys' families were to blame. Mayor Koch took this line when he pointed out that the city government and schools were not capable of controlling these kids, but that "the family has to be accountable." Even Barbara Bush, the First Lady, joined the fray. "Children do things in a group that they would never do [alone]. You ought to know who your children are with."

Another discussion was playing out in feminist circles, where some voices were calling for the rape to be seen as a crime against women, and not be defined in racial terms. In one of the few serious considerations of this perspective, *The Village Voice* dedicated a special section to the case on May 9, and included five pieces by women to highlight their perspective in the discussion. One article noted that "we live in a pro-rape culture. . . . This is not an issue of race, but of gender." Like others, the author pointed out that "there is much less tolerance for racism than sexism in the black community."

Another article in that *Village Voice* issue expressed one woman's complicated reaction as an African-American. She felt torn between her race and her gender. "To bad-mouth the youths means taking a chance that my language might be used against me, against blacks. If I remain silent, or hem and haw about the outrage against women, then again I am in danger." The feeling that a choice had to be made in how to define this terrible crime ignored a central issue. Of course rape is a crime against women, and combating rape and the ways that our society deals with it has everything to do with changing cultural attitudes about women.

And yet this particular case had everything to do with race. While the rape itself was not motivated by racial animus, at least in the narrative of the "wilding" created in the days following the attack, the response to that narrative was all about race. It would never have become the tabloid sensation it did had the boys been white or the victim black. Race not only inspired the extreme reactions to the crime; it also made it easier for so many to believe that these five teenaged boys had committed the crime in the first place, and no one was suggesting that they might, in fact, be innocent.

CHAPTER FOUR

Detective Robert Honeyman returned to the park after his initial visit on the morning of April 20 and photographed the scene once the sun began to brighten the sky. He clicked off shots of the bloodstains, the drag marks, and other evidence. He then turned the pieces of physical evidence he'd collected over to an officer from the Central Park Precinct, who vouchered them into evidence.

The physical evidence was transferred to the police department's lab. Detective Nicholas Petraco, an expert in trace evidence, looked for hairs and fibers and examined the soil samples collected by Honeyman. He looked at Meili's clothing through a microscope, pulling off bits of soil and hair. He examined the fingernail scrapings from Meili but found no evidence there of any value. Petraco also received the clothing from each of the suspects, and samples of their head and pubic hair for the purposes of comparison.

In 1989, hairs could not be individualized, meaning that a hair could at best be called "consistent with" a source and could not be definitively matched to it. Nonetheless, Petraco compared hairs collected from various sources to see what he could come up with. He concluded that a light-colored pubic hair found on Kevin Richardson's shirt was consistent with Trisha Meili's, and that light head hairs found on his underwear and pants were also consistent with Meili's. Other hairs collected from the suspects' clothing clearly did not match Meili's. The pubic hair collected in the rape kit was consistent only with known samples taken from Meili herself.

Not only could hair evidence not be matched at that time; there was not even a probability associated with a conclusion that two hair samples were "consistent," making its reliability questionable. Today, more advanced forms of DNA testing can be applied to hairs, but in 1989 the science of hair comparison consisted mainly of visual inspection of various traits through a microscope, a fairly useless technique except as a way to rule out the source of a hair sample.

Petraco also compared soil samples found on the clothing and sneakers of some of the suspects. Again, only a "consistent with" identification can be made with a soil sample. In these cases, the soil was consistent with soil samples from the crime scene, but soil from other parts of Central Park would also have been consistent, so this comparison provided little helpful data. All it really proved was that the teens with dirt on their shoes had probably been in Central Park.

Mary Veit, a chemist with the serology department of the NYPD lab, examined blood collected from the crime scene and blood samples taken from the victim, the suspects, and Kevin O'Reilly, Trisha Meili's boyfriend. Veit's lab was not equipped to compare DNA profiles, so she could only identify potential DNA samples and determine blood types. As with much of the work done by Detective Petraco, blood typing provided only a general comparison. While someone could be ruled out as the provider of a sample if their blood type was different, having the same type did not constitute a definitive match, as millions in New York City alone could have had the same blood type.

Veit was able to determine blood types for all those involved, based on known samples collected from each individual, but many of the blood samples taken from the crime scene were inconclusive. In some cases, Veit was able to determine only that the sample was human blood. Blood on Meili's shirt, the rock found near the large tree, and other samples from the crime scene did seem to be consistent with type A blood—Trisha Meili's, Kevin Richardson's, and Yusef Salaam's type— but there was not enough information to make a conclusion.

Veit's other responsibility was to search for and identify semen samples and stains and to preserve them and transmit them to the FBI's laboratory, along with blood samples taken from the suspects, so they could be tested using a brand-new technology that compared DNA.

DNA comparison, now an accepted and highly respected form of evidence, was in its infancy in terms of scientific and legal applications in 1989. It was not until the 1980s that the idea of using DNA as a way of differentiating individuals was even conceived. In 1984, Alec Jeffreys, a biochemist studying DNA in Leicester, England, came up with the idea for DNA typing, or "fingerprinting." Two years later, Jeffreys used the technique he'd developed, known as restriction fragment length polymorphism (RFLP) analysis, to help Leicester police solve two rape-murders. It marked the first time DNA testing had been used successfully in a criminal case.

In that case, Leicester police suspected that one man was responsible for two rape-murders, one in 1983 and one in 1986. When a man confessed to the latter crime only, denying involvement in the first, the police used Jeffreys's RFLP test to try to link the suspect to both crimes. In fact, the tests showed that samples from the man who had confessed did not match samples from either crime, a fact that exonerated him instantly. The police went on to test thousands of local men without finding a match. The case got a break only when a woman overheard a man in a bar describing how he had given a second sample on behalf of a friend. Colin Pitchfork had conned his friend into giving blood for him, and when police eventually caught up with him, DNA typing proved that he had raped and murdered both girls. Tellingly, though it eventually linked the true criminal to the crime, the very first DNA test ever in a criminal case actually served to exonerate an individual who had falsely confessed. The era of DNA testing in rape and murder cases had begun.

DNA typing was first used in a court case in the United States in 1987. Tommy Lee Andrews was convicted of rape in Orlando, Florida, based on RFLP DNA testing, after a judge ruled to admit the test results into evidence. Though far more accurate than comparing blood types and looking at hairs under a microscope, this early form of DNA testing was limited by the technology. The test works by taking a DNA sample and producing, through a series of complex procedures, a pattern of bands on X-ray film. But two major problems decrease the likelihood of a successful match. For one, the DNA sample must be large enough and of good-enough quality to create a pattern that is clear. Second, each pattern represents only a single genetic location, which is not enough to prove definitively that two samples have come from the same person. Only when comparing multiple genetic locations and the frequency of each pattern in the population can a definitive match be made, and this requires an even greater volume of high-quality DNA. Despite these limitations, RFLP testing is incredibly useful for excluding suspects, even with relatively small or weak DNA samples. When a single genetic location does not match, an individual can be conclusively ruled out as the source of that DNA.

All the while, Trisha Meili remained in a coma at Metropolitan Hospital. Dr. Robert Kurtz briefed the media frequently on her condition, and it did not look good. The Monday after the attack, April 24, Kurtz told reporters that her odds of surviving had increased, simply because she had made it through the first seventy-two hours, but he warned that her brain might have been deprived of too much oxygen before she was brought to the hospital and that she could have permanent brain damage—if she ever woke up. "In general, the longer people are in comas, the less happy is the outcome." Vigils were held outside the hospital and flowers were placed along the 102nd Street Cross Drive, where Meili was attacked. At one vigil, Mayor Koch spoke: "Millions of New Yorkers of every religion on earth are united in prayer for the young woman who lies comatose. Let ours be the faith that moves mountains as we ask God to heal this young woman."

On April 27, doctors tried to remove the breathing tube that had been inserted during the ambulance ride to the hospital, but Meili couldn't breathe on her own and doctors had to restore it.

On May 1, Meili slowly began to awake from her coma, achieving a semiconscious state. She was able to lift her hand to high-five a nurse, and nodded in response to questions. She could now breathe on her own, and she began working with doctors to redevelop her brain function. Two weeks later, her neurologist wrote an update:

> She presents with signs of severe cognitive dysfunction suggestive of widespread cerebral impairment which is in the process of recovery. At this point, she manifests limitations in all areas of cognitive functioning. Even so, there have been some signs of incremental gains in specific areas over the course of several days. Most limiting at present are problems with attention and concentration, perseveration, memory and construction skills. The severity of the patient's condition raises serious concerns about her prospects for long-term recovery. However, it is far too early to make predictions concerning outcome. . . .

Over the next days and weeks, Meili continued to make progress, but her doctors were unsure of how much cognition she would ultimately recover, and a bout of pneumonia resulted in a temporary setback in her recovery.

Yet slowly she began to regain her memory, identifying objects and remembering moments, but it was not until late May that she began forming memories that would stick. Her last memory before then was the 5:00 p.m. phone call she made to her friend Michael Allen to cancel their dinner plans on April 19, the night she was attacked and raped. Her neurologists said that because of her brain injury, no memories formed at all that evening and that she would never be able to remember what had happened to her in the park.

Identical DNA is found in the nucleus of each cell of an individual, so sperm cells and blood cells from one person exhibit exactly the same

DNA pattern. Prosecutors hoped that blood samples taken from the suspects would match the semen or blood samples found at the scene. Mary Veit, the NYPD serologist, examined each article of Trisha Meili's clothing carefully, searching for stains that might yield useful evidence for the FBI to test. She also checked the teen suspects' clothing, and looked for the presence of semen in the rape kit performed at the hospital. Though she was not equipped to conduct DNA testing, she was able to do a simple test to identify the presence of semen.

Veit found semen near the crotch of Meili's jogging tights, on Kevin Richardson's underwear, on Raymond Santana's sweatshirt, and on Steve Lopez's underwear. Each of these samples she carefully removed from the articles of clothing, froze, and sent to the FBI DNA Analysis Unit in Washington, D.C., along with the samples from the rape kit and blood samples taken from the suspects. What Veit did not find was any blood on the clothing collected from the suspects. Despite the fact that Meili had lost 75 percent of the blood in her body by the time she arrived at Metropolitan Hospital, none of it had apparently gotten onto the clothes of the teenagers nearly everyone believed had brutally assaulted her.

Special Agent Dwight Adams of the FBI received Mary Veit's samples on July 13, 1989. He performed RFLP DNA tests, looking at four different genetic locations for each sample. He found that each of the three semen stains on the teens' clothing matched the DNA of the owner of those clothes. (There was no way to know when the semen had been deposited there, so these tests proved only that these teenagers had managed to get their semen on their own clothing.) The semen on Meili's jogging pants matched that of Kevin O'Reilly, her boyfriend. Meili later explained this result to investigators: the weekend before the attack, she had had sex with O'Reilly before putting on those same pants and going for a jog.

The samples taken from Meili's rape kit were less conclusive. The rectal swab did not produce a band pattern on any of the four tests Adams tried. The cervical swab produced a weak pattern on only one of the tests, and no result for the other three. The one visible pattern was not enough for Adams to even call it a DNA profile. What little result he had didn't match samples from any of the suspects, but Adams labeled the test inconclusive, because if a similarity had been found, it would not have been strong enough to make a match. While preparing for trial that August, Elizabeth Lederer, the lead prosecutor on the case, learned that no matches had been made. "I feel like I've been kicked in the stomach," she told one of the other attorneys assisting with the case. But the fact that the weak pattern that did show up was clearly not a match to samples from any of the suspects did not inspire her to look elsewhere.

In the meantime, Lederer had been successful in getting indictments against eight defendants. A grand jury, convened back in April, had indicted six—Korey Wise, Kevin Richardson, Antron McCray, Yusef Salaam, Raymond Santana, and Steve Lopez—on counts of attempted murder, rape, sodomy, sexual abuse, assault, and riot, stemming from the attacks on John Loughlin and David Lewis as well as the rape of Trisha Meili. The others, Michael Briscoe and Jermain Robinson, who were in the park that night but were not suspected in the rape, or against whom the prosecutors didn't have enough evidence, were indicted only in the attacks on male joggers by the reservoir. Lamont McCall and Clarence Thomas were sent to family court on minor charges.

The arraignment was set for May, when the charges would officially be presented against the eight boys, they would enter their pleas of guilty or not guilty, and bail would be set. They would all be tried in state criminal court as adults, despite their young ages. In the past, anyone under sixteen would have been charged in family court, but a 1978 New York law made it possible for the city to try the fourteen- and fifteen-year-olds alongside those sixteen and older. That law, the Juvenile Offender Act, was created after fifteen-year-old Willie Bosket robbed and then murdered two men on the subway in separate incidents in 1978. Bosket was tried and sentenced in family court to a maximum of five years in a facility for juveniles. The public outrage at his short sentence led to the new juvenile law, which lowered the age of criminal responsibility to fourteen for many violent crimes and felonies, and to thirteen for murder. This paved the way for prosecutors to charge and try all of the Central Park defendants as adults, with the attendant potential for longer sentences.

After providing their statements and hair and blood samples, the teenagers suspected in the Central Park rape were sent to city jail facilities until they could be arraigned. At that hearing, they would be formally charged and have to enter a plea of guilty or not guilty.

Kevin Richardson, Raymond Santana, Antron McCray, Yusef Salaam, and the others who were under sixteen were sent to Spofford Juvenile Facility in the Hunts Point section of the Bronx. In use since 1957, it was the city's only secure detention facility for juveniles. Once convicted, juveniles were assigned to other facilities across the state to serve out their terms, so Spofford was a transient place, full of people not likely to be there long.

The facility had more than two hundred beds and was organized into dormitories, with individual dorms housing up to twenty-four kids, each in a single room. The teenagers couldn't leave, but for the most part they had the freedom to move about the dorm; the doors to their rooms were rarely locked and they could hang out in a common room with a TV and seating area. Still, their schedule was rigid, and several times a day everyone had to be accounted for. They wore a simple uniform of jeans and a T-shirt and were required to keep their rooms unadorned. It was far safer than a long-term prison, especially an adult facility, but there could still be fights and violence. Soon after Yusef's arrival there, another kid in his dorm cut him above the eye while they were watching a movie. His attacker later apologized, explaining that he'd felt that he had to prove his dominance over the new and infamous resident.

Because Korey Wise was sixteen, he was sent to an adult facility, Rikers Island, the sprawling compound that is New York City's largest jail facility. Located on an island in the East River, near Long Island Sound, it is between Queens and the Bronx, next to LaGuardia Airport. Connected to Queens by a bridge, the island houses up to seventeen thousand inmates serving short sentences, or awaiting trial or transfer to state prison facilities, where they serve out longer terms. Rikers is larger than many states' entire prison systems; it is like a small city, with its own transportation system, bakery, laundry, tailor shop, print shop, and even a nursery for women who give birth there. The facility has a mix of dormitory housing as well as more traditional prison cells.

One day early on at Rikers, Korey was in the dayroom, where inmates could watch TV or play cards, and there was a story about his case on the news. He and another teenager charged in the other park attacks were jumped by as many as twenty-eight inmates. The fight was broken up before they were seriously injured, and they were then segregated from other inmates.

By the time they arrived in court for the arraignment, the boys and their families had arranged for representation. As soon as their ordeals in the precincts were over, the young men accused of rape vehemently denied their participation, explaining to their lawyers and families as soon as they could that the incriminating statements that they had provided to the police were not the truth and had been coerced. They would need good lawyers to convince a jury that they had falsely confessed.

Yusef's family called Robert "Bobby" Burns, a sixty-year-old African-American attorney, because he'd done some legal work for someone in the family before. He was not, however, a criminal defense specialist, and in a case like this he was way over his head. He later applied for and received court appointment because Yusef's mother couldn't afford the fees. He received twenty-five dollars per hour from the court for his trial preparation and forty dollars for each hour spent in court.

Elombe Brath, a Schomburg resident and respected community

member, called Colin Moore on behalf of Korey Wise's family. Moore, a black Guyanese activist, had moved to the United States in 1970. After law school in Brooklyn, he'd worked in the Bronx DA's office and then for the NAACP before going into private practice as a defense attorney. His specialty was human rights issues, such as police brutality, but he didn't have much experience with attempted murder and rape cases. Moore worked the case pro bono, and perhaps more than any of the other lawyers, he truly believed that his client should go free.

Michael "Mickey" Joseph was appointed by the court as Antron McCray's lawyer. Joseph was small and wiry, with sandy-blond hair and a beard. He'd spent his entire career working in criminal defense, first at the Legal Aid Society, then as a private attorney. He had more experience than most of the other attorneys when it came to defense work, but his superior skills would be largely overshadowed by the incompetence of the others at trial.

Raymond Santana, Sr., hired an attorney named Peter Rivera. He paid him with a ten-thousand-dollar retainer—his entire savings. Santana Senior liked the fact that Rivera was a Puerto Rican. Rivera had been a city police detective, a DEA agent, and a Bronx assistant district attorney in the Homicide Bureau. At the time, he was in private practice, but he also harbored political ambitions.

Kevin Richardson's family found Howard Diller through a relative, but they were soon unhappy with him. Diller was a rotund sixty-year-old white man with a toupee, and he seemed more interested in self-promotion and ingratiating himself with the media than in defending his client. He'd been an FBI agent earlier in his career but now worked more on drug cases as a defense attorney.

At the arraignment on May 10, Justice Carol Berkman responded to the defense's requests for bail, setting it at $50,000 for Korey Wise and Steve Lopez, and $25,000 for Antron McCray and Yusef Salaam. Kevin Richardson's lawyer asked for a psychiatric evaluation for his client instead of requesting bail, and Raymond Santana's lawyer simply didn't ask for bail at all. The teenagers returned to Spofford and Rikers until bail could be raised.

Yusef's family produced the money quickly, and on May 22 he was released from Spofford. Kevin Richardson made bail in June, when Catholic priest Louis Gigante, brother of famed mobster Vincent "the Chin" Gigante, donated money for him. Kevin and his family had no connection to Gigante, who had apparently read that the Richardson family was having trouble raising the funds and wanted to help. The others would have to wait.

Antron was entered into the system as he had been represented in the media, as Antron McCray, the name he used, but not actually his legal name. Korey was known in court documents and the media as Kharey, a variant spelling of his name that had been used in some school records, though both versions were pronounced the same way. Throughout the trial, Korey would continue to be known as Kharey.

Justice Carol Berkman had also made an unusual announcement at the arraignment. Rather than having her randomly select the trial judge by turning a wheel with names in it, as was the typical procedure, court administrators had directed Berkman to assign Justice Thomas Galligan. A World War II veteran, Galligan was a well-respected judge with fifteen years of experience on the bench. Though the administrative judges who made the decision were within their rights to preempt the random selection by making their own choice, the use of that method was rare, and the defense attorneys were incensed. Galligan had been chosen for his ability to handle the media scrutiny and the inevitable racial politics that would spill into the courtroom, and he proved immediately that he would not back down from the challenge. Galligan had a reputation as a pro-prosecution judge; inmates at Rikers Island, the city's massive jail facility, often referred to it as "Galligan's Island." The defense attorneys quickly submitted motions asking Galligan to step down or send the case back to Berkman for random assignment, but each time he refused, and he would remain the trial judge throughout the proceedings.

The day of the arraignment, Kevin Richardson's lawyer, Howard

Diller, released Kevin's written and videotaped statements. He claimed that the statements exonerated his client, as Kevin denied raping the jogger in each. Nonetheless, releasing the tape, in which Kevin described several boys chasing down, attacking, and raping the jogger, did nothing to help prove his client's innocence, especially when the media cherry-picked the most devastating parts. Diller, for his part, relished the media attention he was suddenly getting, and his dream of one day hosting a talk show may have clouded his judgment when he released the tapes to a hungry news media.

Jermain Robinson's lawyer, Elliot Cook, was an experienced Legal Aid supervisor, and he recognized immediately that his client was in deep trouble. Though Robinson hadn't been accused in the rape, assault victim John Loughlin had identified him, the only identification made by any of the victims in the park. Robinson had also made a statement in which he admitted to participating in the attacks on Loughlin and others in the park. Lederer had a strong case against Robinson, and though he was not charged with the most serious crimes, the robbery and assault charges still had the potential to land him in prison for years. Cook went to a meeting with the other defense attorneys and came away even more concerned. He found that some of the other lawyers had their own agendas, including political aspirations and fame, which did not always coincide with the best interests of their clients.

So Cook made a deal with the prosecution. Because all the media attention was on the rape of the jogger, the other crimes, however serious they'd been, were often forgotten or pushed aside. And Lederer could afford to make a deal, as long as she could be sure that Robinson had had nothing to do with the rape, and a cooperating witness who could testify about the group being in the park could benefit her at trial. As a condition of the plea agreement, Robinson had to submit a blood sample for DNA testing so that it could be confirmed that his was not the DNA found at the scene. He pleaded guilty and received a sentence of one year on October 5, 1989. The significance of the fact that a comparison of Robinson's DNA to the weak sample from the rape kit was enough to exonerate him so that he could plead out, but not enough to exonerate the others accused, was lost on everyone.

Another element of his deal was that he would cooperate with the investigation, and, if asked, testify truthfully at the trials of the other defendants. But there was one problem. Robinson said that the detectives who had come to his home to arrest him had shoved him down to the apartment floor, and he stood by that story throughout his meetings with Lederer. If called to testify as a witness for the prosecution, Robinson's tale of rough treatment by the police would inevitably come up, bolstering any arguments made by the other defense lawyers that their clients had been abused by the police. Though Robinson's testimony might be helpful in placing the defendants in the park, he could not place them at the rape, and his testimony might actually damage the prosecution's case. He never took the stand.

Lederer and her colleagues, frustrated and disappointed with the lack of useful DNA results, continued preparing for trial. Their next challenge was a pretrial hearing set to begin in October of that year, in which Justice Galligan would decide whether to allow the written statements and confession tapes to be admitted as evidence. With no DNA matches or other strong physical evidence linking any of the teens to the crime, the confessions became the only meaningful evidence for the prosecution to take to trial. If the judge threw out the statements, there would be no case, so Lederer knew that the hearing was absolutely critical to a successful prosecution.

The pretrial hearing began on October 10, 1989. Seven defendants were listed: Raymond Santana, Kharey Wise, Yusef Salaam, Antron McCray, Kevin Richardson, Steve Lopez, and Michael Briscoe. Each defendant had his own lawyer, and each attorney presented different arguments to Galligan as to why his client's statement should be excluded. New York State law states that a confession or statement by a defendant "may not be received in evidence against him in a criminal proceeding if such statement was involuntarily made." The law defines an involuntary statement as one obtained:

(a) By any person by the use or threatened use of physical force upon the defendant or another person, or by means of any other improper conduct or undue pressure which impaired the defendant's physical or mental condition to the extent of undermining his ability to make a choice whether or not to make a statement; or

(b) By a public servant engaged in law enforcement activity or by a person then acting under his direction or in cooperation with him:

(i) by means of any promise or statement of fact, which promise or statement creates a substantial risk that the defendant might falsely incriminate himself; or

(ii) in violation of such rights as the defendant may derive from the constitution of this state or of the United States.

Jesse Berman, Steve Lopez's lawyer, had been practicing criminal defense work for more than fifteen years. He'd been hired by a mentor of Lopez from the International Center for Photography, where Lopez participated in a photography class called Community Record. David Spear, the photographer who ran the class, had nominated Lopez for a mayor's award for his volunteer work assisting with the program. Spear paid Berman's retainer, and tried to help Lopez's parents, who had moved to New York from Puerto Rico, throughout the process.

Berman, an experienced trial lawyer, was especially frustrated by Galligan's appointment and what Berman saw as his bias toward the prosecution. Berman proved himself to be more than willing to antagonize Galligan at the pretrial hearing. Once, when he asked a question and Galligan dismissed it, saying, "Even if your understanding is wrong, you have no standing," Berman replied: "That's if your understanding is right."

Galligan retorted: "It happens to be I'm the one who calls the last shot here."

"I don't doubt that, your Honor," Berman replied, but then he added, "at this level."

Galligan seemed no less annoyed by Berman. At one point after sustaining objections to several of Berman's questions, Berman asked the judge, "Are you in pain or something? Are you all right?"

"Not so far," Galligan replied.

"Because you seem to be holding your head down with your eyes closed, and I'm hoping you're all right."

"Is that a sign of pain? . . . It could be boredom, it could be lots of reasons."

Despite his inadvisably contentious banter with Galligan, Berman presented a strong case for his client. Since Steve Lopez had not admitted anything related to the jogger in any of his statements, Berman wasn't particularly concerned about his client's video and written statements being admitted. He argued that the police had not had probable cause to arrest Lopez in the first place, since he'd just been walking down the street and not doing anything illegal when he was arrested. Lopez had been charged with crimes relating to the female jogger because others in custody had named him as a participant, but at the time of his arrest there had not yet been statements incriminating him. He also argued that police should not have produced a videotape of his client after his father told them not to ask any more questions. Berman put Eldomiro Lopez, Steve Lopez's father, on the stand, and he told the judge that he'd asked if he needed a lawyer during the interrogation but that Detective Arroyo had told him that they were "only asking questions."

One element of Jesse Berman's probable-cause argument was something that was rarely recognized in all the coverage of the case. In his cross-examination of Officer Eric Reynolds, an African-American, Berman pointed out that Reynolds had said in his testimony that the radio call he'd heard about John Loughlin's attackers had described them as seven or eight male blacks. When pressed, he said he wasn't sure, but Berman used this to argue that he hadn't had probable cause to arrest a male Hispanic when the suspects were male blacks. It was not a particularly strong argument, since Reynolds was unsure of this memory, and his partner did remember that Hispanics had been mentioned in the call, but it raised a little-mentioned distinction. Black and Latino teenagers were frequently lumped together in the media as poor kids from urban ghettos. Their separate histories, experiences, and, in some cases, languages were overlooked in the rush to find a definable other to blame. That Reynolds and his partner, listening to the same radio broadcast together in the same vehicle, remembered different descriptions of the perpetrators suggests just how interchangeable those racial descriptions had become.

Colin Moore, Korey Wise's attorney, the Guyanese activist working pro bono, saw and tried to exploit the political dimensions of the case. His tactics were not always effective, as he sometimes pushed them too far in arguing for conspiracy theories, such as the idea that Meili's boyfriend or someone she knew had committed the crime, which he spouted often to reporters from Harlem papers.

Though Moore was relatively inexperienced, he presented a multifaceted case, arguing strenuously that his client's statements had been coerced. Korey got on the stand and recounted being slapped and screamed at by Detective Nugent. Moore also tried to prove that Korey had been given the false impression that he could go home if he confessed, and that Detective Hartigan had been coercive when he told him that no jury would believe the story he was telling. He argued that Korey, though at sixteen old enough to be questioned without a parent, was not mentally capable of understanding and waiving the Miranda rights. Korey's mother, Deloris Wise, took the stand and recounted how she had told police about Korey's mental deficiencies while they were interrogating him. "He's in a special ed class and his mentality is like ten years old," she remembers explaining. "You can talk, but he don't understand."

Over the course of about seventeen hours, Korey had given four different statements, two written and two videotaped, and the inconsistencies within them bolstered the case that he had changed his statements to please detectives. Moore got Detective Hartigan to admit that he had raised his voice to Korey, but when he cross-examined Nugent, the detective would not admit to slapping Korey or calling him "a scumbag." When Korey got on the stand, his testimony did not always help his case. When Moore asked Korey about Hartigan's threat, Korey couldn't recall the important details. At one point, Korey flatly refused to answer Lederer's questions. "Ma'am, I don't want to answer any of your questions. Your questions are what got me here."

Howard Diller, the attorney representing Kevin Richardson, also tried to prove that Kevin's statements were involuntary. He accused the detectives of giving Kevin and his family the impression that he would be able to go home, though no detective would admit to that type of coercion. Diller also highlighted Kevin's mother's poor health as she waited for hours in the police precinct. Both Kevin's mother, Gracie Cuffee, and his sister Angela Cuffee testified, but Diller's case was weak.

The case against Yusef Salaam was going to be the hardest to prove for the prosecution, and Bobby Burns, his lawyer, hoped to destroy it altogether. Yusef had not made a videotaped statement, or even signed a written one, and he had been questioned without a guardian even though he was fifteen. Elizabeth Lederer needed to convince Galligan to admit Yusef's oral statements to detectives. Burns's strategy was to prove that the police had known that Yusef was fifteen when they questioned him. Yusef and several relatives all testified that police and prosecutors learned well before they stopped the interrogation that Yusef was fifteen. Sharonne Salaam, Yusef's mother, testified that she had informed Linda Fairstein of Yusef's age as soon as she got to the precinct, and that Fairstein had replied that she didn't need permission to speak to Yusef because he'd shown them a "phony ID." Fairstein denied ever having made that comment, and though she agreed that Mrs. Salaam had told her Yusef's age, she insisted that she'd stopped the interrogation immediately.

ADA Lederer was able to poke holes in the testimony of many of the other defense witnesses, and the detectives who first arrested Yusef denied any knowledge of his age other than the ID card showing him to be sixteen. On the stand, Yusef admitted that he used the card to pass himself off as sixteen to girls.

Some of the other lawyers doubted that Burns was capable of handling the challenge in front of him. And he didn't always cooperate with the other defense attorneys. Once, during Berman's cross-examination of Detective Gonzalez, Berman asked a question about Yusef. Burns jumped up and said, "Don't ask no questions about my client."

Raymond's lawyer, Peter Rivera, a soft-spoken former prosecutor, rarely objected to or challenged Galligan's decisions. Though Rivera was an accomplished attorney, both Raymond and his father felt that he wasn't invested in the case, especially after they saw him talking to the prosecutors as if they were good friends. Rivera, like Jesse Berman, argued that his client had been arrested without probable cause. He called Raymond's father and grandmother to the stand to describe the conditions Raymond had endured and to suggest that police had violated his rights by questioning him in English without a guardian who could understand the proceedings. Raymond's grandmother, Natividad Colon, testified that her English was not very good and that she hadn't understood the Miranda rights or the questions. Detectives Hartigan and Arroyo claimed that Mrs. Colon had told them she understood and that they didn't have to translate, but on cross, Arroyo admitted that when he'd asked how her English was, Mrs. Colon had responded with a hand gesture, indicating "so-so."

Michael "Mickey" Joseph, Antron McCray's attorney, was a seasoned defense attorney who knew when to object and comment on the record, without raising the ire of Justice Galligan. The other attorneys, some of whom were less experienced and competent, often followed suit by joining in Joseph's objections and applications to the judge. For the pretrial hearing, Joseph did not present any defense witnesses. He knew that though there was a case to be made for excluding the confessions, Galligan was unlikely to make that decision, and having Antron and his parents testify would only give prosecutors a sneak preview of his case at trial. It was a gamble, but an educated one.

Michael Briscoe, the last defendant of the seven charged together at the pretrial hearing, was represented by the most combative and politically charged of the lawyers, Alton Maddox. Maddox, a controversial black activist, had already been involved in some of the decade's most divisive cases. He had represented the victims in the Howard Beach case, where Maddox had created a political spectacle by refusing to let his clients cooperate with the investigation until demands for a special prosecutor were met. Maddox had also been on the team that had represented Tawana Brawley in her accusations of rape and hate crimes against half a dozen white men, several of whom were members of the local police department in Wappingers Falls, New York. Maddox, attorney C. Vernon Mason, and the Reverend Al Sharpton had created a frenzy over this alleged incident, inflaming racial tensions with vast conspiracy theories in New York in 1987. After it became clear that Brawley had fabricated the crime, Alton Maddox was suspended from practicing law in 1990 when he refused to testify in an investigation into his conduct in that case.

Maddox did not call any witnesses in defense of Michael Briscoe, but he made a mark in the courtroom with his fiery personality. Earlier, at Briscoe's bail hearing, Maddox had arrived to represent Briscoe, but as he was not yet the attorney of record, Justice Carol Berkman would not allow him to speak. He disobeyed, and created an uproar in the courtroom when court officers approached to escort him out, prompting chants and jeers from supporters in the gallery. As soon as Maddox began his cross-examination of Officer Eric Reynolds at the hearing, Justice Galligan had to jump in almost immediately to tell him not to shout his questions at the officer.

Galligan handed down his ruling on the admissibility of the statements on February 23, 1990. Everyone, Galligan included, was aware that suppressing the confessions would gut the prosecution's case. The defense attorneys knew that Galligan was unlikely to grant the motions to suppress their clients' statements. A decision like that, coupled with the prosecution's lack of physical evidence, might force a dismissal of the charges, leading to the inevitable tabloid headline blaming Galligan for letting the teenagers walk free.

Galligan rejected every argument made by the defense attorneys, found no violations of Miranda rights, and put his full faith in the testimonies of police officers and district attorneys over those of the defendants and their families. In a single exception, Galligan excluded a comment made by Raymond before he was Mirandized. Raymond's lawyer had not even made an argument for excluding it.

Galligan pointed to the boys' insistence on their innocence as evidence that they understood their rights and the charges against them enough not to have been coerced. Kevin's "reluctance to incriminate himself in the most serious of crimes demonstrated both an understanding of his right not to do so and a realistic sensitivity towards law and its consequences," he remarked. He blamed Raymond Santana's father's "cavalier" attitude regarding his son's well-being for any failure to understand or exercise his rights. And Galligan wrote that he found

Korey's testimony claiming that he had been promised to be released if he made a statement "incredible."

With their motions to suppress the incriminating statements denied, the teenagers were headed to trial.

Raymond Santana, Antron McCray, Korey Wise, and Steve Lopez were all still incarcerated after the pretrial hearing in November of 1989, having failed to make bail. Right after the hearing, Alton Maddox and the Reverend Al Sharpton began raising money to help. Antron's family had already come up with nineteen thousand on their own, and the fund gave them the remaining six thousand they needed, so Antron was released on December 8.

The rest of the money Sharpton and Maddox raised was given to Steve Lopez's parents, who were able to put up his fifty-thousand-dollar bail later in December. The money that went to the Lopez family had first been offered to Korey Wise, but his mother turned it down. As a result, Korey would remain at Rikers, housed with adults because he was sixteen, throughout the trial period. Peter Rivera, Raymond Santana's lawyer, who had failed to apply for bail at the arraignment, eventually asked for a reduced bail of ten thousand dollars and later eighteen thousand, but Galligan refused to accept those amounts. Raymond's father couldn't afford the full amount, having spent his savings on the retainer for Rivera, so Raymond, too, remained incarcerated throughout the trial.

The Sixth Amendment to the Constitution guarantees, among other protections, the right of a defendant to "be confronted with the witnesses against him." This posed a problem for trying all the defendants together, because the Fifth Amendment states that no person "shall be compelled in any criminal case to be a witness against himself." Presenting the various statements of the defendants as evidence would mean that codefendants would become witnesses against one another, yet they could not be cross-examined, because this violated their right against self-incrimination. The 1968 Supreme Court decision in *Bruton v. U.S.* established that a jury instruction to ignore one defendant's out-of-court statement as evidence against another defendant did not go far enough in protecting those Fifth and Sixth Amendment rights. However, other courts have allowed such confessions to be presented and defendants who might implicate one another to be tried together when the names of codefendants are removed from any statement or confession.

In this case, the prosecution wanted to keep at least some of the defendants together, believing that weaker cases might benefit from being tried alongside stronger ones. The defense attorneys would have preferred individual trials, giving them the best opportunity to argue their cases without the specter of a "gang" sitting at the defense table. Over objections from the defense attorneys, Galligan gave ADAs Elizabeth Lederer and Arthur "Tim" Clements the chance to propose editing the tapes and statements to sufficiently adhere to the *Bruton* decision.

After a precise and exhaustive review, Lederer and Clements came up with an initial plan to try Yusef Salaam, Raymond Santana, and Antron McCray together. They didn't want all six remaining defendants tried together, because after redacting the names from each individual's tapes, little would be left of them. But combining these three, who rarely mentioned one another in their confessions, would not require inordinate excision. The others would be tried later.

Galligan agreed with the prosecutors and set a date to begin the first trial: April 16, 1990, almost exactly one year after the incidents in Central Park.

Michael Briscoe, who had been charged only with assault and riot and released on five-thousand-dollars bail the previous September, was arrested in March of 1990 for selling drugs to an undercover cop. His lawyer on the new charge arranged for him to plead guilty in both cases, and he received a sentence of one year. He would not have to testify against the other boys in the park.

———

In March of 1990, Mary Veit, the NYPD serologist, was going over evidence while preparing for her testimony at the first trial, set to begin in April. Veit noticed a yellowed area on one of Meili's socks from the crime scene. She immediately thought that it might be a semen stain she had missed, since she knew that bacteria grows on semen, turning it yellow over time. Her tests confirmed that semen was present, and on April 5, she sent this new sample to the FBI lab for testing. Elizabeth Lederer begged Justice Galligan for a postponement of the trial, hoping that this would be the break they needed. Galligan begrudgingly agreed, though he complained that the police lab had been negligent in not finding the stain earlier.

Special Agent Dwight Adams tested this new semen sample from the sock, but he was not able to provide the evidence against the defendants that the prosecutors were hoping for. This time, the DNA was strong and clear, and Adams had to run tests on only two of the four genetic locations before being able to definitively rule out each defendant and all the other suspects who'd been tested. It didn't match the sample from Meili's boyfriend, either. It did match the cervical swab, which had been too weak to be conclusive before, but now echoed this new, stronger evidence. The new test proved that someone else had raped the jogger.

The test was devastating to the prosecution. They were hoping that it would help to convict their suspects; instead, they could no longer refer to the DNA as inconclusive, a technically accurate description that would let them imply that it could be a match if only they had more information. Now their expert would have to admit on the stand that it could not possibly have come from any of the defendants or the other young men they had tested from the park that night.

Only a single DNA profile was found in the sock and cervical swab, not the handful that would be expected in an alleged gang rape. The semen on the pants matched the sample from Meili's boyfriend, and the DNA pattern found in the cervical swab and on Meili's sock were conclusively not a match for any of the suspects tested. Other than the explained presence of Kevin O'Reilly's semen on Meili's jogging pants, the only semen found at the scene had come from a single attacker, who was not any of the teenagers who had been tested.

With this setback, the prosecution needed a new strategy. Yet there is no evidence that anyone considered looking to other suspects or theories of the crime. Despite a prosecutor's obligation to seek justice, it seems that at that moment, winning the case trumped investigating the evidence. The incriminating statements by these five teenagers were so convincing to the detectives and prosecutors that no one felt the need to question their conclusions, which had been so easy to jump to in the hours and days after the rape. In steadfastly sticking to their initial theory of the case, they ignored the fact that in the summer of 1989 there was a serial rapist on the loose, whose crimes took place near where Trisha Meili had been attacked, and who used strikingly similar methods.

Around lunchtime on Wednesday, September 21, 1988, seven months before Trisha Meili was attacked in Central Park, Jackie Herbach was quietly sitting in a pew at the Church of the Heavenly Rest, which is located at Fifth Avenue and Ninetieth Street, facing Central Park. Herbach, a twenty-seven-year-old aspiring actress, was surprised when someone tapped her on the shoulder. She turned, and a young man asked her for the time. He made her nervous, so she moved to leave the empty church. Before she reached the door, the man grabbed her from behind and held a knife to her throat. "If you scream, I'll kill you," he said. He took her to a stairwell leading to the basement, where he demanded her money and jewelry. She recalls, "He went crazy. He became very violent, very scary. He started to choke me." He choked her so hard that blood vessels in her eyes popped. The young man then told her to take off her shirt. She complied, although she realized that he was planning to rape her. She begged him over and over, "Please don't rape me." Finally she told him she had an infection, something he didn't want to catch. That spooked him, and he fled before he had a chance to rape her. Herbach filed a police report, but no arrest was ever made in her case.

Her assailant was just beginning a horrific crime spree, one that would only escalate in violence and terror in the following year.

The man's next known attack occurred in Central Park on April 17, 1989, near the Lasker Rink at the northern end of the park, in an area called Fort Fish, for the War of 1812 fortification that once stood there. A twenty-six-year-old woman was there practicing tai chi exercises that afternoon, and she was alone. He approached and tried to make conversation. The man made her uncomfortable, so she began to walk away. He attacked her, beat her, tore off her clothes, and began to rape her, until a man nearby came to see why she was calling out. Her assailant ran off. The young woman spent at least two nights in the hospital because of her injuries. Her attacker apparently did not ejaculate, so there was no DNA to be collected, but the victim was able to recall a significant detail to the Sex Crimes detective who interviewed her. In addition to identifying him as a Hispanic male, she said she had noticed fresh stitches on his chin. The detective checked local hospital records and found that a man named Matias Reyes, fitting the description given by the victim, had received stitches on his chin a few days earlier at Metropolitan Hospital. Reyes was an eighteen-year-old Puerto Rican who worked at a bodega on 102nd Street and Third Avenue.

Yet Reyes was never questioned with regard to that attack. The victim, who did not want her name mentioned in the press, left New York City soon after the attack and did not cooperate with the police. The detective who had found Reyes's name was transferred out of the Sex Crimes Squad, and the case, unsolved, was closed within months, allowing Reyes to continue his vicious attacks.

Just two days after attacking the woman near the Lasker Rink in Central Park, Matias Reyes committed his most infamous crime. He beat and raped Trisha Meili, the Central Park Jogger, and left her for dead. Despite the proximate locations of these two attacks, there is no indication that the information gathered by police in the April 17, 1989, case was ever communicated to the detectives working the rape that took place two days later. Nor did anyone connect the fact that Reyes had spoken to a police detective he knew as he strolled out of the park on April 19 wearing Meili's headphones.

On April 22, a candlelight vigil was held for the Central Park Jogger at the Church of the Heavenly Rest, where Reyes had attacked Jackie Herbach seven months earlier. More incredibly, six years later, Herbach was working as a personal trainer when Salomon Brothers hired her to work with some of their employees. One of her clients was Trisha Meili, and the two women bonded over their common trauma, though it would be years before either learned that they had been attacked by the same man.

In June 1989, Reyes began to escalate his crime spree. Over the next two months, he attacked five more women, only now he followed them home and surprised them or forced his way into their apartments. On June 11, Reyes followed a woman into an apartment building on East 116th Street. He knocked on her door and pretended to be the son of the building's superintendent. When he got inside, he locked the door behind him and grabbed a knife from the kitchen. He forced her into the shower, raped her, and then raped her again on the bed. He held her face in a sink filled with water, in an apparent attempt to drown her, but she was strong and fought back. Concerned that she would be able to identify him, he stabbed her in several places on her body and around her eyes. Fortunately, the stab wounds were superficial, and the woman recovered, with her sight intact.

Three days later, Reyes knocked on the door of a basement apartment on East Ninety-seventh Street, just off Madison Avenue. Inside were Lourdes Gonzalez, a twenty-four-year-old pregnant woman, and three young children. Her fiancé, Antonio Serrano, was the superintendent of the building, but he was away that day. When Reyes knocked on the door, he asked for the super, pretending he had a question about the building. He said he wanted to leave a message, and he asked when the

102nd Street Cross Drive at night, April 1989
Taro Yamasaki/Getty Images

Tree marked H2 by detectives to indicate one of the locations where Trisha Meili was assaulted
Taro Yamasaki/Getty Images

Detectives observe marks in the grass where Trisha Meili
was dragged from the 102nd Street Cross Drive.
New York Post/*Splash News*

Antron McCray (left) and Korey Wise
are escorted from the 24th Precinct by police.
New York Post/*Splash News*

Schomburg Plaza towers as seen from
Central Park in the spring of 1989
Taro Yamasaki/Getty Images

Yusef Salaam (left) and Raymond Santana duck to avoid being photographed as police move them between precincts.
New York Post/*Splash News*

New York *Daily News* front page, April 21, 1989
New York Daily News/*Getty Images*

New York *Daily News* front page, April 22, 1989
New York Daily News/*Getty Images*

Prosecutor Elizabeth Lederer,
trailed by Detective Mike Sheehan
(right), on her way to
court to cross-examine
Yusef Salaam, August 1990
New York Post/*Splash News*

Yusef Salaam entering 111 Centre Street to hear the verdict in his trial, August 1990
Clarence Davis/Getty Images

Antron and Linda McCray arrive at court as his
trial enters its fourth week, July 1990.
Gerald Herbert/Getty Images

Korey Wise at arraignment with his lawyer, Colin Moore, May 1989
John Pedin/Getty Images

Kevin Richardson and
his mother, Gracie Cuffee,
heading to court on the first
day of his trial, October 1990
Gene Kappock/Getty Images

Demonstrators outside
111 Centre Street call for harsh
punishment for the defendants
during the first trial, July 1990.
New York Post/*Splash News*

Matias Reyes, then known
as the East Side Slasher,
following his arrest in
August 1989, four months
after he raped the
Central Park Jogger
William LaForce, Jr./Getty Images

Raymond Santana spent the
first five years of his sentence at
Goshen Residential Center,
a juvenile prison facility sixty miles
from New York City.
Raymond Santana

Kevin Richardson, incarcerated at Harlem Valley
Secure Center, receiving his associate's degree from
Dutchess Community College 1994
Kevin Richardson

super would be home, establishing for himself a window of many hours before he would be interrupted. After speaking with her for several minutes, Reyes grabbed her by the neck and forced her into the apartment, telling her not to scream. He led the two young boys into their bedroom and locked them in. When he returned to Gonzalez, she was holding a kitchen knife, pointed at Reyes. He grabbed her hand and wrenched the knife away. She begged him to let her take her three-month-old baby into the room with the other kids, and Reyes complied. From inside that room, the children heard as their mother screamed "Don't kill me" and her attacker offered a terrible choice: "Your eyes or your life." Reyes first demanded money, then raped her. Afterward, she began screaming at him, telling him to get out. Reyes stabbed Gonzalcz at least seven times and ran from the apartment. Gonzalez managed to drag herself out to the elevator, but she collapsed there. She died three hours later at St. Luke's–Roosevelt Hospital.

Detectives saw a pattern in these two June attacks. In both cases, the suspect had been described as wearing a blue-and-white-striped shirt, and he had stabbed his victims around the eyes so that they wouldn't be able to identify him. Bruno Francisi, a Sex Crimes Squad detective who dealt with "pattern cases," began to invcstigate.

On July 19, Reyes followed a young woman named Katherine Davis into her apartment building on Madison Avenue and Ninety-fourth Street. Davis, twenty, was a student living at home, but no one else was there. Because of some work being done on the building, the front door was propped open, so Reyes easily slipped in. He followed her up the stairs, and this time he was prepared with a weapon. He had a folding knife in his pocket, which he pulled out just as she was unlocking the door to the apartment. He raped her several times in the apartment and then gave her a similar ultimatum: "I have to kill you or I have to blind you." She begged him to put cloth over her eyes so it would be less painful. He did, and then stabbed her around the eyes, but yet again he failed to inflict permanent damage. Then he offered to call her an ambulance. He left her in the apartment, tied up with three electrical cords, one binding her feet, another binding her hands, and a third wrapped around her head to gag her. Two of the cords were tied together so that her hands were immediately in front of her face, in the same position that Trisha Meili had been found. When he left, he took her ATM card and used it to extract three hundred dollars from her bank account, and he called 911 and gave them her address.

On July 27, 1989, Reyes attempted another attack, this time on a twenty-eight-year-old woman in the hallway of her apartment building at Ninety-fifth Street and Lexington Avenue. He never got into her apartment, and when a neighbor approached, Reyes fled.

On August 5, 1989, nearly a year after he'd attacked Jackie Herbach at the Church of the Heavenly Rest, Matias Reyes struck again. Unarmed, he followed Elizabeth Reynolds into her building on Ninety-first Street between Lexington and Third avenues. He took the stairs and stopped at each floor to see where she got off the elevator. He knocked on her door right after she walked in, startling her into opening it without finding out who it was. He held his hand in a pocket and pretended to have a gun. She screamed and scratched and bit him, but he was stronger. He raped her in her shower and on her bed, then took her ATM card and asked for her PIN code. While he was in another room, Reynolds grabbed a towel and fled the apartment, looking for help. Her doorman and a neighbor subdued Reyes with a broomstick as he tried to leave the building, then held him on the sofa in the lobby until the police arrived. Reyes, known by then to the police as the "East Side Slasher," had finally been caught.

Matias Reyes was born in Fajardo, Puerto Rico, in 1971. When he was just a few years old, his mother moved to New York, leaving him behind with his father. His father was a farmworker, and young Matias often helped him with jobs that included slaughtering pigs. Reyes told a psychologist that his father had abused his mother, and that his grandmother had told him that his father bought him from his mother for four hundred dollars before she moved to New York. He eventually followed his mother to New York City, and he moved back and forth between there and Puerto Rico several times in his early teenage years. He claims to have been sexually abused when he was seven, though, depending on the account, it was either by two male strangers or by family members.

A school report from when he was fourteen noted behavioral problems and labeled him "emotionally disturbed." School records and studies by various psychologists all found his IQ to be in the low or mid-seventies.

According to some reports, when he was fifteen and living in New York, he sexually abused his own mother. He moved back to Puerto Rico for a time and never saw his mother again. By the time he was seventeen, in 1988, Reyes was living in New York and working at a bodega on 102nd Street near Third Avenue, across the street from the 23rd Precinct.

After his arrest on August 5, 1989, Reyes was taken to the 19th Precinct, on the East Side. Though he had not tried to blind his last victim, Elizabeth Reynolds, before he was caught, Detective Bruno Francisi, who had been investigating the serial rapist known as the East Side Slasher, saw similarities in the cases. Francisi had been called in that August day because the rape took place in the same neighborhood as the others, and he recognized other patterns, including the description of the attacker and the fact that one of the other women had also been raped in the shower. Francisi suspected that this man was responsible for the rape of Katherine Davis, the rape on June 11, and the rape and murder of Lourdes Gonzalez. Francisi took custody of him at the 19th Precinct and drove him through Central Park to the Sex Crimes Squad on the West Side.

Francisi told Reyes that he suspected him in some other crimes he was investigating, in addition to that day's rape. "I didn't touch that girl,"

Reyes said. Francisi played him a recording. It was the 911 call Reyes had made after leaving Katherine Davis's apartment. Francisi had, of course, studied that tape, and he had instantly recognized Reyes's voice when they met at the 19th Precinct. When Reyes heard his voice on the tape, he hung his head. "I'm fucked," he said.

He admitted to raping Katherine Davis, but at first he tried to deny the rape that had taken place earlier that day. "What would my grandmother think if she found out?" Reyes asked. Francisi reminded him of the evidence: He had been caught in the woman's building, and she'd identified him at the scene. Recognizing that he was unlikely to be able to deny this one, he confessed anew.

But getting Reyes to confess to murdering Lourdes Gonzalez was a greater challenge. For this, veteran homicide detective Michael Sheehan, who had worked the Central Park Jogger investigation, was brought in. There was no direct evidence yet to link Reyes to the Gonzalez crime, so Sheehan had to rely on his wits and the lies that are standard procedure in interrogations. And Sheehan was a gifted interrogator. One ADA who worked with him recalled that he was "pure insinuation and seduction . . . every inch the promoter, the storyteller, the joker, the charmer."

Reyes's fingerprints had been taken, and Sheehan started by trying to convince him that they had found prints in the apartment on Ninety-seventh Street and it would only be a matter of time before they matched them to Reyes's. But Reyes remained confident that they would not find his fingerprints. After an hour and a half, no progress had been made toward a confession for the murder. All Reyes admitted was that he'd read about the crime in the newspaper, and he asked about whether there had really been a kid in the apartment.

After a break, Sheehan tried something new. Part of his job as an interrogator was to make the suspect comfortable, to convince him that he was a friend or someone Reyes could relate to. Sheehan guessed that, like many sex offenders, Reyes might have been sexually abused as a child. Sheehan asked him if anything bad had happened to him. Alone in the room with Reyes, Sheehan said, "You don't have to be embarrassed. If something happened, you can tell me." Sheehan told Reyes that he'd been propositioned in a public bathroom when he was a kid. He wanted Reyes to believe that they had something in common and that he would take seriously any account of abuse. Reyes admitted that he'd been sexually abused.

"Will you ever forget this guy?" Sheehan asked. "Because I won't ever forget the guy that approached me."

"I'll never forget this guy. I'll never forget him," Reyes yelled.

"Well, do you think this kid at Ninety-seventh Street is ever going to forget the guy who raped and killed his mother?"

Reyes admitted that the kid was not likely to forget. Sheehan then showed Reyes a police sketch of his face. Though the drawing had been made based on the description one of the other female victims had provided, the context in which it was presented suggested that the young boy could perfectly describe Reyes.

"That's me," Reyes said.

Now that Reyes was convinced there was insurmountable evidence against him, Sheehan appealed to his sense of guilt, using classic minimization techniques. "God was there. God was watching. God knows what happened." Sheehan said he wanted to hear from the killer about what had happened. "I think it's you, and if you were there, I hope you tell me the truth. I don't know what happened. I don't know if this was an accident. I don't know if it was a mistake. I don't know if the killer acted in self-defense."

"It wasn't self-defense. She defended her kids. She had the knife. I took it off her easily," Reyes replied.

It was after midnight when ADA Peter Casolaro sat down to record Reyes's confession on videotape. By then, Reyes was defeated, and he hung his head as he answered questions. He waived his Miranda rights and chose not to have an attorney present. He spoke in detail about the murder of Lourdes Gonzalez, recalling specifics about the layout of the basement apartment, and then he described the rape three days earlier. When Casolaro pressed him about two other rapes, the one on July 19 and the one he'd been arrested for the previous day, he stopped talking, saying, "I don't want to keep remembering these things." Twice, the tape stopped as detectives convinced him to speak again. By the end, Reyes had provided detailed confessions, on videotape, to four rapes, including the rape and murder of Lourdes Gonzalez.

Though the confessions to the detectives and ADA Casolaro were thorough and convincing, physical evidence tying Reyes to the crimes would make it a virtually airtight case. Several of his victims had identified him, but the police had chosen to spare Lourdes Gonzalez's young children the trauma of asking them to make an identification. As a result, the only evidence they really had for the Gonzalez murder was Reyes's own confession. Fingerprinting and blood typing were useful tools for investigators, but they could not prove guilt beyond a reasonable doubt. Fingerprints, when they could be collected, only established that an individual had been in a certain location, not what he had done there. Blood typing and hair comparison might rule some people out, but they could not be definitively linked to anyone in particular. But now, prosecutors could take advantage of DNA technology.

FBI laboratories analyzed a blood sample from Reyes and compared it to semen samples taken from the victims in two of the rapes and from Gonzalez. All of the samples were consistent with one another. But ADA Casolaro still had to convince the judge to allow the DNA test results into evidence. Though some courts had embraced DNA technology as the cutting edge, others were skeptical of the potential for laboratory error and the use of race and other factors to narrow down the population considered in the probability calculations. In the case of the Reyes DNA, the FBI calculated that the band patterns they saw were likely to occur in one out of every 49 million Hispanics in the United States. They had used population statistics to further prove the unlikelihood that the DNA found at the crime scene belonged to anyone else.

At a hearing held to determine the admissibility of the DNA evidence, a defense expert argued that using racial or ethnic terms was not justified, while still admitting that the tests pointed to Reyes. The judge assigned to the case, coincidentally, was Justice Thomas Galligan, the very same man who presided over the Central Park Jogger trials. He agreed to allow the DNA tests into evidence. Reyes had caused the delay of his DNA hearing when he shoved his lawyer, who then begged out of representing him. His new lawyer, Richard Siracusa, was appointed so the hearing could proceed, and he represented Reyes throughout the rest of the process.

Siracusa informed Reyes that he was likely to get at least fifty years to life if the case went to trial. With the DNA tests admitted into evidence, and knowing that he was likely to be convicted, Reyes agreed to a plea bargain the day jury selection for the trial was to begin. Galligan had proposed a plea of thirty-three years to life, and the defense and prosecution agreed to it.

On the day of sentencing, November 1, 1991, Reyes had the opportunity to speak. He admitted to the murder but then said, "I am tired of all this bullshit of this Court, for these courts and these lawyers—they are not doing anything for me." He turned and swung at Siracusa, sending him over a chair and onto the floor, before being carried away, fighting, by court officers. After Reyes was escorted out, Galligan commented on his crimes. "It is incomprehensible that any human being would conceive of, let alone commit, such terrible acts," he said. He recommended that Reyes should remain in prison for life, because "if Mr. Reyes is ever at liberty, then civilized people are at risk."

Within days, hours even, of the attack on Trisha Meili in Central Park, momentum had already begun to build toward convictions for the teenagers suspected in the rape. With incriminating statements and videotaped confessions, and a public outcry that had reached a fever pitch, it would be hard to imagine a reversal of course. Yet given the evidence now available to the prosecution on the eve of trial, an opportunity for a reality check had presented itself to investigators and the district attorney's office. Holes in the detectives' and prosecutors' theory of the case had arisen everywhere.

First, there was the fact that the DNA tests pointed to a single rapist, someone who was not any of the kids they'd tested. And though the jogger had bled profusely due to her injuries, none of her blood had been found on the clothing of any of the teenagers. But instead of considering whether the negative DNA results might mean that they had the wrong suspects, the prosecution instead assumed that there must have been a sixth rapist, apparently the only one to ejaculate at the scene, who had been with the other teenagers and simply hadn't been caught.

The time line, as it was originally constructed by the police and quickly disseminated by the media, also looked shaky. That initial time line had been constructed based on the statements of the teenagers to the detectives, but even those statements did not provide a consistent time line for when the rape occurred. Antron and Yusef had placed the rape before the assaults at the reservoir, but Raymond, Kevin, and Korey had listed it as the last event of the night. The detectives settled on the latter explanation early on and shared it with the media. On April 22, *The New York Times* published a map and time line, "Two Hours of Terror," which put the rape at 10:05 p.m., after all the other incidents. *Newsday,* the *Daily News,* and the *New York Post* also published time lines stating that the rape occurred after 10:00 p.m.

But when Trisha Meili awoke from her coma, she was able to tell investigators about her jogging route and pace. From her apartment on Eighty-third Street, it would normally take her about sixteen or seventeen minutes to arrive at the spot where she was first hit on the back of the head and dragged from the path. A neighbor, James Lansing, reported the he'd bumped into Meili and chatted with her at 8:55 p.m. as she left for her run. And her friend Pat Garrett told police that he'd made a plan to meet her back at her apartment at ten o'clock. With all this new information, it was clear that the attack on Meili began between 9:10 and 9:15, almost an hour earlier than previously assumed, and before the assaults of the male joggers near the reservoir.

This new time line left only about ten minutes for the teenagers to have run back up to the 102nd Street Cross Drive after harassing the tandem bikers, committed the brutal rape, and gotten back in time for the assault on David Lewis, at least six hundred yards away, near the reservoir.

Beyond the inconsistencies in the time line, the teens' statements were also inconsistent within themselves, inconsistent with the other statements they had made, and inconsistent with the facts of the case. Antron and Kevin had inaccurately described what the jogger was wearing. Korey said the jogger had been cut with a knife, then said later it was a rock. Kevin, Raymond, and Antron all incorrectly described the attack as having taken place near the reservoir.

And the crime-scene detectives had photographed the trampled grass—leading from the Cross Drive, where Meili was first attacked, to deep in the woods, where she was raped—which measured less than a foot and a half wide, hardly consistent with a gang of youths dragging a woman from the road.

By the spring of 1990, with significant information about Reyes and his other crimes now available, the similarities to the Central Park Jogger rape should have jumped out. While the investigation into the rape of the Central Park Jogger was ongoing, Matias Reyes attacked at least five other women, all clustered on the East Side and within less than a mile of the location of Meili's rape. Reyes had attempted to blind some of his victims, and Meili's worst injuries were around her eyes. Though she hadn't been stabbed with a knife, blunt force to one eye had shattered her socket, damaging her sight permanently. Her long-sleeved shirt had been fashioned as a rope and used to tie her hands in front of her mouth, a manner identical to the one Reyes had used to bind the hands of Katherine Davis with electrical cords. And Michael Sheehan, a veteran detective from the Manhattan North Homicide Squad, worked both cases.

If DNA databanks, which can now be used to search for a DNA match across samples statewide and even nationally, had been available in 1989, Reyes might have been connected almost automatically to the Central Park Jogger rape. But even without this type of system, the myriad holes in the detectives' theory of the case and the evidence linking Reyes to the rape in Central Park should have been enough for them to make that connection on their own. Yet none did.

Beyond the obvious pressure on the detectives and prosecutors to get convictions quickly in a case that had so captured the attention and emotions of the city, the confidence with which investigators embraced the guilt of these young men reflected also the trend toward seeing young minority men as criminals. The assumptions that had pervaded the media's response to the case also blinded those who were responsible for seeing justice done, who were unwilling or unable to recognize the flaws in their case against the teenagers from Harlem. One of the detectives who worked on the case later explained to a reporter why he believed the teenagers were able to talk about the crime on videotape so callously: "In that race, in that society, rape is no big deal."

These same assumptions could be seen in another sensational crime, one that occurred in Boston that same year, as investigators and a whole city eagerly believed the story concocted by Charles Stuart. Stuart and his seven-months-pregnant wife, Carol, both white, were shot in their car during an apparent robbery attempt on a dark street near a housing project in the mostly black neighborhood of Mission Hill. Carol was shot in the head and pronounced dead at the hospital, and her baby was delivered two months early, but the infant had been without oxygen too long and had suffered too much brain damage. He was taken off life support seventeen days later. Charles Stuart spent six weeks in the hospital while recovering from the gunshot wound to his abdomen and several subsequent surgeries.

As with the Central Park Jogger case, the murder of Carol Stuart provided rich fodder for the local papers. A sensational photograph of the victims in the car was captured at the scene and printed in the next morning's *Boston Herald.* Fueled by a war for circulation between the *Herald* and *The Boston Globe,* reporters painted a lurid picture of the crime. The Stuarts were an "all-American couple," and accounts compared their charmed lifestyle to Camelot. The location of the shooting reinforced fears of "black on white" crime. Calls to reinstate the death penalty were heard in response.

Once Stuart was out of intensive care a few days after the incident, he calmly and in great detail told the police about how a black man had jumped into their car as they were heading home from the hospital, forced them at gunpoint to drive to an empty street in the Mission Hill district, and then demanded their valuables. Stuart described how the assailant had suspected him of being a cop and had then shot Carol in the head before aiming the gun at him. He described the shooter's size, features, clothing, and voice in detail. The Boston Police Department, under pressure to solve this particularly public crime, put more than a hundred officers on the case, canvassing and searching the Mission Hill projects.

After frisking and harassing many local residents, police got a tip that led them to Willie Bennett. Bennett was already infamous, having served time for shooting a cop. Charles Stuart eventually picked Bennett out of a lineup, and though the tipsters who'd claimed Bennett confessed to them later recanted, the Boston police were sure they'd found their murderer.

It soon fell apart. Charles Stuart's brother, Matthew, told the authorities that he had collected a bag containing jewelry and a gun from Stuart immediately after the shooting, believing he was helping his brother with an insurance scam. It turned out that Charles Stuart had carefully planned to murder his wife to cash in on a life-insurance policy, concocting an assailant he knew would be plausible to the police. Stuart's invention was so plausible, in fact, that Willie Bennett was nearly prosecuted for a crime he hadn't committed. Stuart jumped to his death from the Tobin Bridge in Boston just as police were heading to his house to arrest him.

Charles Stuart believed that he could get away with this heinous crime exactly because he knew that the crime he staged would make sense to people. He chose his location and the description of the attacker based on the assumptions he knew the media, the public, and the police would make. And it almost worked.

The term *racial hoax,* coined by law professor Katheryn Russell-Brown, is used to describe this type of deception, when a crime is either invented or committed and then blamed on someone of a different race by the perpetrator. Charles Stuart was by no means the only one to have the idea to commit a crime and blame it on a person of color. In fact, Russell found forty-seven cases between 1987 and 1996 in which a racial hoax was perpetrated by a white person accusing a black person of a crime. The vast majority of racial hoaxes are white-on-black ones and prey on whites' fear of violent crime by African-Americans. In many of these hoaxes, innocent people were arrested or detained, and some hoaxes lasted months or even years before the truth was revealed.

In the Central Park Jogger case, the narrative that was so quickly swallowed whole by the media and public relied on the same assumptions that encourage white-on-black racial hoaxes and make them so successful. Charles Stuart knew that many people in Boston would willingly believe the story of a black man in a tracksuit robbing and shooting a white couple, perhaps even see it as inevitable. By the same logic, the rape of a white woman in Central Park by a group of minority teenagers from Harlem did not stretch the imaginations of fearful New York residents, even when the actual evidence contradicted the popular narrative.

CHAPTER FIVE

On the evening of August 23, 1989, just four months after the rape in Central Park, another racially charged incident added to what seemed like a growing pattern in New York City. Four black teenagers went to the mostly Italian neighborhood of Bensonhurst, in Brooklyn, to look at a 1982 Pontiac that had been advertised for sale. A group of white teenagers from the neighborhood were out with baseball bats, awaiting the arrival of some other black kids who were rumored to be coming for the birthday party of a girl from the neighborhood. When the four young men walked past, the group surrounded them. Someone had a gun. One of the four, sixteen-year-old Yusuf Hawkins, was shot twice in the chest and was dead before he reached the hospital.

Demonstrators organized by Al Sharpton walked the streets of Bensonhurst in protest. Local residents turned out to taunt and jeer them, hurling racial epithets. Some yelled, "Niggers go home," "We don't want you here," and even "James Earl Ray," the name of the assassin who killed Martin Luther King, Jr. Others took up a chant: "Central Park, Central Park," in reference to the jogger case. Some held up watermelons. Sharpton's protesters retorted by chanting, "Howard Beach, Howard Beach." The name of Tawana Brawley, the black teenager who had falsely alleged that several white men had raped her in her upstate New York town, was also yelled during the confrontation. These terrible crimes and incidents, each of which had ratcheted up racial tensions in the city, were so inextricably linked in the minds of New Yorkers that one could not occur without everyone instantly thinking of those that had come before.

In the fall of 1989, David Dinkins beat incumbent three-term Mayor Ed Koch in the Democratic primary and went on to become the city's first African-American mayor. Mayor Koch's outspoken and sometimes racially divisive politics fell in favor of a candidate the city hoped would mend those fractured bonds. Many credited the Hawkins murder and the overt racism that followed in its footsteps with helping Dinkins win the election.

The Bensonhurst case came to trial quickly, and in May 1990, nineteen-year-old Joey Fama was convicted of second-degree murder in the killing of Yusuf Hawkins. But more protests ensued when Keith Mondello, another leader of the gang, was acquitted on the most serious charge of murder. Al Sharpton complained at a rally that Mayor Dinkins was a "sissy" for not focusing more on race relations.

Twelve days after Trisha Meili had fully awakened from a coma and began forming new memories that would last, she was transferred to Gaylord Hospital, a rehabilitation center in Wallingford, Connecticut. There she continued physical and mental recovery from the traumatic brain injury she had suffered. She'd already had surgery to repair her shattered eye socket, and her bruises were beginning to heal, but at Gaylord she relearned basic skills, like walking and speaking normally, and worked at regaining her ability to remember words and ideas. She never completely recovered her sense of smell, and doctors determined that she would never have any memory of what had happened to her the night of April 19, 1989. Her brain had been so badly damaged that night that long-term memories from the hours before she lost consciousness were never even formed.

But through her determination and efforts at Gaylord, Trisha Meili continued to amaze her doctors. She started jogging again with the Achilles Track Club, a running group for people with disabilities. In September, Salomon Brothers asked her to do some work for them from a desk in her room at Gaylord. In November, she returned to New York

City, moving into an apartment set up by her employer, and returned to work there after Thanksgiving.

The trial of Antron McCray, Yusef Salaam, and Raymond Santana started on a Monday morning, June 25, 1990. The trial was held in a courtroom on the seventh floor of 111 Centre Street, a square beige building largely unadorned except for a few stripes of windows and close to the cluster of courthouses and other municipal buildings near City Hall.

The courtroom was packed with reporters, including not only the crime-beat reporters from the city papers but also others from across the country. Lines formed outside each day of those wishing to fill the rows of seats behind the family members and reporters. Some were the usual court watchers, including people who wandered in off the street because they had nowhere else to go. Others were just curious about the famous case, or came to see who else would show up. John F. Kennedy, Jr., then working at the DA's office, was sometimes spotted in the audience. A number of black activists appeared in court with their followers, whom the press dubbed "the Supporters." Though these groups came to show support for the defendants and rail against the justice system, many were more concerned with promoting their own political agendas than arguing against the actual merits of the prosecution's case.

Outside the courthouse, others voiced their desire for swift and harsh punishment of the teenagers on trial. Members of the Guardian Angels, a group made up of volunteer civilians who combat crime through patrols and citizen's arrests, demonstrated as the trial began, holding signs that said ADULT CRIMES, ADULT PUNISHMENT; JUSTICE FOR THE JOGGER; and THERE IS NOTHING MINOR ABOUT RAPE.

The Reverend Al Sharpton, who had been advising the families and was often present at the pretrial hearing, was not in the audience at the start of the first trial of the Central Park defendants. Instead, he was downstairs in the same courthouse, having been on trial himself since

March, accused of stealing money from a charitable organization he'd founded.

The jury for the trial of McCray, Salaam, and Santana was made up of four white members, four black members, three Latinos, and one Asian-American. Only two were women. They had been selected from a pool of about three hundred New Yorkers. The group included a former Methodist minister, a repairman for a utility company, a former reporter and speechwriter, a filing clerk, and a housewife.

That June morning, as the jurors filed into the crowded courtroom in front of Justice Thomas B. Galligan, they saw all three defendants sitting together at one side of the defense table, their lawyers at the other end. Savvier defense attorneys would have separated them, lest their physical proximity imply a deeper connection than their lawyers would have wished to suggest.

Elizabeth Lederer, the serious and competent assistant district attorney in the Sex Crimes Prosecution Unit, deftly wove a tale of mischief and mayhem in Central Park on April 19, 1989, in her opening statement, describing the weak evidence the prosecution had as if it were strong and dismissing the lack of DNA matches as inconsequential. Presenting her case calmly and without emotion, she laid out a time line of events in the park, and though she chose not to specify the exact times of each incident, she placed the attack on Trisha Meili between the harassment of the tandem bikers and the assaults on the joggers near the reservoir.

Lederer admitted that the witnesses and victims from the park could not identify their assailants (with the exception of Jermain Robinson, who had already pleaded guilty), but she argued that the witnesses' stories would confirm admissions by the defendants. Lederer told the jury that tests performed on the teenagers' clothing would bolster her case, and she explained that a hair found on Kevin Richardson's clothing "matched and was consistent with" hair from the jogger, greatly exaggerating the conclusiveness of hair testing. Though Kevin Richardson was not a defendant in this trial, she mentioned him often. The physical evidence against him was strongest because of the hair samples, and each of the three on trial had named him as a rapist, so Lederer wanted to tie the defendants to Kevin as firmly as possible. If she could make him seem like a vicious predator, without a defense attorney to object to that characterization, he might make the defendants actually in the room look guilty by association.

She did admit to the negative DNA results, but argued to the jury that the lack of DNA evidence was not inconsistent with their guilt, suggesting that these young men did not ejaculate but were otherwise participants in the rape. ADA Lederer placed the most weight on the confessions, telling the jury about what they would see on the videotapes and hear from detectives about the teenagers' admissions. With a detached manner, she described the crime scene in graphic detail. "As the police officers approached, they saw a young woman whose hair was matted with blood and mud, who was naked but for a jogging bra. Who was tied up with a blood soaked shirt that went around her mouth, her neck and her wrists. And she lay there thrashing in the mud, groaning. . . . Her left eye was swollen shut, her right eye was opened and stared blankly."

The defense attorneys went next, presenting their theories as to why the jury shouldn't convict. Each had a different style and approach. Mickey Joseph, Antron's lawyer and the most experienced criminal defense attorney among them, focused on reasonable doubt in the absence of physical evidence and accused the detectives of crossing the line in the interrogations. He pointed out the artifice of the videotaped statements, since so many hours had elapsed before the recordings began, but he did not provide the jury with an alternate theory that might actually prove his client's innocence.

Bobby Burns, Yusef's attorney, played up the political angle of the case by suggesting that the police were especially motivated to extract confessions. "After the female jogger's body had been discovered, the entire character of the investigative activity into the case began to escalate into a degree of excitement and intensity." He described how many high-ranking members of the NYPD had been involved. "You had sergeants, you had captains, you had brass. . . . So there was a strong motivation to solve and close out this crime as quickly as possible." Burns tried to suggest that the police went too far because of this pressure, but he stopped short of accusing them of misconduct or coercion.

Finally, Peter Rivera, Raymond Santana's lawyer, presented a brief narrative of his client's ordeal, arguing that police had had no right to arrest Raymond in the first place and that they had held him for far too long in order to force a confession out of him. He asked the jury to be skeptical of the testimony of the police officers, and stated most clearly and emphatically that his client had been coerced.

The next day, the *Daily News* published a column by Bob Herbert commenting on the first day of the trial. He assessed the opening statements and described the scene in the courtroom, depicting the teenaged defendants as "mutants." Herbert mocked their dress and appearance, describing Antron McCray as "little, a tiny-headed, frightened, wimpish pipsqueak." He made fun of Yusef Salaam's "pistachio ice cream"–colored socks, and the fact that Raymond Santana's family hadn't been able to afford bail or a jacket for him to wear to court. The assumption of guilt and the tendency to portray the defendants as freaks that permeated the mainstream media was so powerful that even Herbert, the African-American journalist known for his critical columns on race relations, fell prey to it. Like most journalists, he failed to turn a skeptical eye to the inconsistencies in the teens' statements or the utter lack of physical evidence against the Central Park defendants. Nearly everyone in the city believed wholeheartedly in the narrative that the NYPD and now the district attorney's office were promoting.

As the testimonies began, Elizabeth Lederer and her cocounsel, Tim Clements, presented their witnesses as chronologically as possible, hoping to weave a clear narrative of the complicated events of April 19 and 20. Their half of the case took almost four weeks. They began by establishing the presence of a large group of black and Hispanic teenagers in the park through the testimony of Officer Raymond Alvarez, who had driven through Central Park and scattered the group by shining his light at them just after 9:00 p.m.

Then the park victims testified. First Michael Vigna, then Gerald Malone and Patricia Dean, the tandem bike riders, followed by the male joggers at the reservoir: David Lewis, David Good, Robert Garner, and John Loughlin. Each described his or her experience of being harassed and attacked by the teenage gang, and, whenever possible, the time it had happened. It was a strong lineup, and it drew attention to the racial rift in the courtroom. Other than in the front rows, which were reserved for the media, an almost entirely black and Latino crowd of supporters sat behind the defendants. Behind the prosecution's table, the spectators were almost all white, as were most of the victims who paraded in front of the jury. The park witnesses represented exactly the educated, employed, and white part of the city that found the specter of "urban crime" so frightening.

The contrast to the defendants in that segregated courtroom was especially apparent. Mickey Joseph had fought to keep all but Lewis and Loughlin off the stand, arguing that the defendants had not been charged with crimes related to the other witnesses, but Galligan agreed to let them testify because they could speak to the more general riot charge and could help corroborate the admissions of some of the defendants.

Missing from that early parade of victims were Antonio Diaz, who was often referred to as "the bum," and Trisha Meili. Diaz, a former heroin addict on methadone, was in the hospital when the other victims testified, but he did eventually tell his story, through a Spanish interpreter, at a later date. Meili would take the stand later, after doctors had described her injuries, and when her testimony could stand alone and make a greater impact.

In the midst of testifying, one of the victims, Gerald Malone, noticed something he never had before. In trying to make a point about how the victims had not been able to identify anyone from the park, Peter Rivera presented the witness with some of the photos he'd been shown that first night for identification. But this time, Malone recognized something in one of the pictures: a logo on a jacket, which he recalled having seen on one of the kids blocking his path in the park that night. The photo was of Kevin Richardson, and though he was not a defendant in this trial, Malone's discovery bolstered the prosecution's case that Kevin had been the ringleader. Rivera's mistake in handing the witness photos that the prosecution had not brought out was compounded when Patricia Dean, Malone's fellow tandem biker, also admitted that the logo looked familiar—from the windbreaker of a kid who had grabbed at her legs and tried to knock her off the bicycle.

The defense lawyers' cross-examinations of these witnesses revealed their rhetorical styles and varied skills. Mickey Joseph, Antron McCray's attorney, often made good arguments, trying to keep the most devastating and graphic descriptions from the jury, but sometimes failed to emphasize his best points to the jury, and he faced a strict judge, one who was unlikely to grant his objections and requests. Peter Rivera was quieter, objecting less often and asking fewer questions than the other defense attorneys. Robert Burns, who represented Yusef Salaam, would often concur with the objections of Mickey Joseph during the direct examinations, objecting just after he did. But on cross-examinations, Burns did more damage than good. With the victims from the park, Burns asked so many questions that each witness effectively repeated his or her entire description of events, often highlighting especially negative testimony, with no apparent purpose. Burns encouraged John Loughlin to explore in detail the shape and texture of the object that had been used to hit him in the head. One reporter commented, "The result [of Burns's cross-examinations] is that the prosecution is enjoying an unintended windfall: the highly unusual opportunity of having its case presented to the jury twice."

After the victims, several police officers who had been in the park that night testified about having heard calls on the radio about a group of teenagers and then searching for them throughout the park. Officers Reynolds and Powers testified about the arrests of the teenagers who were caught in and around the park. Peter Rivera got in one good point when cross-examining Officer Reynolds. Under pressure, Reynolds admitted that paperwork he'd filled out later had inaccurately described Raymond as having resisted arrest by running away, having been advised of his rights early on, and having refused an offer for a phone call after his arrest, though none of those things had actually occurred. It was the first small chink in the credibility of the police.

Vinicio Moore and Carlos Colon, the two construction workers, told the jury about finding a bloodied, flailing body while walking through the park. By asking Moore about the beers he and his friend had consumed that night and whether the police had ever taken blood or tissue samples from him, Peter Rivera tried to suggest that they ought to be considered suspects. It wasn't a strong point, but it was the only time any of the defense lawyers attempted to suggest an alternative theory of the case. The defense attorneys were not required to present alternatives to the jury, but a case without them is usually a weak one.

The defense attorneys did achieve one small victory when Justice Galligan ruled that a series of charts created by the prosecution could not be shown to the jury. The exhibits reflected the forensic tests of hair, semen, and blood samples, but Mickey Joseph argued that they were potentially confusing to jurors, pointing out, "It does say 'positive for sperm,' but cannot say whose sperm." Galligan concurred and excluded the charts.

The officers who first arrived on the scene and the EMTs who treated Trisha Meili testified as to her grave injuries. The gory details seemed to have an effect on the jury. They were shown dozens of large color photographs of the injuries to the jogger, and they sometimes betrayed their disgust, shaking their heads or frowning.

Doctor Robert Kurtz, the director of the surgical intensive care unit at Metropolitan Hospital, who had overseen Trisha Meili's treatment, described in excruciating detail the degree and severity of her injuries. He told of the multiple surgeries she had endured and mentioned her bout with pneumonia in the hospital during her long and slow recovery. With his clear and dramatic testimony, the jurors came to see a picture of just how life-threatening Meili's situation had been. "She hung on to life by a thread. I think it's close to a miracle that she survived," he told them.

The defense pointed out that there was little medical evidence that the victim had been raped at all, but Kurtz argued that it was common in rapes to see no trauma to the vaginal area. Both Burns and Joseph tried to get the doctor to admit that a rape victim who fought back would have bruises or scars to show for it, but Kurtz's confident rejection of their claims neutralized what might otherwise have been a strong argument.

Detective José Ramón Rosario was the first detective to take the stand. He had not played a major role in the investigation, but he had made the fateful call from Metropolitan Hospital, telling the desk sergeant to hold the teenagers who had been arrested in Central Park, and he had joined other officers in picking up Antron McCray and his family and taking them to the Central Park Precinct. During his cross-examination, Antron's lawyer focused on Detective Rosario's interaction with the McCray family at their apartment. Antron had not been read the Miranda rights there, and Mickey Joseph pressed Rosario to admit that Antron was being arrested as a suspect and therefore should have had his rights read to him. Despite having participated in a briefing about the case earlier on the day that he arrived at the McCray household, Rosario played dumb.

"You knew that Antron McCray was being brought down to [the] Central Park Precinct and was going to be questioned about some very serious crimes, didn't you?" asked Joseph.

"No, sir."

"You didn't know he was going to be questioned about that?"

"I didn't know what his role was in the investigation."

When pressed further, Rosario said he "assumed he was not a suspect." With that, incredulous supporters could be heard murmuring and scoffing in the courtroom. The idea that a group of police officers would go to Antron's apartment and pick him and his parents up to take them to the precinct without any idea of his involvement or whether he was even a suspect was hard to swallow.

During Robert Burns's cross-examination of Detective Rosario, Mickey Joseph jumped up to object several times. It was unusual, given that defense attorneys, though independently representing their own clients, are essentially on the same side. Joseph was trying to prevent Burns from rehashing more gory details of Meili's injuries, but the interruptions created the impression that the defense lawyers were nowhere near being on the same page.

After Rosario, Detective Robert Honeyman testified about the crime scene. During direct examination by Elizabeth Lederer, Honeyman identified several photographs he'd taken at the crime scene, including a photograph of the path marked in the wet grass where Trisha Meili had been dragged off the road. Lederer asked him to point out the width of the drag mark, which he did. "Approximately sixteen to eighteen inches," he said. No one in the courtroom seemed to realize the significance of this testimony. None of the defense attorneys pointed out that a group of at least five teenaged boys, a wild gang, if the prosecution was to be believed, would probably not have walked in a single file line as they dragged a victim into the woods. None asked Honeyman whether a narrow path such as this might indicate a single attacker rather than a group. Mickey Joseph even objected to the photograph being placed into evidence, arguing that the yardstick proving that the path was narrow was not there during the attack and should not have been in the image.

The prosecution's case rested on the written and videotaped statements, and the testimonies of the detectives who interviewed and interrogated the teenagers would be crucial, an opportunity for the jury to consider how those confessions had been obtained and whether they could be trusted. Studies have shown that confessions are a uniquely persuasive form of evidence when presented to a jury, even in the face of contradictory physical evidence. Juries believe confessions because they cannot imagine a situation in which anyone would confess to something they hadn't done, though the interrogation tactics regularly used by law enforcement can and do lead to false confessions. The introduction of the confessions began on July 12.

The way that Lederer ordered and presented the detectives' testimonies would be vital to how the jury would receive them. Though it might have been most logical to have the pairs of detectives who conducted an interrogation together testify one after the other to most clearly explain what had happened, instead Lederer split them up. Detectives Gonzalez and Hildebrandt, who had interrogated Antron, and Detectives Arroyo and Hartigan, who had interrogated Raymond, testified several days apart from each other in both cases. By doing this, Lederer was able to paint her version of the story and present the most damning evidence, the written and videotaped statements, without the scrutiny that might have come from a more direct comparison of the detectives' descriptions of the interrogation process.

Detectives Carlos Gonzalez and Harry Hildebrandt, who had participated in the interrogation of Antron McCray, testified five days apart. There were no glaringly huge inconsistencies between their testimonies, but many small ones existed. They disagreed about whether Antron's mother, Linda, had spoken to Antron during the interview, whether she had been in the room when the statement was written out, and who had suggested that she leave the room so that Antron could speak more freely. Hildebrandt testified that it was Bobby McCray's idea, whereas Gonzalez said that he and Detective Hildebrandt had proposed that Linda leave the room. They also disagreed on when the rape first came up during the interrogation process, and who mentioned the victim first. In his cross-examinations, Mickey Joseph also called attention to small contradictions between testimonies in the pretrial hearing and the trial testimonies of both detectives.

On many points, the detectives agreed. Both denied that there had been any discussion of Antron's going home or promises made to him for confessing. And they agreed that Hildebrandt had only asked questions like "What happened?" and never yelled or cursed. Both detectives tried to prove that they had known very little about the case going into the interview, Hildebrandt especially. He wouldn't admit to having seen any media outside the precinct, though others testified to the massive nuisance they created just outside the doors. When Mickey Joseph asked, "And you elected in this particular case, you're telling us, to find out no information whatsoever as to what occurred prior to speaking with the individual, is that right?" Hildebrandt simply replied, "I was following orders." Hildebrandt testified that the only fact of the case he knew before he walked into the interview with Antron was that a female jogger had been raped. Detective Hildebrandt didn't even admit that he'd been sure Antron was a suspect.

Gonzalez said that he didn't know if Antron was under arrest when they began his interview, though at least he agreed that Antron was a suspect. And he admitted that none of the detectives in the room made any written record until an incriminating statement had been made, many hours into the session.

Hildebrandt's unwillingness to acknowledge any effort to familiarize himself with the details of the case made it look like he was hiding something. If Gonzalez and Hildebrandt were to be believed, Antron suddenly admitted that he had raped the female jogger, having only been asked, "What happened?" as soon as his mother was out of earshot.

Mickey Joseph, in his cross-examinations, asked the detectives why they hadn't written down Antron's denials, when he claimed he had not seen a female jogger in the park at all. Detective Hildebrandt explained that they hadn't written them down because they weren't true. Joseph pressed, and he managed to point out to the jury that the detectives had had a preconceived idea of what the truth was and were not going to stop until they heard what they wanted.

During her direct examination of Hildebrandt, Lederer had used his testimony to bring into evidence Antron's written and videotaped statements. The power of the video was indisputable. In it, the jurors saw Antron, with his parents, detail the events of that night, including the rape of the jogger, and nothing on the tape indicated that Antron had been forced to speak.

"We charged her and like we got on the ground, everybody started hitting her and stuff and she was on the ground. Everybody stomping and everything. And she got hit, then we grabbed each, like I grabbed one arm, this other kid grabbed one arm and we grabbed her legs and stuff. And then we like all took turns getting on her, like getting on top of her."

The vivid description of the rape emotionally outweighed anything exculpatory to be found in the video. Though Antron incorrectly described the attack as having happened on the jogging track around the reservoir, near the tennis courts, and the jogger as wearing blue shorts, those were far less salient details than the gruesome recounting of a violent attack. Mickey Joseph tried to ask Hildebrandt about a visit he made to Central Park with Antron, and whether Antron had directed the detective toward the reservoir rather than to the actual crime scene. Joseph didn't even get far enough into his questions to give the jury an idea of what he was getting at; Galligan sustained Lederer's objections immediately and would not allow the line of questioning. Though detectives were able to repeat admissions by defendants in court, in these circumstances exculpatory statements were inadmissible under the hearsay rules. Joseph knew that Antron would have to testify in order for the jury to hear his comments at the crime scene, and that was not a decision to be taken lightly.

Detectives Humberto Arroyo and John Hartigan each played an important role in Raymond Santana's interrogation, though, like the detectives who had testified about Antron's statements, they appeared in court several days apart. Much of their cross-examinations by the defense lawyers revolved around how well Raymond's grandmother spoke English and whether she'd understood what was going on well enough to represent Raymond's interests. Both detectives agreed that she had told them they didn't need to translate for her, and both said that it had been Raymond's idea to speak with Hartigan alone. The jury learned from Hartigan that Raymond first made his incriminating statements during the period he was alone with the detective. Hartigan, like Detectives Gonzalez and Hildebrandt before, said that they had only asked questions like "What happened next?" During Arroyo's cross-examination, Bobby Burns pointed out that getting confessions is normally like "pulling teeth," but Arroyo denied that it had been difficult to get a confession from Raymond.

These detectives presented a much more overlapping version of what had happened inside the interrogation room than Gonzalez and Hildebrandt had, but Rivera, Raymond's lawyer, still managed to press an important point. He asked Hartigan whether he'd used specific words, such as *faggot* and *fuck*, while questioning Raymond. "Did you ever turn to my client and ask my client if he ever fucked Patricia Meili?" "No." "Did you . . . ask my client if he was looking at Kevin Richardson's dick?" "Never." "Did any of you call my client a faggot?" "No." Rivera was not only asking Hartigan about specifics of the interrogation; he was also pointing out for everyone in the courtroom the shock value that words like that could have. He implied that Raymond confessed because he felt bullied and offended by the things the detectives said to him. Hartigan denied that the interview was anything like what Rivera was suggesting, but the jury still heard a plausible version of how a detective might intimidate a fourteen-year-old suspect. Hartigan reinforced that image when he explained that he'd been standing over a seated Raymond as he signed the statement.

The prosecution's case against Yusef Salaam relied mostly on the testimony of Detective Thomas McKenna. A twenty-four-year veteran on the force, McKenna was part of the elite Manhattan North Homicide Squad. He'd led the interview of Yusef Salaam in the third-floor Sex Crimes office of the 20th Precinct before Yusef's mother interrupted it. Since there was neither a videotaped statement nor even a signed written statement, McKenna's credibility was of the utmost importance to Lederer's case. On the stand, McKenna told his version of Yusef's description of the events of that night.

If Burns's job was to attack McKenna's credibility, to suggest that McKenna had either made up what he claimed Yusef had said or had browbeaten him into saying it, the attorney failed miserably. He entered McKenna's notes into evidence, hoping to point out slight inconsistencies in timing and the fact that the notes taken in the room featured fewer details than the report McKenna wrote later. But the notes, which Lederer could not have brought into evidence herself, were now fair game, allowing her to provide the jury with even more incriminating evidence in her redirect examination. And as he had with other witnesses, Burns repeated questions, dragging out the incriminating facts over and over, and failed to make a point with his convoluted series of questions. He often paused between questions and stared at the ceiling. McKenna deflected any suggestion of inconsistency easily, and Burns ended up digging himself deeper into a hole.

McKenna did describe how he'd lied to Yusef about how they'd been able to take fingerprints off the shiny pants of the jogger, the only time any of the detectives admitted using deception. But McKenna's trick was by the book and raised no legal questions as to the admissibility of Yusef's statement.

That most of these detectives claimed on the stand that it had required little more than asking "What happened?" in order to get incriminating statements out of the defendants, despite interrogations that lasted hours, was highly implausible. And the minor inconsistencies in their testimonies were beginning to add up. Though McKenna did admit to lying to Yusef about the fingerprints, his behavior was not only typical but also perfectly legal, and nothing for him to be ashamed of or have to hide from. But no detective admitted to yelling, cursing, or browbeating in any way, nor did they ever say that anyone had given the boys or their families the sense that they could go home if they confessed or became witnesses, which is not allowed because of the danger of causing false confessions. Yet all of the boys had cited a desire to go home and a belief that they could if they gave the police what they wanted. The young men thought that they could be witnesses, even saw themselves as helping the police close the case. The belief that confessing to a serious crime will lead to being released, however irrational, is commonly cited as a reason for falsely confessing, especially among younger suspects.

That they universally believed they could go home and felt intimidated and desperate enough to make such an irrational decision as confessing proves that there was more to the interrogations than simple, friendly questions such as "What happened?" But it is not entirely shocking that the detectives all testified to such an incredible version of the interrogations. A 1994 study of police corruption in the NYPD, commissioned by the city's mayor, found not only limited extreme acts of corruption by police officers illegally gaining from the drug trade or stealing money but also a wider pattern of perjury among police officers. The commission found that officers commonly committed perjury, often enough to have a nickname for it—"testilying"—when they believed that their testimony would help put guilty criminals in prison. The study concluded that "despite the devastating consequences of police falsifications, there is a persistent belief among many officers that it is necessary and justified, even if unlawful. . . . This attitude is so entrenched . . . that when investigators confronted one recently arrested officer with evidence of perjury, he asked in disbelief, 'What's wrong with that? They're guilty.' "

On July 13, in the midst of the detectives' testimonies about the interrogations, FBI agent Dwight Adams presented the results of the DNA tests. He first explained to the jury how restriction fragment length polymorphism (RFLP) DNA testing works, then described the series of tests he'd performed. He told the jury of the matches between semen found on Antron's and Raymond's clothing and their blood samples. But all that those tests proved was that two teenaged boys had had a bit of their own semen on their clothing. The most significant tests were of the samples taken from Trisha Meili and her clothing. The stain on her jogging pants matched the sample from Kevin O'Reilly, her boyfriend. The rectal swab from Meili's rape kit produced no DNA profile whatsoever. Adams explained how he had done four different tests on the semen from the cervical swab and had gotten only a weak DNA pattern on one of the tests. In his direct testimony, he said that "no conclusive results could be obtained from the semen stain found on item Q-11, which was the cervical swab," and that he had decided that this single band pattern was not even worth comparing to the DNA from blood samples. This echoed the media reports that had surfaced the previous October, describing the tests as "inconclusive," rather than negative.

The semen sample found on Trisha Meili's sock by NYPD chemist Mary Veit just before the trial was to begin proved most revealing. Adams explained that he only needed to look at the results from two tests to find that the "DNA profile from that semen stain did not match any individual" whose blood sample he compared it to, which included the defendants, other kids who had been in the park that night, and Meili's boyfriend. He also admitted that the test from the sock was a stronger version of the same result he'd found on the test from the cervical swab, suggesting that a match might be made between the semen on the sock and the semen from the swab. These results were detrimental to the prosecution's case, but Lederer chose to call Adams to present the negative tests rather than allow the defense to bring it out later. As she had in her opening statement, Lederer quickly moved past the revelation that the DNA did not match that of any of the defendants currently on trial or that of any of the other kids from the park that night who had been tested.

Under Mickey Joseph's cross-examination, Adams agreed that Antron McCray was conclusively not the source of the semen found on the pants, socks, or cervical swab taken from Trisha Meili. Though the district attorney and Agent Adams had focused on the inconclusive nature of the tests, it was now clear that while no match could be made, other than to Kevin O'Reilly, the tests were not actually inconclusive. In fact, they proved that none of the defendants in this trial or any other could possibly have been the source of the semen. It was a breakthrough for the defense case, and the media finally took notice.

The article from *The New York Times* was titled "Semen Tested in Jogger Case Was Not That of Defendants," and the *Daily News* ran a story entitled "DNA Prints Fail to ID Jogger's Attackers." In the latter article, reporter Lizette Alvarez referred to this information as "a revelation, wrested from an FBI expert under cross examination" and noted that it was "hailed by the defense as a major setback for the prosecution." It may have been, but the title of that article still referred to the defendants as the "jogger's attackers," underscoring that more setbacks would be needed for the mainstream media and public to begin to doubt the prosecution's version of events.

Two *Newsday* columnists had noticed the mounting holes in the case against Antron, Raymond, and Yusef. Jim Dwyer and Carole Agus each wrote a column the following week noting the lack of forensic proof. "We are waiting to see if there is any believable evidence that will connect these kids to the crime. So far, we haven't heard any," Agus wrote. When referring to Raymond's statement, which had been read into the record by Detective Arroyo, both columnists placed quotation marks around the word *confession,* expressing skepticism that it was authentic. Dwyer concluded that "nothing close to the words in this statement supposedly uttered by Raymond Santana ever sat on the lips of a 14 and a half year old. No New York jury is going to be convinced this confession contains the language of a New York kid." Yet their doubts and concerns were unique among the mainstream press, and the questions they raised did nothing to alter the overwhelming sense that the teenagers were guilty.

On July 16, 1990, Trisha Meili took the stand. Lederer had hoped to spare her the trauma, but the physical evidence was by no means ironclad and they needed her to explain how Kevin O'Reilly's semen had gotten onto the jogging pants she was wearing that night, to dissuade those who might be tempted to believe "the boyfriend did it" theory. Lederer also knew that Meili would impress the jurors, and give them a tangible victim to feel sympathy for. Meili had been counseled not to take the stand by family and friends concerned about her psychological well-being, but she understood that her testimony might be crucial, and she bravely decided to face the crowded courtroom and the young men she had been told had attacked and raped her.

Early that morning, Trisha Meili had arrived at the courthouse in a van with tinted windows, delivered by a police escort via an underground garage in the building so that the media and crowds couldn't see her. She wobbled as she approached the witness stand, escorted by an officer of the court. Her shakiness and a distinctive scar around her once-shattered eye were the only visible remnants of her injuries; her short blond hair had grown back over the scars on her scalp. She spoke calmly and confidently as she answered ADA Lederer's questions. She explained her habit of jogging in the evenings because of her grueling work schedule, and how she had no memory whatsoever of the events of that night past five o'clock in the evening. Meili also described the lasting effects of the attack:

I have problems with balance when I am walking, and coordination. At times as I'm walking down the hall or down the street, I'll veer off either to the right or to the left. I also have a great deal of trouble going down steps, and I have to hold on to the banister, or if there is another person there, I'll grab onto them. I also have lost my sense of smell completely and totally, that hasn't come back at all. I also suffer from double vision and I compensate for it when I'm reading by holding papers, whatever I'm reading, over to the left.

Her privacy and anonymity were protected by the ban that was already in place on cameras in the courtroom, and the courtroom sketch artists were ordered not to draw her face.

All three defense attorneys chose not to cross-examine Meili, recognizing that they could only sow more sympathy for her with the jurors by putting her on the spot any more. She was on the stand for less than fifteen minutes.

As Meili left the courthouse in the van with tinted windows, angry supporters of the defendants hurled insults, calling her "whore" and "prostitute." They'd been using similar language to try to intimidate Elizabeth Lederer throughout the trial, forcing her to walk to court every day from her office with a phalanx of police officers surrounding her. The wise decision of the defense attorneys not to cross-examine Meili was also unpopular with the supporters, who jeered the defense attorneys as they left the courthouse that day, accusing them of "selling out."

Columnist Mike McAlary of the *Daily News* pointed out the racism and offensive conduct of the supporters, citing parallels to cases like Howard Beach, when local whites tried to defend their neighborhood from charges of racism by suggesting that four blacks could have been there only for some criminal reason. McAlary quoted a woman who sat in the courtroom: "Why would the jogger be over in that part of the park?" she asked. "She wanted drugs."

Of the supporters filling the rows behind the defendants and crowding the streets outside the courthouse, there were several different factions. Some were the families of the accused, sitting quietly behind them in the courtroom. Others included the Reverend Al Sharpton and his devotees, who were just as likely to be out on the sidewalk chanting, "No Justice! No Peace!" as sitting inside. The most radical group were those who spouted "the boyfriend did it" theory and screamed curses and threats at Elizabeth Lederer.

But not every supporter was so extreme. The Reverend Calvin O. Butts III, the pastor of the Abyssinian Baptist Church in Harlem, had been reluctant at first to support the teenagers, frustrated, too, at the crime epidemic he saw devastating his community. But he eventually came to the trial to show his support. "The presumption of innocence was lost in the rush to judgment," he said. "People are not saying they forgive the crime. They're not saying they don't have compassion for that woman. All they're saying is, there is a considerable amount, an overwhelming amount, of reasonable doubt."

Most of the faces of those sitting behind the defense tables and supporting the defendants were black. The Latino community did not have a vocal response to the case, and Raymond felt abandoned, that he was supported by the black community but not his own. At that time, African-Americans had a much longer history and memory of police misconduct and abuse, and there was a sense among activists that it was possible that a group of minority teenagers could be framed, or at least railroaded. The Latino community, somewhat newer to New York, tended to accept the authority of the police more and was less comfortable actively battling with the establishment. In this case especially, the crime was so heinous and the narrative of what had happened developed so early that only a small subset of political activists was willing to get involved on behalf of the defendants.

The defense attorneys were often frustrated with Galligan's lack of leeway on their requests and objections. Mickey Joseph had been court-appointed, which meant that he was paid by the court and needed the judge's approval to hire experts. Joseph had wanted an expert to testify about Antron's susceptibility to a false confession, but Galligan had denied his request several times, though the doctor did meet with Antron. His test suggested that Antron's intellect was below average and that he would have been easily pressured, but the jury never heard anything about it.

Detective Nicholas Petraco, the criminologist with the NYPD's forensics lab, testified about his findings from hair and soil samples collected from the defendants and at the crime scene. Lederer had suggested that hairs found on Kevin Richardson's clothing were a match to Trisha Meili's, but Petraco did not entirely back her up. Though he described two samples taken from Kevin's clothing as being "consistent with" Meili's, he also explained that there is no such thing as a "match." Tim Clements, Lederer's cocounsel, helped him get the point across: "So, you cannot make individualized determinations as to the source of a particular strand of human hair, say the way you can with fingerprints?" "No, you cannot," Petraco responded.

The prosecution called their last witness, Detective Michael Sheehan, on July 25. Sheehan was the Manhattan North Homicide Squad detective who had escorted Raymond to the crime scene and helped in the investigation. He introduced Raymond's written and videotaped statements to the jury. Raymond's video was even more shocking than Antron's had been. In it, Raymond described arriving on the scene after Kevin Richardson had already begun struggling with the "lady," and how Steve Lopez had cursed at her and hit her in the head with a brick. Raymond denied raping the jogger, but he said that while the others raped her, he was "grabbing the lady's tits."

Peter Rivera, Raymond's lawyer, got Sheehan to admit that though Raymond had said that he'd knelt while feeling her breasts, there had been no mud whatsoever on his clothing. Sheehan could also not provide a logical explanation for why they never asked Raymond about the inconsistencies in his statement. But Sheehan knew how to testify, and, like McKenna, he charmed the jury and came away looking very credible. With that, Elizabeth Lederer rested her case. Though some contradictions and unbelievable claims had begun to damage the credibility of a few of the detectives, the written and videotaped statements of the three defendants were powerful and had clearly made an impact on the jury.

Mickey Joseph presented Antron's case first. He considered having Antron testify, so that Antron could describe his visit to the crime scene, when he'd said "I'm not lying anymore. I don't know anything about any woman." But the risk of damage to his case during a tough cross-examination was too great. In the end, only Bobby and Linda McCray would testify on Antron's behalf. Joseph's goal was to prove that Antron had been coerced into giving an incriminating statement through threats and promises that he could go home.

The McCrays described a very different interview from the one Detectives Gonzalez and Hildebrandt had. Bobby said Linda was crying and speaking loudly during the interrogation, and that Gonzalez had repeatedly asked about the "woman," in contradiction with the detectives' testimonies. He also said that the detectives told Antron to "put yourself right with them and you may be a witness and go home. If not, [you are] going to jail." He said that they yelled at Antron and called him a liar. Bobby believed that Antron was telling the truth about not knowing anything about the woman, but he thought that doing what the police wanted would actually help his son. In private, he told Antron, "I know you're telling the truth. You tell these people what they want to hear and you'll go home." When Antron said he wouldn't lie and say he was there when he wasn't, Bobby "got upset and angry, and threw a chair across the room, because I was trying to get my son to tell a lie." Both he and Linda described their feelings of powerlessness at the police precinct. Linda hadn't known what to do or what rights she had: "I was scared. I was upset. I didn't know what to do. They were the police." Bobby said, "I didn't have no right to say anything, I was in the precinct."

For his case, Bobby Burns tried to prove that the detectives had interrogated Yusef in bad faith, without a parent present. Yusef's sister Aisha and relatives Marilyn Hatcher and Vincent Jones told of how Aisha and Marilyn had both informed various detectives that Yusef was only fifteen much earlier on than any prosecution witness had admitted. Sharonne Salaam, Yusef's mother, testified that she'd informed Linda Fairstein immediately that her son was fifteen, and she accused Fairstein of wasting time in order to keep her from her son.

Burns's final witness was Yusef himself. The other defense attorneys tried desperately to convince Burns not to call the defendant, knowing that he would make all three look guilty if he didn't hold up under pressure. The morning of Yusef's testimony, reporters overheard Joseph and Rivera arguing with Burns over his decision in the hallway outside the courtroom.

Yusef strode to the witness stand with poise and carried with him a copy of the Koran. He was tall, over six feet, and looked older than his sixteen years. He told his version of the story, in which he'd entered the park with a large group, witnessed some other assaults in the park but had not participated, had lost track of the group when they crested a slope ahead of him, and he said he knew nothing about the rape of a female jogger. He did admit that he had carried a length of pipe with him. He was well spoken and coolly denied admitting anything to McKenna at all.

Yusef remained calm during the cross-examination as he flatly denied Lederer's accusations. But sometimes her questions were enough to get her points across. She challenged his assertion that he'd lost track of the other kids in the park, suggesting that his claim that he'd gotten tired after a few minutes of walking was absurd. There was a clear hostility in the air between Yusef and Lederer as she asked specific questions about his whereabouts and activities that evening, clearly referencing the statements of other kids in the park. "And do you recall telling Michael Briscoe as you were standing with him in the ballfields, as you saw police cars driving, you told him to 'chill out, they're not coming, they're just going to the place to help the bum we beat up?' . . . Isn't it true that you were with Kharey when, in Kharey's words, you were playing with the female jogger?" Yusef denied each accusation.

Yusef's responses often came across as defiant and sarcastic, as if he wasn't taking the whole process very seriously.

"You went into the park that night. You weren't going there for a picnic, were you?" Lederer asked.

"No, I wasn't," he replied. "I don't have a picnic in the nighttime."

"And you went in with a pipe and you thought it would be fun, isn't that right?" she asked.

"Yes."

Peter Rivera's defense of Raymond consisted of only two witnesses. Natividad Colon, Raymond's grandmother, spoke through a Spanish interpreter and explained that she was illiterate and spoke only Spanish. In the cross-examination, Colon continued to insist that she spoke no English at all, but Lederer reminded her that she'd told reporters to leave her alone in English when they'd come to her door, and she was forced to admit that she understood "some things." Rivera did not even ask her about intimidating factors in the interrogation room, such as detectives yelling at Raymond, in order to establish some kind of coercion defense.

Raymond Santana, Sr.'s, testimony did not help the case much, either, and may have even aided Lederer in suggesting that he had been indifferent to the seriousness of the situation his son was in. He did describe what Raymond had said during a visit to the crime scene: "Then we went downhill like, and [the detective] said, 'Raymond, you was here,' and Raymond said, 'No, I never been here.' Raymond said he was on the other side of the park." Despite this recollection, Rivera had failed to make a strong case that Raymond Jr.'s confession was coerced, the only real shot they had at an acquittal.

Once the defense attorneys rested their cases, Lederer called several rebuttal witnesses, mostly detectives who corroborated earlier detectives' testimonies or challenged defense witnesses' statements. The most dramatic element of the rebuttal case came when Lederer called Linda Fairstein, the ADA in charge of the Sex Crimes Prosecution Unit. Lederer needed her to contradict the claims by Yusef's family members that they had told Fairstein early on about Yusef's true age. Fairstein seemed calm and comfortable as she described her part in the drama that had unfolded at the precinct. As she did so, Sharonne Salaam, who had previously been content to glare silently at Fairstein, leapt up and yelled, "You're lying, you're lying. My son already took a lie detector test. He's innocent!" Yusef had, in fact, taken and passed a lie-detector test, administered by a forensic polygraphist at the behest of his lawyer. He answered no to questions about whether he'd witnessed or participated in the assault or rape of the female jogger, and the polygraph indicated that he was telling the truth. But the results were inadmissible, so the jury would never see them. Galligan threw Mrs. Salaam out of the courtroom and would not let her back in for the remainder of the trial, despite repeated apologies and beseeching. He admonished the jury to ignore her outburst.

After Fairstein's testimony, the prosecution rested. Mickey Joseph began his summation: "There is not one piece of physical evidence or scientific evidence that established that Antron committed any crime whatsoever." He asked the jury to reject his client's statements, "because they were obtained improperly . . . [and] are therefore unreliable." He accused Detectives Hildebrandt and Gonzalez of lying on the stand and using threats and promises to obtain Antron's incriminating statement. Joseph listed for the jury the many inconsistencies between the detectives' testimonies and argued that the McCrays' version of the story "is consistent with common sense." Joseph also pointed out the inconsistencies between Antron's statement and the facts. He posed a question to the jurors: What if a witness came in and told them that the female jogger "was here by the reservoir and she was running around in short pants and she wasn't dragged anywhere, and her hands were never tied together," as Antron had claimed? He answered his own question: "You people, based upon the location and based upon the facts, would say, 'That person doesn't know what they are talking about.' "

Bobby Burns went next. He began with a lengthy apology of sorts to the jury, pleading with them not to hold him and his behavior against Yusef. Burns argued that there was no proof a rape had even occurred, given that Meili had no memory of the attack, and he implied that she might have had consensual sex that evening that she didn't remember. His explanation of the interactions in the precinct when Yusef's family arrived and spoke with various detectives and with Linda Fairstein was befuddling and roundabout. Burns emphasized Yusef's truthfulness, suggesting several times that because Yusef admitted to taking a pipe into the park, he must be telling the truth.

Peter Rivera was the last of the defense attorneys, and he took the most time rambling through his summation. He denied that Raymond had even witnessed any of the attacks in the park, suggesting that Raymond only got the details right about John Loughlin because the cops knew those details early on and intentionally planted them. He pointed out the errors Raymond made relative to the facts in his videotaped statement, and suggested that the detectives had to have been lying when they claimed that they only asked questions as simple as "What happened?" Rivera emphasized the length of time that Raymond had been questioned and the hardships of his interrogation. "I submit to you, ladies and gentlemen, that Raymond's will was broken, that Raymond's will was broken several times by promises that were made to him, by veiled threats, by coercion on the part of all the officers that questioned Raymond Santana. And that's why Raymond cooperated."

Finally, the prosecution had their chance to conclude. Elizabeth Lederer methodically responded to each point from the defense attorneys in the same rigid and flat voice she'd used throughout the trial. Why weren't the teenagers covered in blood and mud? Because the attack was brief and took place up above where she was found, where it wasn't so muddy. Lederer explained to the jury that Meili lost all that blood after they left, and had rolled down the hill into the mud puddle where she was later discovered. If the detectives had been yelling at Antron as the McCray family claimed, wouldn't they have ended the interview? The cops couldn't have been feeding them information, because the teenagers all knew details of the other crimes in the park.

She highlighted the places where their statements agreed with the known facts of the case, often reading from the written statements and even replaying bits of the videotaped ones. She went further than the forensics expert would go, stating unequivocally that the hairs found on Kevin Richardson were Patricia Meili's. She argued that the sperm that was found in Meili's cervix proved that she had been raped, and that the fact that no match was made simply meant that these three had not ejaculated in the victim. She reminded the jury that "ejaculation is not an element of rape. There is no legal requirement that ejaculation occur for the crime of rape to be committed."

While Lederer described the attack on Antonio Diaz, someone in the audience knocked loudly, and a row of people sitting behind the defendants stood and silently walked out of the courtroom in protest. The group included Linda and Bobby McCray, as well as the remaining members of Yusef's family, Sharonne Salaam having been barred from the courtroom for her earlier outburst. The group marched into the hallway of the courthouse and then stood in a circle in protest. Afterward, Galligan would not let them back into the courtroom, despite pleas from the defense attorneys, for the remainder of the trial.

Lederer, though reserved and calm throughout her closing argument, betrayed her disdain for the defendants in her voice at times, especially when talking about Yusef's testimony. "That story makes no sense at all. It's absolutely incredible. . . . I submit to you that [it] is an insult to your intelligence and to your common sense. Nothing about what Yusef Salaam told you from the witness stand has the ring of truth." She finished her summation: "The only fair and just and true verdict in this case, based on this evidence, is a verdict of guilty as to each of the defendants on each of the counts."

After a six-week trial, the case went to the jury, and they deliberated for ten days, often returning to the courtroom to have portions of the record reread or videotapes replayed. Newspaper articles published nearly every day of deliberations noted the jury's specific requests, and quoted the prosecution and defense lawyers as they tried to guess as to the leanings of the jury.

It was 7:15 p.m. on August 18, 1990, when jury foreman Earle Fisher announced the verdict. Antron McCray, Yusef Salaam, and Raymond Santana were each convicted of rape, assault, robbery, and riot, but acquitted of attempted murder. Antron's parents hugged each other and cried. Antron sat stunned at the defense table, realizing for the first time how real it was. Though he'd understood the gravity of the trial, he'd never truly believed he would be convicted until that moment. In the moments after the verdict was read, Antron turned to Mickey Joseph and said, "Thank you very much for all of your efforts." Joseph was touched and surprised by this rare display of respect and thoughtfulness from a client, especially a teenager facing the devastating reality of years in prison.

Yusef, who had been portrayed in the media as angry and defiant, sat in astonishment. He, too, had never actually believed that he would be convicted, even during the trial, and the moment the verdict was read, he was more confused than anything else. It was like *The Twilight Zone,* he said. Like Antron, he'd believed even up until that moment that he could not be convicted of something he hadn't done. He broke down in tears as he was led away.

Raymond Santana's father was not in court that day, nor had he sat in the courtroom for any of the trial, except when he was called to testify. Instead, he'd sat on a bench in the hallway just outside the courtroom. He knew that his son had been convicted in the court of public opinion, and he had no interest in attending a trial whose outcome was already assured. The day the verdict was read, he was home, not wanting to hear in person what he could already predict. A mob of reporters came to his building, but he ignored them. The following day, during a press conference staged by Al Sharpton outside the apartment building where the McCrays lived, Bobby McCray knocked over a microphone stand with a baseball bat and yelled at reporters and others gathered to "get out of here."

The jury's deliberations had not gone smoothly. The jurors had agreed to convict on the lesser charges quickly, but they reached a stumbling block when they came to the sex crimes. Ronald Gold, a white sixty-year-old former entertainment reporter and speechwriter, tried to convince his fellow jurors to acquit Antron for the rape charge, finding the inconsistencies in his statements too much to stomach. Pedro Sanchez, a Latino bus driver, defended Santana. After considering a hung verdict on the rape charge for Antron, Gold backed down after watching his videotaped confession for a fifth time.

As soon as the verdicts were read, Antron and Yusef, who had been living at home, out on bail during the trial, were taken into custody. Raymond, now fifteen, was returned to Spofford, where he had been since he was first arrested, unable to raise the money for bail.

Reactions were mixed. The detectives in the case celebrated in the back of the courtroom. The *Post*'s headline the next morning was JOG-GER THRILLED. Those supporters of the defendants who had protested throughout the trial were especially cruel to Lederer as she left the courthouse. One shouted, "The devil herself, she's going to pay for it." Others screamed at the defense attorneys, unhappy with their subpar performances. At his press conference, Al Sharpton railed against their incompetence.

Mayor Dinkins characteristically equivocated. "The jury served our criminal-justice system well," he said. "It was a difficult decision for them, considering the ages of the youths and the seriousness of the charges leveled against them."

C. Vernon Mason, a controversial black activist lawyer, quickly replaced Mickey Joseph as Antron's attorney, and William Kunstler, the famed white radical attorney, took over for Bobby Burns in time for Yusef's sentencing. Mason immediately started bad-mouthing his predecessor, but Kunstler wouldn't, believing that a white lawyer should not criticize a black lawyer, whether he'd failed miserably or not. Kunstler's instinct may have hurt Yusef's appeal, since an argument about Burns's ineffective counsel might have had some success.

Sentencing took place a few weeks later, on September 11, 1990. The new, more politically active attorneys tried to make it a forum on racism in the justice system, calling for Justice Galligan to step down from the case and referring to the proceeding as a "legal lynching." Antron, Raymond, and Yusef had the chance to speak for themselves and to plead their cases to the judge. Antron and Raymond each did, briefly, proclaiming their innocence and thanking their families. Yusef read a prepared statement and performed a spoken word poem he'd composed for the occasion, likening himself to such assassinated and persecuted black leaders as Malcolm X, Martin Luther King, Jr., and Nelson Mandela. "I and many other people know I told the truth," he said. "It's only those who are ignorant that fail to see this. Why would I lie on or go against the holy Koran? That's the same as lying on the word of God. I would never disrespect my own religion of which I was born into. I think my debt to society has been paid if this is the price to pay for being a black man living in America." The *Post* ridiculed his arrogance with a front-page headline: SALAAM BALONEY!

Galligan, for his part, was unimpressed. "The people of this city have the right to enjoy freedom, the freedom to walk its streets and parks unmolested, but today these freedoms are being challenged. The quality of life in this city has seriously deteriorated. There was a time when youngsters would take baseball bats to the park to play baseball. But now a twelve-inch length of pipe has become an instrument of fun."

He sentenced each of them to three to ten years for the rape and assault of Trisha Meili, and three to ten years for the robbery of John Loughlin, to be served consecutively. All three were under sixteen on April 19, 1989, and though they had been tried as adults, Galligan didn't bother handing down a ruling at all for the lesser convictions because the juvenile-sentencing regulations set their maximum time at five to ten years. Their ages also meant that all three would serve in juvenile facilities until they turned 21, when they would be transferred to adult prisons.

Now ADA Elizabeth Lederer, exhausted and drained from a year of working on such a high-pressure case, immediately had to turn her attention to the three remaining defendants. Lederer and her colleagues did not want Kevin Richardson, Korey Wise, and Steve Lopez tried together. Because both Kevin and Korey mentioned Lopez often in their statements, they would have to redact Lopez's name from the documents and videos if they were on trial together. Lederer proposed to Justice Galligan that they first try Kevin and Korey together. This would also give them more time to find other witnesses and build a stronger case against Lopez, who had confessed to being with the group as they harassed and assaulted joggers and bicyclists but who had refused to admit anything at all relating to the female jogger.

The People v. Kevin Richardson and Korey Wise began on October 22, 1990, just six weeks after the sentencing of the first three defendants. In many ways, the trials would be similar, with the prosecution laying out essentially the same case against these defendants.

The major difference from the first trial in Elizabeth Lederer's opening statement was her presentation of the time line for the crimes in Central Park. At the first trial, Lederer described the rape as having happened before the assaults of male joggers at the reservoir, but both Korey's and Kevin's statements placed the attack on the female jogger after the reservoir attacks. Lederer couldn't tell the jury that Patricia Meili had been attacked when the teens said she was, because the evidence didn't support it, but stating definitively that it had happened earlier would only make it look like the defendants didn't really know about the crime, or that detectives had planted the information back when they believed the attack had happened later. Rather than investigate the reason that the defendants' statements were incorrect, she chose to present an opening statement that simply hid a glaring contradiction from the jury.

Otherwise, Lederer's opening was the same clear narrative that she had used so successfully in the first trial. She explained to the jury exactly what they would hear and see, and confidently argued that the lack of a DNA match was not inconsistent with the case she was going to prove.

Korey Wise, now eighteen years old, had been in jail since his arrest in April 1989, unable to make bail. As he sat and listened to the district attorney describe him as a rapist and violent criminal, he became agitated, shaking his head and mumbling to himself. As Lederer walked across the courtroom at the end of her presentation, Korey muttered, "Lies, lies, lies." As the jury filed out of the courtroom for a recess, Korey couldn't contain his emotions any longer. He burst forth with a torrent of cries while pounding his head with his fists. "No. No. No. Can't take this. Oh, Lord Jesus. No. It's not all right. . . . It's wrong. No. No. Woman's lying. Oh, Lord Jesus. She's lying."

The defense attorneys were up next, and they could not have presented their cases more differently. Kevin's lawyer, Howard Diller, was a stout, white, middle-aged defense attorney, who had been hired by the family for a five-thousand-dollar retainer, leaving him with little resources to invest in the case. But he loved all the media attention he got with such a high-profile defendant. When he'd released Kevin's videotaped statement to the media months earlier, he'd argued that Kevin never admitted to raping the jogger and that the tapes should actually exonerate his client. He followed the same tack in his opening statement. Rather than trying to convince the jury that Kevin's statement had been coerced, Diller suggested that the jury assume it was true, but he said that the jurors should note that Kevin described the events as a spectator, not as a participant. Diller's presentation was disjointed and unclear, and he went on to say, "There's nothing in the statement really that says that he did anything acting in concert with anybody, except the words. We submit that those were fed words." Other than this argument, which he undercut in the very same sentence, Diller provided little in the way of alternative theories or facts that might exonerate his client.

Colin Moore, a black activist lawyer from Guyana, argued vociferously that Korey had been coerced, a task made easier by Korey's four contradicting statements, and that the whole prosecution was part of a racist conspiracy. Whereas Diller was friendly and polite when cross-examining the prosecution's witnesses, Moore was hostile and implicated everyone in the conspiracy he alleged was working against his client. He often took this strategy too far, playing to the more radical supporters in the audience, and sometimes alienating the jury. But Moore made legitimate points about the facts of the case, poking holes in the prosecution's theories and highlighting those inconsistencies within Korey's statements.

In his opening, Moore reconstructed the time line, showing that there had not been enough time between the assaults on the bikers and Antonio Diaz near 102nd Street and the attacks by the reservoir for the rape to have been committed by the same people. His logic was sound, but he had to skirt the fact that he was essentially admitting that Korey and the group had committed the other crimes in the park. He maintained that no rape had occurred at all, citing the lack of "external signs of trauma in her genital areas." Moore also stressed the lack of DNA and other physical evidence. "All of the scientific evidence in this case will fail to link any sperm or any hair or any fingernail clipping or any evidence in this case with the defendant Korey Wise." He described Korey as a "confused young man," and pointed out how he'd gotten the details wrong and changed his story about a rock used to hit Meili when pressed by Elizabeth Lederer in one of the videotaped interviews.

Moore delivered his comments with a Caribbean accent and with much more confidence than Diller had mustered. He referenced film director Steven Spielberg when comparing Lederer's opening to an illusion, and he ended with a quote from Shakespeare's *The Tempest,* reasoning again that the prosecution's case was a fantasy.

After the opening statements, Kevin Richardson's doting mother and older sisters were especially disappointed in Howard Diller. He had already released Kevin's videotaped confession to the press, and now he had given an opening that did little to convince them he had any arguments that might work at trial. Colin Moore's fiery opening and his powerful rhetoric in front of the press outside made them long for an attorney who seemed more invested in a positive outcome for Kevin. They decided to fire Diller and hire C. Vernon Mason, the activist lawyer who was already representing Antron McCray on appeal.

Mason was no stranger to high-profile racial cases in New York, having represented Tawana Brawley and the family of Michael Griffith, the young man who died after being hit by a car in the Howard Beach incident. He arrived in court on the fifth day of the trial, ready to demand a mistrial so that he would not be burdened by the mistakes Diller had already made. Not only did Galligan not declare a mistrial; he would not allow Mason to take over for Diller at all. Mason had already announced to the press his intention of presenting a case more like Moore's, including cross-examining Trisha Meili and highlighting the racial aspects of the case. The activist supporters in the audience were disappointed and outraged by Galligan's rejection of Mason. Diller, too, was unhappy. He now faced representing a client whose family was uncooperative with his trial plan and who did not want him on the case at all. Kevin's mother and sister Angela announced to the judge that they would not testify, leaving Diller without his main witnesses.

Many of the same witnesses from the first trial testified for the prosecution: the other Central Park victims, police officers who had been in the park that night, medical personnel who had arrived at the scene and those who had later treated Trisha Meili at Metropolitan Hospital, detectives who had interrogated the defendants, and forensics specialists in DNA and hair samples.

As at the first trial, a cadre of supporters of the defendants filled one side of the courtroom, often responding with murmurs of approval when Colin Moore posed questions and made statements, and hissing at Elizabeth Lederer and her witnesses. Justice Galligan often had to reprimand the supporters for their noise and inappropriate behavior in the courtroom. Once, he threw out a man wearing a T-shirt that read MY BROTHER ANTRON MCCRAY IS INNOCENT. He later ejected another supporter for talking. The man responded, "This is a racist court then. The bench is racist. Black folks sitting here want justice."

On November 2, 1990, Trisha Meili testified. Fewer members of the media attended the second trial, since it seemed somewhat redundant to the first, but Meili's presence in the courtroom increased the excitement and tension. Colin Moore had long been telling the press and the defendants' supporters that he was going to ask tough questions of the jogger, particularly about her boyfriends and her sex life. In his examination, he started by going over her recovery, pointing out that she was back to working long hours again and even occasionally jogging in the park as she had done before the attack, trying to prove that her injuries were less serious and permanent than the prosecution had suggested. Moore then went over her jogging route to establish the probable time that she had reached the 102nd Street Cross Drive, something Lederer had avoided in her opening and in her direct examination of Meili. But Moore knew the time line was important, and in questioning Meili, he established that, given her normal pace and jogging route, she would have arrived at the location of the attack at around 9:10 or 9:15.

Next, Moore began asking about the men in her life, first suggesting that Michael Allen, with whom she'd canceled a dinner date earlier that evening, might have come over after 5:00 p.m. Then he implied that Kevin O'Reilly, her boyfriend, might be a suspect because he knew what route she took when she jogged in the park. Then Moore asked her whether she had said something to a nurse at Metropolitan Hospital that implicated someone she knew in the crime. When Lederer objected, Moore explained that the nurse would testify about Meili's comments. But he claimed the date of this alleged declaration was just three days after the attack, when she was still in a coma and intubated, unable to speak. After that, things continued to deteriorate. As Moore asked questions about whether Meili had had any relationships that were violent or if there had been "altercations," Galligan sustained objections to nearly every question. Moore eventually gave up after only thirty-five minutes, a relatively short cross-examination compared to what he'd promised the supporters and media. Some newspapers criticized Moore for his questions and treatment of Meili. An editorial in the *Post* accused him of ulterior motives: "His goal is to use the case as a means to pursue his own agenda—sowing racial discord in New York City. . . . The questioning [of the jogger] seemed designed [to] further humiliate a woman who has already experienced extraordinary pain and suffering." Moore had scored few points, except perhaps with the defendant's most ardent supporters.

When Pat Garrett, a colleague and former roommate of Meili, took the stand to explain how he'd gone to her apartment the night of the attack and found she wasn't there, Moore implied that something unsavory had been going on. He called it an "intimate setting" because Meili had joked to Garrett that she would be in her pajamas by the time he arrived at 10:00 p.m. Moore even called Kevin O'Reilly to the stand to ask him about Pat Garrett and Michael Allen, and to imply that he, too, had been a suspect. Galligan didn't allow most of the questions.

In the midst of the trial, Elizabeth Lederer announced a surprise witness. The defense attorneys fought her inclusion, but since Lederer had not known about the witness until well into the trial, Galligan allowed it. When Melonie Jackson came to court to testify, it was clear that she didn't want to be there. Jackson, twenty-nine, knew Korey through members of her family who lived at the Schomburg Plaza, and she didn't want to do anything that might hurt him. But she told the jury that she had been visiting her sister and nephews in July 1989 when Korey called from Rikers. She said she had gotten on the line with him and asked him about what had happened, and he'd told her he didn't rape the female jogger. When Lederer pressed, Melonie, teary-eyed, replied that Korey told her that he had held the jogger's legs. It was a devastating blow to Korey's case. Moore tripped her up a bit when she claimed during the cross-examination that Korey said he'd "fondled" the jogger's legs, rather than held or touched them, as she had previously said. *Fondled* did not seem like the kind of word that a learning-disabled and mostly illiterate kid would have used. But though Moore tried to call her motives into question, it seemed clear that she did not want to testify against Korey, making her damaging claims that much more believable.

Given Korey's innocence and the fact that there was no clear motive for Jackson to lie, her testimony is puzzling. If Korey did make that statement to Jackson, it may have been because he did not understand the "acting in concert" laws and still believed that an admission that he'd been a witness, as long as he hadn't actually raped the jogger, might even help his case. It was a common idea planted by the detectives—that the young men could be witnesses against the others—and Korey may have just been continuing to play along, hopelessly unaware of the realities of the justice system.

———

When Colin Moore took over the cross-examination of Detective John Hartigan, he wanted to show that Korey had been coerced into confessing. He pointed out that Hartigan had successfully gotten many statements over the course of his interrogations, and that the detective was particularly adept at gaining confessions. Moore also asked Hartigan about the many inconsistencies and mistakes in Kevin's and Korey's statements, such as the fact that Kevin had said the jogger's pants were gray and had gotten the direction the jogger was running wrong, and that Korey had said that she'd been cut with a knife. Though Moore represented only Korey, at times it seemed that he was trying to defend Kevin, too, especially where Kevin's lawyer was lacking. There was clear antagonism in the air as Moore tried to paint Hartigan as a bully who had intimidated the young men in order to gain a confession, but Hartigan deflected many of Moore's questions. Moore finally got to the heart of the matter toward the end of a long cross-examination.

"You wanted [Korey] to tell you that he was involved in the rape of Patricia Meili, that's what you wanted, isn't it?" he asked, pressing the detective.

"I wanted him to tell the truth," Hartigan replied, in a refrain familiar from many of the detectives' testimonies.

"This was your version of the truth, right?"

"That's what I believed to be the truth," Hartigan said finally.

When Detective Nicholas Petraco testified this time, more was on the line than at the first trial. Two hairs that had been found on Kevin's clothing were similar to Patricia Meili's hair, giving the prosecution their only direct physical evidence that corroborated the confessions. The problem was that comparing hair samples was an inexact science, and unlike with DNA, it was impossible in 1989 to conclusively make a match. Petraco described how he'd compared the hairs found on Kevin's clothing to known samples from Trisha Meili by using twenty separate characteristics. But he knew better than to call it a match, and he told the jury that the hairs were "similar in all physical characteristics to the known sample." On cross-examination, both attorneys suggested other ways that hairs might have gotten on the clothing, pointing out that the teenagers might have picked up blond hairs at school, or that hairs might have been transferred after the clothing was confiscated by the police. The best they could do was point out that there was no way to make a "match," and that the hairs, therefore, could have come from someone else. "It's possible that it comes from another source than Patricia Meili?" Diller asked. "Yes," Petraco replied.

As at the previous trial, Elizabeth Lederer used the various detectives who testified to bring in the written and videotaped statements, which were read and played to the jury. In the first videotape, Korey had said only that he'd been a witness to the rape. The jurors heard Lederer pressuring him about how the jogger must have been hit in the head with a rock or brick, and Korey changing his story to agree with her version. Lederer said, "I don't want you to think that you have to say that" and "Are you saying that because I am asking you?" The jury had seen enough to suspect that Korey might have been confused and easily pressured. Yet Korey also admitted more than the others in his final videotape session, saying at one point, "This is my first rape." He admitted to "playing with her," and described in detail how Steve Lopez had cut her legs with a knife and hit her with a rock, and how Lopez and Raymond were "fucking her."

In his videotaped statement, Kevin described how they chased the jogger down and how Antron, Raymond, and Lopez had had sex with her. Coupled with the graphic photos they'd seen earlier, the jury members had a vivid and gruesome picture painted for them. It was clear to everyone in the courtroom that the tapes made a powerful impact on the jurors, as they alternately grimaced and shook their heads.

Once the prosecution rested, Diller presented Kevin's defense first. His case consisted mainly of character witnesses, especially because he could not count on Kevin's family to testify, given his rocky relationship with them. Two people who were not family members testified about Kevin's reputation as a caring and respectful person. Paul Richardson, Kevin's father, briefly described his time at the precinct and how he had believed Kevin would be allowed to go home if he signed the statement. He also said that he had asked to go along with Kevin to the park and had been denied, in direct contradiction to what Detective Hartigan had said on the stand.

Gracie Cuffee, Kevin's mother, also decided to testify on her son's behalf, despite her previous indication that she would refuse to cooperate with Howard Diller's defense strategy, and she described a scene in which detectives would berate her son as soon as she left the room. She, too, had believed throughout the ordeal that Kevin would be going home soon. Kevin's sister Angela remained steadfast in her refusal to cooperate with Diller. It was not until Diller had already rested his case that it became clear that her failure to appear might actually damage her brother's case.

When Angela eventually did testify, she described to the jury how Detective Hartigan had told Kevin what to write in his statement, and how Hartigan had not allowed her to go along with them to the park when he took Kevin there. Under cross-examination by Elizabeth Lederer, Angela denied that the signature in Hartigan's memo book was hers. Lederer brought out several samples of Angela's signature, suggesting that she could prove forensically that Angela had signed the page, but Angela would not budge. Lederer later called a police handwriting expert to contradict Angela's denial.

Colin Moore also trotted out character witnesses for Korey, including a Catholic nun, a community leader who worked as a consultant for the local ABC News affiliate, and Bill Perkins, a city assemblyman who was also chair of the Schomburg tenants' association, but he also did something that no other lawyer had: He tried to present an alibi defense. Korey's girlfriend's foster mother, her granddaughter, and a security guard for the building all testified that they had seen Korey in and around the Schomburg towers around the time the rape was taking place. Though Lederer was able to poke small holes in these testimonies, she could not do anything to damage the credibility of Helene Brathwaite, another resident of the towers and a respected member of the community, who testified that she had spoken to Korey outside the building at 9:30 p.m.

Deloris Wise, Korey's mother, also testified that her son had come home just after 9:30, but on cross-examination she became agitated and hostile toward Lederer and her questions. Galligan had to ask her not to "holler," and she glared and seethed at the prosecutor, once calling her a "lying snake." After agreeing to behave better, Wise refused to answer questions or to read aloud a document, and Galligan threw her out, striking her entire testimony and telling the jury to disregard everything she had said.

Moore also called Dr. Vernard Adams, who had testified for the prosecution at the first trial. Dr. Adams, a forensic medical examiner, had observed the injuries to Trisha Meili, and he testified that none of her injuries had come from a sharp blade, contradicting Korey's statements that Steve Lopez had cut the jogger with a knife. Adams's testimony supported the defense's argument that Korey hadn't known what he was talking about when he confessed, but it also gave ADA Lederer the opportunity to rehash the terrible injuries that were inflicted on the jogger, gruesome color photos included.

Finally, Korey Wise took the stand in his own defense. Moore was taking a risk, given Korey's childlike nature, but if Korey could express how overwhelmed he'd felt, he might make an impression on the jury that he'd been coerced. Also, since Korey was sixteen and had not had a relative present during questioning, no one else could describe what had happened in the interrogation room that made him confess. Korey described the events of the evening, admitting that he'd gone into the park but saying that he'd left soon after, without having participated in any assaults. He explained that he'd then gone over to his girlfriend Lisa's place for most of the rest of the evening. He described being taken to the police precinct, and he accused Detective Nugent of slapping him and swearing at him, and telling him that he could go home if he lied and said he'd been there.

Korey admitted that he couldn't read or write very well, and that he had difficulty hearing, adding to the sense that he would not have been capable of withstanding the intense pressure of an interrogation.

During her cross-examination, Lederer drove home his intellectual disadvantage when she asked him to read something and he could not. Lederer asked about Korey's truancy from school, putting records in front of him that proved he'd been absent often. At first, he tried to explain that he'd been threatened by other kids and was scared to go to school, but he got frustrated with the line of questioning. "What does this have to do with my case? . . . Come on, man. I'm tired of hearing this." Galligan asked him to answer the questions and sit down, and when he did not cooperate, Galligan sent the jury out of the courtroom. As they filed out, Korey blew up. "I'm facing fifty-seven years over this, man. She's playing herself, man, bringing up '85. I was twelve years old back then. What does this have to do with Central Park? '85? The reason why I wasn't in school because I was threatened not to go back to school. People putting guns to my head, that's why." Korey eventually calmed down and Galligan allowed him to continue his testimony.

Lederer asked him about many of the specific things he'd said on the tape and whether they had been his words. Korey continued to claim that the police had made him say those things, sometimes testing his credibility with the jury, as when he said that detectives had told him to say that he suggested to the others that they drag the "bum" off the road so he would not get hurt. Lederer pressed him by showing him a portion of the videotaped statement where he demonstrated a punch as he described the other boys punching the jogger.

"Did the police make you do what you did on the videotape, punching with both fists?"

"Somehow."

"Did they tell you when in the videotape you were supposed to do that?"

"No."

"Did they tell you how you were supposed to do it?"

"No."

"So you figured that out on your own, did you?"

"I wanted to go home."

"Mr. Wise, the police didn't make you do that, did they?"

"I tell you, I wanted to go home."

"The police didn't make you do that punching?"

"No. I did it myself."

Howard Diller's closing statement, like the presentation of his entire case, was disjointed and sloppy. He began by talking about how the victim had become a celebrity, with everyone wanting quick justice, comparing Trisha Meili to Charles Lindbergh when his son was kidnapped. He challenged the validity of the hair samples but failed to emphasize the weakness of the prosecution's physical evidence, especially the negative DNA results. Diller accused the detectives of conning Kevin into confessing, thinking he could go home, and pointed out where the language in the statement was clearly not that of a fifteen-year-old. In his opening, Diller had admitted that Kevin was in the park but was not acting in concert in the rape because he did not participate in any way, but Kevin's family had insisted that Diller not acknowledge Kevin's presence there at all in his closing. His hands were tied, as he was left with only a coercion defense to present, and a summation that ignored a significant claim of his opening statement.

Colin Moore described a vast white conspiracy to frame the first minority kids who came along. He contrasted the powerful detectives and prosecutors with the powerless teenagers and their families, unable to withstand the intense interrogations. "These young men did not have a snowball's chance in hell," he said. He showed clips of the video-taped confessions, carefully pointing out to the jury where Lederer had coached answers out of Korey. Moore suggested that Korey had given concrete answers only when Lederer provided him with names or asked about specifics, whereas with open-ended questions, he hadn't had anything to say. Moore's strongest argument was that Korey had been confused and was easily coerced, and the fact that Korey had given four different statements to the police and prosecutors only served to make that point. "Which one are you supposed to believe?" Moore asked. Clearly, Korey was not himself a credible witness, so Moore told the jury they had to reject all of his statements, not cherry-pick the incriminating parts, as the district attorney wanted. "And that leaves you with no evidence."

Lederer's closing repeated much of what she'd said at the first trial, but she also had to contend with Moore's and Diller's specific arguments. She insisted that the case had nothing to do with race, as Moore had indicated, pointing out that many other black and Hispanic teenagers had been questioned and then released. Lederer spoke of Korey's lack of understanding, referring to his admission to Melonie Jackson that he didn't rape the jogger and only touched her legs. "He still doesn't get it," she said, and she was right.

In her summation, Lederer denied that Kevin and his family had been misled by the police, insisting that they had only told him to tell the truth. She ended by contradicting Moore's claim that the police were powerful and the teenagers their victims, suggesting instead that Korey, Kevin, and the others in the park that night were the powerful ones. "And look at how they wielded that power. Look what they did to their victims."

The jury began their deliberations on Friday, November 30, and continued through the weekend. This jury was made up of seven women and five men and was just as diverse as the jury at the first trial, with five whites, four African-Americans, two Latinos, and one Asian-American.

They deliberated for twelve consecutive days before reaching their verdict, which shocked both the defense and the prosecution. On December 11, 1990, as the verdict was read, the courtroom erupted into a frenzy. Kevin Richardson was convicted on every count, including attempted murder, rape, and sodomy. His mother fell to the ground as the verdict was read, and supporters screamed at the judge and prosecution, calling them racist, and yelled that the jogger was a "whore." The jury had to be removed to another courtroom to finish reading their verdict. Korey was convicted only of first-degree assault, sexual abuse, and riot. He was acquitted on the charges of rape and attempted murder. Korey and Kevin cried and hugged, but Korey also had some angry words for prosecutor Elizabeth Lederer. "You bitch, you'll pay for this. Jesus is going to get you," he hissed.

The verdicts were surprising because they were so different for the two defendants. As the jurors began speaking with the media in the days after the verdicts, their reasoning became clearer. They believed that the hairs found on Kevin that were similar to the jogger's were a significant piece of evidence, and while in the jury room they had noticed grass and dirt stains on Kevin's underwear, which led them to believe that he had pulled his pants down and was therefore guilty of the rape.

The verdict on the charges against Korey came after lengthy deliberations. The jurors agreed to ignore completely the testimony of any witness they did not believe was credible, including Melonie Jackson. Many also found Korey himself not credible, especially in the second videotape. The reactions of the jurors ran the gamut, with some believing everything in the second tape and wanting to convict on every charge, and others believing that Korey had been coerced and maybe even abused by the police. Lingering in the back of their minds was the sense that Korey faced a much longer sentence as an adult than anyone else tried in the case, which they knew because Korey himself had blurted it out in one of several outbursts during the trial.

Mostly, the contradictions in Korey's four statements made it hard for them to know what to believe. In the end, they reached a compromise, convicting Korey of only one of the assault charges, stemming from "depraved indifference," because they believed he had been there and done nothing to help, leaving the jogger there to die. The jurors eventually agreed that Korey's admission that he'd touched the jogger's leg was valid, hence the conviction for sexual abuse. And though it was not meant to be relevant in their deliberations, one juror later conceded to the press that their belief that Korey was remorseful had affected their decision in his favor.

At sentencing in January, the Richardson family finally got their wish, and C. Vernon Mason replaced Howard Diller as Kevin's lawyer. He railed against the verdict, arguing that Kevin had had "ineffective assistance of counsel." Moore, too, asked that the verdicts against his client be set aside, presenting a well-reasoned argument about the inconsistencies in the case, but unsurprisingly, Galligan denied each claim. Both teenagers spoke briefly, thanking their families and declaring their innocence before Galligan ruled on their sentences. Galligan used strong words to denounce both young men. "Such wanton and depraved action by each defendant demands the most serious condemnation of society," he commented. "Wise's strident and ardent behavior at the time the verdict was rendered, his belligerent and offensive conduct as a witness, speak volumes about who he is."

Justice Galligan sentenced Kevin to three and a third to ten years for each of the major counts, to be served consecutively, but like the defendants in the first trial, because of Kevin's status as a juvenile, his term would be limited to five to ten years. Because Korey was sixteen at the time of his arrest and therefore not eligible for juvenile sentencing, though he was convicted of lesser crimes, he faced up to twenty-six years. Galligan, in a surprising decision after his harsh words for Korey, applied the sentences concurrently, so that only the lengthiest sentence, of five to fifteen years for the assault, would apply.

With five convictions under her belt, Elizabeth Lederer turned her attention to Steve Lopez. She had always believed that Lopez was the leader of the group and one of the more violent attackers in the jogger's rape, based upon the statements of the others already convicted. But because those statements were not admissible against Lopez, she would need someone to testify against him, and no one was willing to do that. Lopez had given statements to the police and the assistant district attorney, but he had only admitted to witnessing the attacks on Loughlin and Diaz, and he had not been willing to say anything at all about the female jogger. Unless she could find someone to testify, the case was a loser.

On the eve of the trial, Lederer offered a plea to Jesse Berman, Lopez's lawyer. After a few days of deliberation, Lopez and his family accepted the offer—to plead guilty to robbery in the Loughlin assault and receive a sentence of one and a half to four and a half years. Steve Lopez joined Jermain Robinson and Michael Briscoe, both of whom had already pleaded guilty to lesser charges unrelated to the rape. Two others, Orlando Escobar and Antonio Montalvo, were arrested and charged only in the assaults on Antonio Diaz and John Loughlin. Both pleaded guilty to attempted robbery.

Kevin Richardson, Raymond Santana, Korey Wise, Yusef Salaam, and Antron McCray would be the only defendants convicted of crimes related to the rape of Trisha Meili, and they would come to be known as the Central Park Five.

CHAPTER SIX

For a time back in 1990, in the months leading up to his trial, Korey Wise was incarcerated at Rikers Island. Matias Reyes, the man who had actually raped the Central Park Jogger, was there as well, in the same housing block. Reyes was awaiting trial on the other rape and murder charges that would eventually lead to his life sentence. One day, the two got into an argument over the TV in a common area. Reyes knew that he was facing one of the boys charged in a rape he'd committed, having seen the newspaper headlines in the bodega where he worked, but he revealed nothing to Korey. They would not meet again for a dozen years.

Meanwhile, the Central Park Five were serving out their time in prisons across the state of New York. Because Antron, Kevin, Yusef, and Raymond had been considered "juvenile offenders," tried as adults but sentenced as juveniles, they were incarcerated in juvenile facilities until their twenty-first birthdays, when they were transferred to maximum-security adult prisons. Korey, who at sixteen was ineligible for the protections afforded by the juvenile laws, was sent immediately to a maximum-security facility, which housed adult violent offenders, where he served his entire term.

Kevin saw violence and riots, and he was even involved in a few fights himself while at Harlem Valley, a maximum-security juvenile prison in Wingdale, New York, where he served for almost five years. But after his twenty-first birthday, he was transferred to an adult maximum-security prison, Coxsackie Correctional. There, the violence was more serious, often instigated by men serving life sentences and with little to lose. Kevin was lucky to avoid physical harm there, but the experience was terrifying nonetheless.

Raymond had thought that after the year and a half he spent at Spofford during the trial, he knew what to expect in prison, but Goshen, the juvenile facility where he spent his next five years, was a far less friendly place. When he turned twenty-one, he was moved to Downstate Correctional, where the guards were tougher and the inmates got into fights with knives and other weapons. Raymond avoided those conflicts, motivated by a hope of being paroled or released before serving his entire sentence. Though his favorite activity as a kid had been drawing, Raymond began lifting weights, and he became a bulkier version of the fourteen-year-old who'd entered prison.

In 1993, Raymond was allowed out of Goshen, the juvenile facility where he was then incarcerated, to visit his mother, who was dying of cancer. She was so sick that when she tried to speak, she could only grunt, so they just sat there looking at each other. At her wake, some family members treated him as a pariah.

Antron passed his five years as a juvenile at Brookwood, which was set up like a dorm, with individual rooms rather than cells. He then served two years at Clinton, a maximum-security adult facility, where he found a much more "hardcore" environment. He was surrounded by lifers in traditional cells and had little privacy. Like Raymond, Antron changed physically while in prison. At fifteen, he'd been five three and scrawny, and though he gained only a couple of inches in height, he put on nearly a hundred pounds during his incarceration, evolving from a skinny kid to a solidly built young man. On a few brief occasions during his sentence, he was at the same facility as other members of the Central Park Five, but mostly he knew no one.

Before his arrest, Antron McCray had been closer to his stepfather than to his mother. Linda McCray was the disciplinarian in the house, and Antron felt more comfortable with his stepfather, Bobby, who coached his baseball team and whom Antron considered his best friend. But Bobby, thinking he was helping, had encouraged Antron to confess. Afterward, Bobby was heartbroken and had a difficult time dealing with his stepson. He withdrew and didn't keep in touch as well while Antron served his time. Linda, however, proved stalwart, remaining at her son's side throughout his trial and encouraging him to remain strong in the face of it all. During his incarceration, she visited him every weekend, traveling by train, bus, or car to wherever he was.

Yusef's prison experience was similar to that of the other boys, though he served his time at another facility, called Harlem Village. It was somewhat more dangerous than Goshen or Brookwood, but even that was much safer than what was happening in the adult facilities, including Clinton Correctional, where he went when he turned twenty-one. "What you see in a youth facility, you think is the worst of the worst, until you get to adult prison," he recalled. Though Yusef saw terrible violence in those prisons, the Muslim community he connected with at each location largely insulated him from it. He'd always been committed to his religion, and though he felt that the other members of the community were interested in him at first because of his notoriety—his name and image had often been in the newspapers—they soon saw that he was serious and knowledgeable when it came to Islam, more so than some members who had converted while in prison. He found there was safety in numbers and was protected from much of the violence around him. He rose to become a respected leader of the religious community in each facility where he served. Islam also gave him something meaningful to connect to during his incarceration, and it helped him manage his anger at being wrongly convicted.

Korey was incarcerated at maximum-security prison facilities Clinton, Attica, Wende, and Auburn, which were scattered across the state of New York. Though eighteen by the time he began serving his prison term, he was only five five, and his mental and emotional capabilities were limited by his learning disabilities and hearing loss. He was careful not to break any rules or cause trouble, and he survived, but with everlasting scars. It was hard being so far away from home, so while he was at Attica, in western New York, he requested a transfer to a facility closer to the city. Instead, he was moved to Wende, in Alden, New York, even farther west, a six-hour drive from his family. Korey's father, Victor, a maintenance man, who started drinking more heavily after his son was convicted, died during Korey's incarceration.

Despite the hardships of the various juvenile and adult prisons where Antron, Raymond, Korey, Yusef, and Kevin spent their adolescent years, each had access to educational programs that allowed them to continue their studies. All five achieved high school equivalency diplomas and then matriculated into college programs. Raymond received an associate's degree in science. Kevin completed an associate's degree through Dutchess Community College while he was at Harlem Valley and then started a bachelor's degree program through Mercy College. Antron and Korey began associate's degrees, and Yusef completed one. Their educations were all cut short in 1995, when Governor Pataki banned inmates from participating in New York's Tuition Assistance Program, effectively canceling the college curricula at most prisons across the state.

William Kunstler, the famed civil rights attorney, filed an appeal on Yusef's behalf not long after sentencing. His argument centered on Yusef's separation from his family during his interrogation. A panel of judges reviewed the case for the Court of Appeals of New York and upheld Yusef's conviction, but one judge disagreed. In a dissenting opinion, Judge Vito Titone argued that Yusef's statement should have been suppressed because the police and Linda Fairstein had denied Yusef access to the family members and friends who were downstairs in the precinct, hoping to counsel him. "Indeed it is apparent that the authorities' purpose was to obtain the evidence they wanted before permitting [the] defendant to speak with an adult who might interfere with the investigators' absolute control over his person and environment."

As the Central Park Five served their sentences, the city they had left behind was going through a transformation. The crime rates that had increased throughout the 1970s and 1980s and the despair that stemmed from the deterioration of New York City began to turn around. The economy was improving, both nationally and locally; the use of crack cocaine decreased as a younger generation saw the terrible impact of the drug on their parents and older siblings, leading to less drug-related violence; and new strategies and initiatives provided ways to combat crime throughout the city.

Mayor Dinkins was able to secure funding to put more than 5,000 additional cops on the street in the first years of his term, bringing NYPD strength up to 31,000 officers by 1994, the highest levels ever. And the poor—mostly black and Latino—communities that had been hit hardest by the bad economy, drugs, and violence of the past decades began fighting back through tenants associations, PTAs, and community organizations, policing their own neighborhoods, promoting after-school programs and sports leagues, and working to improve their local schools.

The NYPD also had a new strategy that contributed to the city's extraordinary turnaround. In 1990, William Bratton had been hired as the head of the New York City Transit Police. In this position, he implemented a strategy based on the "broken windows" theory of social disorder and crime, which posits that if a broken window is left unfixed, it will appear that no one cares, and more windows will be broken. This theory advanced the idea that by vigorously addressing relatively minor infractions and quality-of-life issues, other, more serious crimes would ebb, as well. Bratton applied this to the subways, cracking down on turnstile jumping, arresting offenders and keeping them handcuffed together in the stations to send a message to other would-be fare beaters. The transit police also enforced laws against panhandling and erased graffiti from subway cars right after it had been painted, not only cleaning up the cars but also discouraging the graffiti artists by eliminating their work before others could see it.

These efforts began to help. Officers discovered that when they arrested fare beaters, one in seven had an outstanding warrant; others were carrying concealed weapons, leading to arrests and convictions on more serious charges. In 1994, Rudy Giuliani campaigned on a tough-on-crime platform and won the mayoralty, unseating Dinkins after one term. He installed Bratton as commissioner of the NYPD, and Bratton brought his strategy with him. He also promoted Jack Maple, a lieutenant in the transit police, to deputy commissioner. Under their watch, the NYPD began cracking down on so-called quality-of-life crimes throughout the city, making arrests for public urination, drunkenness, and disorderly conduct. Maple, an eccentric cop famous for his bow ties, bowler hats, and spats, grilled the precinct commanders on their methods in regular meetings, which were called "COMPSTAT" sessions, for the computerized crime statistics used to target problems and needs within specific precincts of the NYPD. In 1990, there were 2,245 murders in New York City, the highest ever. By 1995, the murder rate had dropped to 1,177, the lowest number since the 1970s, and it continued to fall. By the late 1990s, crime in New York City had been cut nearly in half since the end of the 1980s.

The crackdown in New York City may have helped to improve the crime rates and contributed to the overall turnaround of the city, but it also created a greater rift between the police and the residents of neighborhoods with large minority populations, where much of that crackdown occurred. Mistrust of the police only grew in those neighborhoods, where residents often felt under siege. Beginning in the 1980s, but expanding in the early 1990s under Police Commissioner Lee Brown, New York had implemented a strategy known as "community policing," which aims to create more respectful interactions between police and communities so that local residents can assist the police in their investigations and feel more secure in their neighborhoods. But that wasn't always enough to restore trust between minority communities and the police.

Central Park, which in 1989 had been in a sorry state of disrepair, with brown grass and graffiti-covered landmarks, was also being transformed. The Central Park Conservancy, a nonprofit organization that spearheaded the improvements, had been founded in 1980. A few projects had been completed before 1989, but there was much work still to be done, and the park remained a devastating reminder of the beauty it once held. In 1993, a restoration of the Harlem Meer, the large body of water just inside the park and not far from the Schomburg Plaza, was completed, and by 1997 the massive Great Lawn at the center of the park was brought back as a grassy green meadow where people could picnic, stroll, and play games. These efforts restored the beauty of the park and brought New York City residents back to Central Park, reversing its negative image.

After five years of incarceration, the minimum time on their sentences, the Central Park Five became eligible for parole. At a parole hearing in September 1995, Kevin Richardson was criticized for attending his required sexual offender counseling without admitting guilt. "One of the problems is when you deny the crime, participating in sexual offender treatment doesn't have productive results," the board reprimanded. Kevin asked to read a poem to the panel. "My Life: If I could turn back the hands of time, I would reverse this life that has been mine. I would not be led down the wrong path, I will only do things that make people laugh. I will make no mistakes, I would be great, but today reaching the age of 21, my life has just begun. If you can sense my true sense of pride, there would be no question of the goal that I strive: to love and honor and cherish every little thing, in what the rest of my life will bring." His parole application was denied.

All four of the other Central Park defendants also refused to admit to any part of the rape. Each was denied parole. None was likely to receive an early parole without admitting guilt for the crimes he had been convicted of. Instead, each would have to wait for his conditional release date, which occurs when a convict's accrued time off for good behavior equals the remaining time left on his sentence. A conditional release is not at the discretion of a parole board, which can choose to punish the applicant for his attitude or unwillingness to confess and express remorse. Conditional release dates began to arrive for the four young men who'd been sentenced as juveniles beginning in 1995. Raymond was conditionally released in December 1995, followed by Antron in September 1996. Yusef and Kevin received conditional releases in March and June of 1997, respectively. They had served between six and more than eight years for the rape of the Central Park Jogger.

When Kevin was released from Coxsackie Correctional Facility, his sisters and other family members came to pick him up. His mother had stayed in New York, too sick to make the trip, waiting for him to come home to the Schomburg Plaza. His sisters brought him nice new clothes to wear, and they cried and jumped for joy when he walked through the gates, finally a free man. He was so happy and relieved that he kissed the ground.

Korey, whose maximum sentence was fifteen years rather than ten because he was sixteen at the time of the crime, would have to wait another five years.

Following that joyous reunion with his family, Kevin, then twenty-two, struggled to settle into his life on the outside. He'd forgotten what handling his own money was like, and he'd never seen a MetroCard for the subway. Kevin and the others, now registered sex offenders, had to pay to go to group counseling sessions for sexual predators, and Kevin was horrified by the stories of the other members. He and Yusef attended the sessions together and shook their heads at the terrible things the other men had done, knowing that they should not be there. Yusef was kicked

186 · Sarah Burns

out of one group for denying the crime he was supposed to have committed, and instead he had to pay for private counseling. Raymond had a difficult time breaking his habits from prison. When he first got out, he was constantly on guard and acted aggressively so as not to appear weak.

Antron McCray had an especially hard time adjusting to life back in New York. When he was released from Clinton Correctional Facility, way upstate in Dannemora, New York, he took a bus home by himself and almost walked past the front door to his parents' building because he didn't remember the place. His relationship with his stepfather remained strained, and though Bobby apologized many times, Antron had lingering anger toward his stepfather over the role he'd played in encouraging him to confess. Bobby had kidney problems and was on dialysis at that time, and he eventually died from kidney failure in 1997, just a year after Antron's release. Antron still regrets that he never had a chance to tell Bobby he forgave him while he was alive.

Antron wanted to keep his head down and work hard in order to prove that people who thought he was a bad guy were wrong. He felt that even members of his own family didn't believe him. Antron had three sons but did not maintain long-term relationships with their mothers. In July 1999, he moved to Maryland, where a cousin lived, and used his legal name to apply for jobs. Because his conviction had been entered under Antron McCray, his record didn't come up on background checks, and so he was able to get a job without mentioning his incarceration, the only way he was likely to find work. In Maryland, he worked as a forklift operator in warehouses.

All these young men had a tough time finding decent jobs. Because they were registered sex offenders, few would hire them. Yusef worked construction for a while, but when they cut back his hours and he asked if he could go to school part-time, they fired him. Kevin's brother-in-law helped him get a job as an usher at a movie theater at one point, and he also spent time as a construction worker, deliveryman, and a bouncer. When he applied for a job at the post office, they told him that they would have hired him if not for his record.

For Raymond, finding a job proved impossible. He got the impression that his parole officer was itching to send him back to jail. A year and a half after being released, Raymond was charged with robbery related to a fight between another man and a local woman over drugs. He'd had nothing to do with it, and the charges were dropped, but he was instead accused of a parole violation—for breaking his curfew—and sentenced to two and a half years. He served twenty months in a maximum-security facility upstate—Great Meadow, in Comstock, New York—which was worse than anything he'd seen during his previous stint. Still unable to find work after his release, he turned to selling drugs. Six months later, he was caught with crack and pleaded guilty to criminal possession of a controlled substance with intent to distribute. Given his previous experiences with the justice system, he believed that fighting the charges would only lead to a longer sentence. Because of his prior conviction, he received a sentence of forty-two months to seven years.

Yusef married a woman three months after they started dating; they had three daughters together in the span of less than three years, but the marriage soon fell apart. Yusef believes that he might not have ended up divorced so soon if he hadn't rushed into it, trying to make the most of his time on the outside.

In late 2001, after being denied parole three times, Korey was still incarcerated at Auburn Correctional Facility, near Syracuse, New York. Before his first parole hearing, a counselor had let him know that showing remorse and admitting his guilt would make the parole board go easier on him, but he'd been unwilling to admit that he'd ever even seen the female jogger, just as the other four young men had refused, even if it cost them an earlier release. After being denied a second time, Korey boycotted his third hearing. He was frustrated that after being so careful to act as a model prisoner, it seemed that his good behavior meant nothing to the parole board unless he lied and confessed to something he hadn't done.

———

Matias Reyes was also incarcerated at Auburn then, and one day toward the end of 2001 he approached Korey out in the yard. He apologized for the fight they'd had years earlier over the television at Rikers, and he asked if things were okay between them. Korey told Reyes that he harbored no grudge, that it was all in the past. They went on to have a friendly conversation, talking about religion and their experiences. Reyes mentioned that he was aware that Korey had always maintained his innocence throughout his incarceration, though Reyes continued to keep quiet about his own involvement with the crime that had sent the young man to jail. Korey didn't think much of it, but Reyes left their meeting feeling guilty that Korey was still serving time for something he'd done. Soon after, Reyes confessed to a prison employee that someone else at the prison was serving time for a famous crime that he had in fact committed.

His shocking admission began wending its way through the justice system as higher-ups in the department of corrections began to hear that someone else had admitted to raping the Central Park Jogger. By January of 2002, Reyes was interviewed by someone from the state inspector general's office, the department that polices state officials. In early February, the inspector general's office turned the case over to the Manhattan district attorney's office.

Nancy Ryan, the very same assistant district attorney who had originally wanted to try the Central Park Jogger case before Linda Fairstein wrested it away for her Sex Crimes Prosecution Unit, was assigned to reinvestigate Reyes's explosive confession and whether it had any impact on the convictions of the Central Park Five. The media loved to play up the supposed rivalry between Ryan and Fairstein, and some saw Ryan's involvement in the reinvestigation as an opportunity to get even with Fairstein for stealing the case out from under her in 1989. In 2002, Linda Fairstein retired from her career as a prosecutor and focused on writing a series of novels featuring a sex crimes ADA, but she continued to share her thoughts on the case with the media, remaining steadfast in promoting the guilt of the Central Park Five.

Nancy Ryan and another ADA, Peter Casolaro, began the reinvestigation by looking back at the DNA evidence. When Reyes pleaded guilty in 1991 to his other crimes, DNA had connected him to several of the crime scenes, though no one had ever checked to see if his DNA matched the profile from the Central Park case.

This time, Reyes's DNA was compared to the single profile established in 1989 from a cervical swab and from Meili's sock. In May of 2002, they received the results: It was a match.

As soon as the DNA evidence gave credence to Reyes's claim, the district attorney's office moved ahead cautiously, checking his whole story and his assertion that he had raped the jogger alone. Until then, his confession had been kept under wraps, but once the DNA test connected Reyes to the case with certainty, the news began to leak out. In June 2002, *The New York Times* reported that the DA's office was investigating a claim by Reyes that he'd raped the Central Park Jogger, but there was still doubt as to what it meant for the teenagers who had already served their sentences.

Korey was finally eligible for a conditional release in August 2002, after serving more than thirteen years. His mother and a television producer from ABC News, who by then had heard about Reyes's confession and was following the new developments, came to pick him up. It was an emotional reunion, and Korey seemed shaken to be out after so long; he was dizzy and unsteady on his feet.

ADAs Ryan and Casolaro had interviewed Reyes several times in May 2002, trying to piece together his claims and see if they could be corroborated. By now, they knew that Reyes had raped the jogger; DNA proved that much. What remained for them to determine was whether Antron, Raymond, Yusef, Kevin, and Korey had been wrongly convicted or if they, too, had been there and abetted Reyes's crime. They conducted interviews with many police officers, inmates, and other players and revisited the details of the original case and Reyes's history in the justice system. In all of their investigations, Ryan and Casolaro were unable to find evidence of any connection between Reyes and the teenagers who'd been convicted, other than Reyes's brief encounters with Korey at Rikers and Auburn. None of Reyes's associates, with whom he used to commit robberies as a teenager, knew any of the teens from the park. In their statements and confessions, the defendants in the jogger case and the others arrested from that group had named many people without ever mentioning Reyes.*

In June, NYPD investigators working with the DA's office interviewed Raymond and Kevin, telling them they were there for another purpose and leaving them in the dark about Reyes's admission and the reinvestigation. Kevin admitted that he'd been in the park that night, but he continued to deny any involvement in the rape, telling the investigators that he'd been tricked into confessing by promises that he could go home. Raymond admitted having gone into the park with the intention to assault and rob people, but he denied anything having to do with the rape. He said, "Hartigan and Arroyo okey doked me with that good cop bad cop routine. . . . So I made up the story you see on the tape to satisfy them." Kevin and Raymond, as well as others who'd been in the park that night, were shown a photograph of Reyes, and no one recognized him.

Ryan also went back and looked at the evidence collected at the crime scene, including photographs. She noticed the narrow drag marks etched in the wet grass leading off the road and concluded that "the pathway is sixteen to eighteen inches wide, and appears to be more consistent with a single attacker dragging an inert form than with a group." The hairs found on Kevin Richardson's clothing, which an expert witness had testified at trial were similar to Trisha Meili's hair—the only physical evi-

*The name Tony, which had been one of Reyes's nicknames at the time, did come up in some of the statements, but there was also an Antonio "Tony" Montalvo from the group of thirty-three interviewed in conjunction with the case back in 1989.

dence that directly linked any of the defendants to the crime—were also reexamined. An FBI specialist determined that the hairs should never have been presented at trial because they were too undifferentiated to make a comparison given the techniques available at the time. Since that time, however, newer forms of DNA testing had been developed, and it was now possible to extract DNA from individual hairs. Using that technology, experts compared the hairs found on Kevin Richardson's clothing in 1989 to Meili's hair. They did not match.

Reyes's narrative of the crime fit accurately with the evidence gathered back in 1989, including his description of the crime-scene location, as well as the injuries sustained by the jogger. Reyes told the investigators that he went into Central Park that night from the bodega where he worked on 102nd Street, intending to commit a crime. He saw the jogger first on the East Drive, heading north, and followed her for a while, waiting to see where she was going. He remembered correctly that she had been wearing dark jogging pants. Once Meili turned onto the dark and quiet 102nd Street Cross Drive, Reyes began to draw closer. He grabbed a large branch with both hands and then quickly caught up to her, aware that her headset would prevent her from hearing his approach. He slammed her with the branch from behind, sending her facefirst to the pavement, and her headphones flew off. Reyes explained that she was so stunned that he was able to drag her off the road without her fighting back at all, through the grass and into a more overgrown area. He recounted raping her there and said she then broke away and ran, half-naked. When he caught up to her, he picked up a rock and hit her face. He found her keys in a small zippered pouch and demanded to know her address, planning to steal from her apartment, but she wouldn't give it to him and he beat her savagely.

The evidence at the crime scene suggests that Reyes remembered the location of the rape incorrectly, because Meili's clothing was found near the second location rather than the first, but otherwise his description conforms perfectly to the forensics. Meili's injuries would be consistent with being hit by a branch in the back of the head and with a rock around the face, and the drag marks leading toward one location where some blood was found and the existence of a second location with a large pool of blood also corroborated his story.

Reyes's recollections shed new light on evidence gathered at the crime scene in Central Park back in 1989. Reyes remembered that he had taken Meili's radio headset, which was never found at the crime scene or in the possession of any of the accused. He said that he took her keys and the small pouch attached to her shoe that held them. In 1989, investigators had looked for the keys, but they did not know about the carrying case until Reyes told them. When asked in 2002, Meili recalled having a case that attached to her shoe, which explains why one of Meili's sneakers was found at the scene with the laces undone. Meili also had a strange cut on her cheek, the source of which was never identified. The injury was shaped like a cross, and Reyes indicated that he wore a ring at the time with a three-dimensional image of Jesus on the cross.

Reyes also described other crimes he'd gotten away with before his arrest later that summer of 1989. Ryan and her team were able to corroborate some of those stories, such as the rape of Jackie Herbach at the Church of the Heavenly Rest back in 1988, and the April 17, 1989, assault of a woman in Central Park, not far from where Meili was attacked just two days later. He also told investigators about bumping into a detective he knew, nicknamed "Blondie," on his way out of the park the night of the Central Park Jogger rape. Though the officer did not recall his meeting with Reyes, he was, in fact, heading into Central Park that night and driving in a taxicab with another detective who was not his usual partner, just as Reyes had described.

In addition to the growing sense that Reyes's story was credible, similarities between his other crimes and the rape of Trisha Meili pointed to the likelihood that that crime was part of a pattern. Several of Reyes's other victims had been stabbed around their eyes or threatened with blinding. Though Meili was not stabbed, Reyes had used a rock to batter her eyes, doing serious damage to her eye socket and causing permanent vision problems. And Reyes had tied one of his other rape victims with an extension cord exactly as Meili had been tied with her shirt. His other known crimes had been committed on the Upper East Side of Manhattan or in Central Park, all within less than a mile of the Central Park rape.

And he always worked alone.

Ryan and Casolaro's investigation revisited the contradictions and inaccuracies in the statements of the teenagers. They found that "analysis shows that the accounts given by the five defendants differed from one another on the specific details of virtually every major aspect of the crime—who initiated the attack, who knocked the victim down, who undressed her, who struck her, who held her, who raped her, what weapons were used in the course of the assault, and when in the sequence of events the attack took place." They also noted that no one got the location of the attack right in their videotaped statement, with the sole exception of Korey Wise, who had already been taken to the crime scene by detectives, but that "the defendants were not similarly confused about the locations of the other crimes they described."

The ADAs also noted the problems with the time line of incidents in the park. "Given the times when each of those events were estimated to have occurred, it is difficult to construct a scenario that would have allowed the defendants the time to interrupt their progression south, detour to the 102nd Street Transverse, and commit a gang rape."

Besides the glaring inconsistencies among the various statements given by the Central Park Five, other factors added to the growing sense that the "confessions" could have been coerced. Of the five teenagers who implicated themselves in the rape, only Korey Wise was sixteen at the time and not considered a juvenile in the state of New York, but his low IQ and hearing loss prevented him from being able to understand and waive his Miranda rights or fully comprehend his situation. The others were just fourteen and fifteen years old at the time of their interrogations and false confessions.

The fact that each of the young men—and some of their parents—later said that they believed they could go home if they cooperated suggests that the detectives had somehow given them that sense, even though confessions obtained using explicit or implied promises should be considered coerced and therefore not admissible in a court of law. Though the statements have often been referred to as confessions, in each case the young man was clearly trying to diminish his own culpability, even as he made admissions that were terribly damning. Most of the boys admitted to witnessing the crime and participating in some more minor way, while directing the blame for the rape at other boys who had been accused. Rather than confessing, each boy had believed that he was cooperating and might help the police by becoming a witness, thereby leading to his release.

Ryan concluded that the small details that Reyes got wrong about the crime were understandable in light of the amount of time that had passed and given the fact that his account hewed so closely to the facts of the case. Considering the contradictions in the statements of the Central Park Five, the new DNA tests, the credibility of Reyes's account, and the similarities between the rape of the jogger in Central Park and Reyes's other crimes, all of which he committed by himself, Ryan, Casolaro, and District Attorney Robert Morgenthau were satisfied that the convictions of Raymond Santana, Antron McCray, Korey Wise, Yusef Salaam, and Kevin Richardson should not stand.

As the reinvestigation by the district attorney's office was concluding, lawyers working on behalf of the Central Park Five filed a motion in September 2002, asking a judge to vacate the original convictions based on Reyes's confession and the evidence that corroborated it. The defense attorneys had been alerted to Reyes's confession by the article in *The New York Times* in June and had set about getting an affidavit from Reyes that they could use as evidence to present with their motion.

ADAs Nancy Ryan and Peter Casolaro filed their affirmation on behalf of the People on December 5, joining with the defense lawyers' motion. The fifty-eight-page document outlined their reinvestigation in detail and concluded that, "based on the facts and for the reasons set forth below, the People consent to the defendants' motion to set aside the verdicts on all the charges of which they were convicted." The DA could have simply not opposed the defense's request, but he chose to submit the extensive report documenting exactly why the convictions should be vacated, explaining the facts that Reyes provided, the results of new forensic tests that exculpated the Central Park Five, and Nancy Ryan and Peter Casolaro's review of both the original case against the teenagers and Reyes's earlier crimes. Justice Galligan had retired from the New York State Supreme Court by then, so Justice Charles J. Tejada was assigned in his stead.

On December 19, 2002, Tejada called the lawyers into the courtroom. The Central Park Five were not in attendance, their lawyers having suggested they stay away. But many of their family members were there, including Kevin Richardson's sisters, Linda McCray, and Raymond Santana, Sr., who had stayed out of the courtroom during the original trial because he knew the outcome would be a bad one. This time, he had a good feeling. The judge took only a few minutes to announce that the motion to vacate the convictions was granted in full.

The ruling, which essentially affirmed that the defendants would not have been convicted at trial if Reyes's confession had been available at the time, fell short of truly exonerating them, leaving the district attorney free to reprosecute them for any and all of the charges in the original indictments. The DA's office quickly dispelled any fears of a new trial by immediately responding to Tejada's decision with an oral motion to dismiss the indictments. Tejada responded, "The motion is granted. Have a very Merry Christmas and a happy New Year."

The Central Park Five's convictions had been erased. The courtroom, filled with family members and other supporters, erupted into a joyous celebration, with weeping and shouting all around. Their families rejoiced, hardly able to believe that their hopes had finally been fulfilled.

"I think I stopped breathing for a minute," Kevin Richardson's sister Angela Cuffee told a reporter. "I can't even tell you—it doesn't feel real. I can't even speak." Linda McCray thanked Jesus, and Sharonne Salaam called Yusef in Georgia, where he was then living, to tell him the news. Kevin was home with his mother watching NYI, the local news channel, where he first heard that his conviction had been vacated. Moments later, he got a call from his sister at the courthouse, and he and his mother held each other and cried. Korey felt great that Morgenthau had come through for them, but to him it was just "a moving along step" to justice.

Raymond was still serving his sentence for a drug charge at Franklin Correctional Facility when the rape conviction was vacated. In the afternoon, when he was sure the hearing was over, he called his father from a pay phone. As soon as he heard the news that his conviction had been vacated, he announced it to his fellow inmates, who were crowded around. They broke into cheers and applause. Raymond would never have been given such a lengthy sentence in the drug case if not for his prior guilty verdict, so within a week of the conviction being vacated he was resentenced as a first-time offender. Because of the time he'd already served, Raymond was immediately released, just two days before Christmas in 2002. His father was waiting to take him home from the processing center in Queens, where a crowd of media had gathered outside the front door. A corrections officer offered Raymond the option of leaving through a back entrance to avoid the crowds, but he chose to walk out with his head held high. "I'm a free man. I'm going out the front," he said.

Others were not so pleased. Though the district attorney's office had supported the vacating of the convictions with their affirmation, the NYPD had a different perspective. With reputations on the line, Police Commissioner Ray Kelly had called together an independent panel in November 2002, including private attorney Michael Armstrong, who had previously investigated police corruption, Jules Martin, and Stephen

Hammerman, to do their own simultaneous reinvestigation. Though the DA's report had not accused the NYPD of misconduct directly, any admission that the Central Park Five were innocent of the rape automatically raised questions about how and why they had confessed.

Members of the police department felt frustrated that the district attorney's office had not included them more in the reinvestigation and had allowed the judge to make a ruling before the police report had been completed, though their inclusion was not required or expected. In fact, the convening of a panel by the NYPD was a highly unusual move, one that reflected deep concerns over the outcome of the case. An attorney for the detectives' union publicly accused the DA's report of "patent errors" and implied that Nancy Ryan had done a poor job. "If Nancy Ryan's preparing an inaccurate report, she's deceiving the court," a vice president of the union commented. But Morgenthau backed Ryan up, pointing out that many prosecutors had teamed up to reinvestigate and that ultimately he was responsible for their work. "It's my decision," he said. "The buck stops here." He also admitted that they had made a mistake back in 1989.

The report to Police Commissioner Ray Kelly was released in January 2003. It concluded that "there was no misconduct on the part of the New York City Police Department in the arrests and interrogations of the defendants." In defending the actions of the police, it made complaints about Nancy Ryan's work, pointing out how the NYPD had been excluded from her reinvestigation, and noting that Matias Reyes had never been given a polygraph or asked to testify under oath as to his claims. The NYPD report took issue with some of the findings in the district attorney's affirmation, trying to debunk the arguments that demonstrated the innocence of the Central Park Five. It denied that a new jury would find any differently with the Reyes evidence available. But the language of the panel was less firm than that of the DA's report, describing the opinions of the panel as theories rather than facts, often using phrases like "we believe that" or "we adopt the view," and describing what they thought to be "the most likely scenario."

Without seriously reconsidering the interrogations and statements themselves in light of the newly discovered evidence, as the district attorney had, the panel simply cited Galligan's original decision in the pretrial hearing as proof that the statements had not been coerced. They came up with a new theory of what had happened that night in the park, essentially ignoring the version that Reyes had told in his confession. They suggested instead that "the defendants came upon the jogger and subjected her to the same kind of attack, albeit with sexual overtones, that they inflicted upon other victims in the park that night. Perhaps attracted to the scene by the jogger's screams, Reyes either joined in the attack as it was ending or waited until the defendants had moved on to their next victims before descending upon her himself, raping her and inflicting upon her the brutal injuries that almost caused her death."

They admitted that the evidence "could afford a reasonable basis for maintaining that Reyes did, indeed, commit an attack on the jogger by himself," but they based their "theory" on "the consistencies found in the defendants' statements, the informal remarks made by the defendants at various times, the corroborative testimony of other witnesses, the absence of convincing motive for Reyes and suspicion of his general credibility." According to the report, Reyes should not be considered believable, mainly because he was a criminal, but they also highlighted the minor inconsistencies in his statements as evidence that he was lying. This was in strange contrast to their use of the discrepancies in the teenagers' statements as proof of guilt and the lack of coercion, noting, "It would seem that consistency [in the teenagers' statements] would be a feature of planted rather than spontaneous evidence." And again they used the fact that the problems with the statements had been considered at the pretrial hearing and dismissed by Justice Galligan as a reason not to reexamine them.

As for Reyes's motive in coming forward when he did, the report rejected Reyes's claim that he felt guilty after discovering that Korey was still in prison. Instead, they developed a theory based on the idea that Korey or friends of his had threatened Reyes, though even they acknowledged that their own opinion was based on little fact. "Such scraps of information, some of them of highly dubious reliability, certainly do not add up to proof that Reyes was motivated in coming forward by fear of threats," admitted the panel. A third theory, that Reyes confessed because he wanted a transfer to a more "favorable prison assignment," seems possible, though not a reason to discredit Reyes's reliability. In all likelihood, he was angling for a more comfortable or safer prison, but there is no evidence that such a goal would cause him to lie about the involvement of the teenagers.

The issue of Meili's headset was also raised in the police review. Ryan's investigation had pointed to Reyes's description of the victim's Walkman as a new development that proved his accurate knowledge of the crime. The NYPD report noted that, in fact, Korey had mentioned the female jogger as having a Walkman during one of his interviews, describing a "pouch for Walkman on her belt." The report used Korey's statement as proof that he, too, knew details about Meili that he could only have witnessed in person. However, what Meili owned was not, in fact, a Walkman, but a radio headset that would not have needed a pouch, since the entire device rested on the jogger's head. Reyes's description was accurate; Korey's was not.

The narrow drag marks in the grass, which contradicted the NYPD report's theory that the teenagers had attacked Meili before Reyes did, were ignored. When asked about the drag marks by a reporter after the report was released, Michael Armstrong commented that "we focused on that at one point, and then we didn't follow it up. If it's wide enough for one person to drag a body, and the others followed behind, so what? We didn't bother to address it, because it didn't seem to be a major point." The report tried to indicate that the many footprints visible around the drag marks were significant, but a detective had explained in his testimony at trial that those had all been created by the detectives who examined the crime scene.

The report accused Reyes of being wrong when he said that after he raped the jogger, she broke free and ran, half-naked, to a second location, where he caught up and eventually beat her within an inch of her life. The report cited Detective Honeyman, who had testified at the trials, as saying that there were drag marks found between the locations of the first and second assault. If this were the case, then Reyes had incorrectly described his victim as running, when, in fact, he had dragged her several hundred feet. But the authors of the report had misread the detective's testimony. The truth is that the only drag marks Honeyman found led from the road to the location of the first part of the attack. From there to the second site, there was no evidence of drag marks, and Reyes's description of dragging the jogger off the road and then her running from him exactly fit the crime-scene evidence.

Though the NYPD report got this fact wrong, the tabloid papers seized it, and reporters wrote repeatedly about how Reyes's story was unreliable and full of holes, because he "does not recall how he dragged the woman almost 300 feet." The *Daily News* and the *Post,* whose lurid headlines had encouraged the original rush to judgment, clamored to see who could better cast doubt on Reyes and the district attorney's investigation. Even before the district attorney's office submitted their findings to the judge, comments by former detectives and prosecutors were finding their way into the press.

The tabloids often quoted anonymous "law enforcement sources" to discredit Reyes's story or Nancy Ryan's investigation. One *Daily News* article cited several anonymous sources, who claimed that Reyes's confession "omits key details," and who noted that "if Reyes did all he claimed, he would have been drenched in blood, not just on his pants, as he said." But the newspaper failed to note that the teenage defendants had not had any blood at all on the clothing they wore that evening. The article concluded that "a dominant opinion is that the teenagers started the attack on the jogger, then Reyes showed up and continued it." Those inside the district attorney's office were not commenting to the press, so the tabloid quotes were confined solely to those sources who maintained the guilt of the Central Park Five.

The New York Times did their own investigating, rather than relying only on "law enforcement sources." Jim Dwyer, a veteran reporter who had raised questions about the prosecution's case in a *Newsday* column during the first trial, wrote a series of articles for the *Times,* along with several colleagues. They covered Reyes's other crimes and their similarities to the jogger rape, the significance of the drag marks, and the many contradictions and inconsistencies in the teenagers' statements. The *Times* articles also noted some of the inaccuracies in the report commissioned by the NYPD.

The reversal of the convictions outraged many of those who were invested in the guilt of the Central Park Five. "To vacate every one of these charges seems to me an act of moral cowardice and political correctness in the worst degree," said one former state police supervisor. Michael Sheehan, one of the detectives who had worked on the case, criticized the DA's office. "This lunatic concocts this wild story and these people fell for it," he said. Linda Fairstein, who had assigned her deputy Elizabeth Lederer to prosecute the original convictions, was furious. "It's completely outrageous—unbelievable that you're going to overturn these convictions without a hearing," she said. "I think that Reyes ran with that pack of kids. He stayed longer when the others moved on. He completed the assault," Fairstein explained. "I don't think there's a question in the minds of anyone present during the interrogation process that these five men were participants . . . in the attack on the jogger." Fairstein also disparaged the district attorney's reinvestigation for excluding her. "I've never been interviewed or invited to discuss the case," she said of their investigation. "I'm puzzled by it. I've made myself available, but it hasn't happened."

The press called attention to the supposed rivalry between Nancy Ryan and Linda Fairstein. In addition to coverage in the *Daily News,* the *Post* featured an article, "Legal Eagles' Rivalry Behind Jogger Probe," that again cited many anonymous sources who spoke of the "power struggle" between the two women. A sidebar within the article listed biographical facts about each one, mentioning that Ryan was divorced, while Fairstein was "married to a prominent lawyer," and quoting an unnamed colleague who described Ryan as "not easy to get along with." The article painted Fairstein as "tall, blond and striking . . . a media darling," in contrast to

Ryan, who was "dark-haired and serious." It was even rumored that an angry and unflattering character in Fairstein's successful series of novels was based on Ryan, and Fairstein herself claimed in an article that Ryan had bad-mouthed her in a background check as she was being vetted for the position of attorney general under President Clinton, a job she did not get. The article suggested that Ryan was jealous of Fairstein and was using the reinvestigation to tarnish her rival's reputation. The article was cowritten by Andrea Peyser, a columnist for the *Post,* who repeatedly expressed her view in those pages that the teenagers were guilty of the rape. The pages of the *Post* were littered with articles and columns quoting only sources who denied that the teenagers might have been innocent and referring skeptically to Reyes's "confession."

An editorial in the *Daily News* complained that the lesser charges for other assaults in the park should not have been thrown out along with the rape convictions. Though the time served by each defendant was more than they would have received for the lesser crimes unrelated to the jogger, some argued that their now-clean records did not do justice to their guilt for these other crimes. In fact, the convictions had to be thrown out in full, because the only significant evidence presented at trial for any of the crimes were the statements of the defendants themselves, which had to be disregarded in full after Reyes's confessions and DNA tests called into question their validity. Once one part of a confession is deemed false or coerced, the entire confession should be considered tainted. The district attorney could certainly have reprosecuted for the lesser charges of assault and riot, though it would have been a tough case to prove without any identifications or confessions. Even if they had been convicted again, it is not likely that a judge would have sentenced them to serve any time, given that they had already served far more than their share for the other offenses.

When the convictions were vacated, Ann Coulter, the right-wing columnist and political commentator, was particularly vocal in rejecting the possibility that the Central Park Five were innocent of the rape.

Probably feeling "humiliated," in 1989, a mob of feral beasts descended on Central Park to attack joggers and bicyclists. They brutalized a female jogger while incomprehensibly chanting "Wild Thing" in their ghetto patois.

In her syndicated column, Coulter railed against the *Times* and the liberal media for believing that "every criminal is innocent," and she criticized the efforts of those who would seek to exonerate anyone already convicted of a crime. "The odds of an innocent man being found guilty by an unanimous jury are basically nil. When the media assert a convict was 'exonerated,' they mean his conviction was thrown out on a technicality," she wrote. "It is more likely that the Central Park jogger was raped by space aliens than that Matias Reyes acted alone," she concluded. "But through their loud-mouthed lobbying in the media, criminal defense lawyers are determined to turn these beasts into their latest Sacco and Vanzetti case." In describing the young men, *feral* and *beast* were not the only words she used that hearkened back to a time when lynchings were common; Coulter also called them "animals," "primitives," and "savages" repeatedly.

The resistance to considering the possibility of the Central Park Five's innocence by police, former prosecutors, and some in the media reflected a desire not to let go of the original narrative, which had become so powerfully entrenched, as the accepted version of what had happened. Some who had actually worked on the case did not want to believe that they might have made a mistake, just as when contradictory or nonexistent evidence failed to inspire a fresh look at the time of the original investigation. Others simply found the narrative of a gang rape by black and Latino teenagers from Harlem so compelling, so believable, and so part of the public consciousness that they refused to let it go.

And though the convictions were vacated, erased in the court system as if they had never existed, the media coverage that told the new story was nowhere near as noisy as the original reporting had been. The *Daily*

News and the *Post* published articles citing Linda Fairstein and NYPD officials defending the original convictions, so much of the information that was printed hardly broadcasted their innocence. To this day, many people who read the papers in 2002 assume or were led to believe that the convictions were vacated on a technicality, or that the new evidence did nothing to contradict the guilt of the Central Park Five.

The question remains: How to prevent wrongful convictions? Groups dedicated to this very goal, such as the Innocence Project, recommend several changes. They call for better protections to be built in to eyewitness identification procedures to prevent misidentifications, which have been all too common in many of the wrongful-conviction cases that have been overturned by DNA testing. They also ask for better funding and oversight of forensic sciences to avoid the errors, overstatements, and even misconduct that can contribute to wrongful convictions. In order to prevent false confessions and protect those most vulnerable, the Innocence Project recommends videotaping all stages of custodial interrogations, not just the final portion, after questions have been asked and statements signed. By taping interrogations, suspects are better protected from coercive techniques and investigators are protected from false accusations of abuse or coercion. The record then also allows juries to see just what goes on in interrogations and for detectives to understand how it is possible for them to inadvertently give a suspect information about a crime that can later be worked into a false confession.

In this case, if the interviews and interrogations had been videotaped in full, not just after the confessions were bullied out of the kids and rehearsed for the camera, the jury could have seen the real techniques the detectives used, not just the ones they admitted to. Or perhaps the detectives, aware that their words and actions could be reviewed, would have behaved differently. But it was not only aggressive interrogation techniques that led to the false confessions, which then provided the basis for the convictions of the Central Park Five. As soon as the police leaked their version of the story to the media, the public absorbed it, believing immediately that these young men had gang-raped a woman in Central Park. The tabloids fanned the flames, but few considered even for a moment that they might be jumping to conclusions. There is no way to prove that the reaction would have been different if the races of the supposed perpetrators or that of the victim had been flipped, but it is hard to believe that the same attention would have been paid. Certainly things are different today than they were in 1989, but even in an era that has seen the election of the country's first black president, the underlying racism and old fears are not gone. In order to truly prevent these miscarriages of justice in the future, the country must continue working toward changing and ultimately destroying those deeply held attitudes and prejudices that were at work in the Central Park Jogger case.

Two days after the Central Park Jogger rape, Mayor Ed Koch commented to the media, "I think that everybody here—maybe across the nation—will look at this case to see how the criminal justice system works. How will this be handled? This is, I think, putting the criminal justice system on trial." He was, like many New Yorkers, enraged by the horrific crime that had occurred, and he hoped to see swift and decisive "justice" meted out to those that he—and nearly everyone else—believed were responsible. The convictions were won, but the verdict for the system that sent Antron McCray, Raymond Santana, Kevin Richardson, Korey Wise, and Yusef Salaam to prison was anything but a success.

If the police and prosecutors working to convict the teenagers in the Central Park case had considered for a moment the possibility that their suspects were innocent and that they should be looking elsewhere, it would not have been difficult to discover Matias Reyes. His victim in an attack two days before Trisha Meili was raped, also in Central Park, had described her assailant's fresh stitches, and a detective was able to discover his name from hospital records. Yet no connection was made, and Matias Reyes remained free, not only to rape Trisha Meili but to attack at least five other women before being caught. One, the pregnant Lourdes Gonzalez, was stabbed to death in her apartment, with three young children in the next room. These crimes might have been prevented if the police had bothered to consider anything but the narrative of the case they instantly formed and then clung to, or if they had paid enough attention to the glaring inconsistencies in the statements of the young men they had in custody.

But they were blinded by the same assumptions and preconceptions that persuaded much of the media and the public when news of the terrible crime in Central Park first broke. In a city filled with gangs, drugs, violence, and racial tensions, with cases like those of Bernhard Goetz, Tawana Brawley, Howard Beach, and Eleanor Bumpurs, it seemed obvious and almost inevitable that a group of "wilding" black and Latino teenagers could and would commit such a disgusting crime. The fact that the victim was white and successful only increased the sense of outrage and the pressure to convict. The racist language and calls for the death penalty that evoked memories of southern lynchings added fuel to the fire and proved that post–civil rights America was still struggling to live out, as Dr. Martin Luther King, Jr., said, "the true meaning of its creed."

Those struggles continue as the idea that these teenagers could have been wrongly convicted is met with skepticism and denial, and still more racism. Though New York and the country have changed—in many ways for the better—since 1989, who is to say that a rush to judgment like this one could not happen again?

EPILOGUE

When Trisha Meili returned to work after months of rehab at Gaylord Hospital in Connecticut, she tried to regain something of the life she'd had before the attack. As part of her rehabilitation, she exercised constantly and went to several psychotherapy sessions each week. She also began dating again, going to plays and concerts. Gradually, she was able to take on more responsibilities at work; Salomon Brothers promoted her to the position of vice president.

Meili became more involved in the Achilles Track Club, a running group for people with disabilities, and joined the board of advisors for SAVI, the Sexual Assault and Violence Intervention program at Mount Sinai Hospital in New York.

In 1995, with the support of the Achilles Track Club, Meili ran the New York Marathon, which ends in Central Park, not far from the spot where she'd been attacked six and a half years earlier.

That same year, Meili met Jim Schwarz, a consultant living in Connecticut. They were married on September 15, 1996.

In 1998, she left Salomon Brothers and briefly worked for a nonprofit before turning to public speaking. She began by giving a talk at a Brain Injury Association conference. Without revealing her identity as the "Central Park Jogger," Trisha Meili spoke about her experience as the survivor of a traumatic brain injury. When she was finally ready to tell her whole story and allow her name to be made public, she wrote a book. Published in 2003, *I Am the Central Park Jogger: A Story of Hope and Possibility* detailed Meili's life before the brutal attack that left her near death and her remarkable path to recovery. By then, Reyes had confessed to being her sole attacker, but since she has no memory of the attack, she chose not to explore the details of the crime in depth in her book.

Since then, she has continued her career as a motivational speaker, giving lectures on the theme of "hope and possibility," which she explored in her book.

Korey Wise, whose sentence was five years longer than those of his co-defendants and who served his entire term in maximum-security facilities, despite being the least intellectually and emotionally developed of the group, also had the most difficult time getting his life together. Though he completed a high school equivalency program and started taking some college courses while in prison, his learning disabilities and hearing problems remained unaddressed. He speaks loudly and with an impediment that calls to mind the speech patterns of a deaf person; he still leans in when someone is speaking to him, trying to better understand what they are saying. His speech is jumbled and he often repeats words, struggling to express ideas more complex than his communication skills allow.

He's found work where he can, sometimes in Al Sharpton's office, cleaning up, other times on construction jobs. Lately, there hasn't been much construction work available, so he stays with friends, living off unemployment and the little money he saved from those previous jobs. He tries to talk to kids and help them, to tell them his story, in the hopes of changing the direction of their lives. He tells them about his experience in prison, and describes how you have no control over anything there but that "out here you have control over everything." Though he's frustrated and bitter, he remains gentle and chivalrous, anxious to move on to "bigger and better things" in his life.

Once his conviction was vacated, Kevin Richardson was able to apply for better jobs than those he had scraped by on with a criminal record.

He lives in New York City and works in environmental services at a geriatric center. He's not satisfied there, but it's a stable job, he has good benefits, and it "pays the bills." He's still close to his mother and older sisters. They all gather every Friday at the apartment on the thirty-fourth floor of the Schomburg tower where Kevin grew up and where his mother still lives. Most weekends, the family is there together, sharing meals, but every one of them is still affected each day by what Kevin went through. His mother's and sisters' eyes well up when talking about the ordeal.

Kevin has grown up; he's tall but still baby-faced. He's savvier now, understands better what happened to him and why. He talks about the pressure he knows police were under to solve the case quickly: "They [had] to make it look good," he says. He's studied the politics and culture of that time and talks about how racial tensions and the media influenced the outcome for him. He says that he used to be angry and bitter about what happened, blaming the detectives and DAs who put him in jail, but now he's trying to think about it less often.

After Raymond Santana's conviction in the Central Park Jogger rape was overturned, he was ready to start over. Since then, Raymond has had better luck finding jobs and getting back on his feet. The hours he spent lifting weights in prison proved to be the beginnings of his new career. He now works as a personal trainer and assistant manager at a gym in New York City. He works long hours, but he calls it "the best job in the world."

His daughter was born in 2004. She lives with her mother in Brooklyn, but she spends every other weekend with Raymond in Harlem, and he visits her in Brooklyn on his off weekends. He spends a lot of time with his father, who still lives in the same apartment on 117th Street where Raymond lived in 1989.

Raymond is shy and even-tempered. His father says he's more serious than when he went to prison, and less trusting. Raymond often stays in the Bronx, happy to avoid the acquaintances who are convinced that he will soon receive financial compensation for his wrongful conviction.

Though Yusef Salaam is divorced from the mother of his three young daughters, he sees them often and his family continues to grow. He and his fiancée have a daughter, who was born in January of 2009, and his fiancée's three children also live with them.

Yusef is gregarious and outspoken. He loves to talk and share his story, and he often speaks and reads his poetry at various events and on college campuses, campaigning against the death penalty and injustice. He smiles easily and dresses well. His early interest in computers and how things work have translated into a job; he works for New York–Presbyterian Hospital as a desktop auditor, keeping track of the computers and software for the hospital.

He's frustrated by the discrimination he still sees every day, the way that black men are treated differently on the street by the police. His Muslim faith is still very important to him and it helps him remain grounded about the difficulties he's faced in life.

Antron McCray's three older sons live in New York City, but he, too, has expanded his family since his conviction was vacated. He's married to a woman he met in Maryland. They have since moved and live with their three young children.

He still works as a forklift operator, and though his job pays the bills, he desperately wants a new career with the potential for upward mobility and better pay. While still living in Maryland, Antron applied for a job as a corrections officer, but he was turned down because of his old conviction, even though, in theory, the vacating of his conviction should have erased his record. More recently, he tried to take the police officers' exam, but he was told he wouldn't be hired, regardless of how he did on the test. His mother, Linda, who had stood by his side throughout his incarceration, couldn't understand why he would want to apply for jobs that would put him back into a criminal justice system that had treated him so unfairly. He explained to her that it was all he knew. She broke down and said, "I'm so sorry."

What he wants most is to have a complete exoneration, so that no one can doubt his innocence and he can move on with his life. He says he just wants "to be a good role model for my kids" and to have a chance at a real career.

Antron is still shy and private. Living far from New York allows him to avoid contact with people who know his history, and even there he doesn't engage much. He spends most of his free time at home with his family. "I wasn't born rich," he said; "I was born in the struggle."

On December 8, 2003, civil rights attorneys representing Antron McCray, Kevin Richardson, Raymond Santana, and their families filed a lawsuit in New York federal court against New York City, the NYPD, the district attorney's office, and many individuals involved in the case, including Linda Fairstein, Elizabeth Lederer, and more than a dozen police detectives and supervisors. Yusef Salaam and Korey Wise soon filed similar suits. The lawsuits demand fifty million dollars for each former defendant, alleging a violation of their civil rights by those who helped land them in jail, and include some of their family members as plaintiffs, as well. The team of lawyers representing the Central Park Five are an experienced group, including Myron Beldock, one of the lawyers who helped to exonerate Rubin "Hurricane" Carter, and Michael Warren and Jonathan Moore, who represented grafitti artist Michael Stewart's family after his death at the hands of the NYPD.

They will have to prove that the civil rights of the teenagers and their families were violated in order to prevail. The suit alleges violations of the young men's Fourth, Fifth, Thirteenth, and Fourteenth Amendment rights, accusing the city and its agents of malicious prosecution based upon racial animus and a conspiracy to deprive them of their constitutional rights.

Though the case was filed in late 2003, progress has been slow. In late

2007 a decision was rendered on the defendants' motions to dismiss the case, keeping intact many of the arguments made in the original civil complaint. Discovery has since begun, but it has moved slowly. A jury trial, if the case proceeds that far, could begin in late 2011 at the earliest, almost eight years after the suit was filed.

In April 2010, twenty-one years after the Central Park Jogger rape, New York City's mayor, Michael Bloomberg, used the word *wilding* to describe a violent incident in Times Square in which several people were shot. Newspaper articles evoked the Central Park Jogger case as the source of the word, and reporters wrote of the fear that in the current economic downturn, the city might revert to the "bad old days." According to the media, late on Easter Sunday hundreds of young men and women, "gang members," as Mayor Bloomberg called them, created a disorderly scene in and around Times Square. Four people were shot, three injured by bullets and one by a BB gun, though none of the injuries was life-threatening. At least thirty-three people were arrested. Though most of the articles did not specify the race or ethnicity of the "gang members" arrested by the police, the mayor's use of the word *wilding* and its reprinting in many newspapers tell us everything we need to know about their skin color and about how little progress we've made since 1989. The Central Park Jogger case and the fear of crime from the 1980s still haunts the memories of many New Yorkers, and the use of animal terms to describe disorderly minority teenagers continues without reflection or remorse.

ACKNOWLEDGMENTS

I owe a deep debt of gratitude to the Central Park Five: Yusef Salaam; Antron McCray; Kevin Richardson; Raymond Santana, Jr.; and Korey Wise, without whose cooperation I could not have written this book. That they have come out of this experience without bitterness or anger, despite the hardships they have faced, truly amazes me. I want to thank them for entrusting me with their powerful stories.

I also want to thank their families, especially Linda McCray; Raymond Santana, Sr.; Angela Black; and Gracie Cuffee, for allowing me into their homes and lives. They have had to put up with more than their share of prying journalists over the years, and I am grateful that they were willing to once again revisit such dark and difficult memories. I am deeply touched by their ability to remain so strong in the face of this painful injustice.

I would not have written this book if not for my experience working for Jonathan Moore and Bill Goodman, two very principled lawyers who first introduced me to this miscarriage of justice. Thanks also to many of the other lawyers and paralegals working on the civil suit for the Central Park Five: Michael Tarif Warren, Everyn Warren, Roger Wareham, Myron Beldock, Karen Dippold, Sofia Yakren, Janice Badalutz, Jane Byrialsen, and Sid Thaxter, all of whom have helped me along the way.

Many others provided their invaluable recollections in interviews, including several of the defense lawyers who were involved in the case: Mickey Joseph, Colin Moore, Elliot Cook, Jesse Berman, Richard Siracusa, and Ron Kuby; and journalists who covered the case then and now: Tim Sullivan, LynNell Hancock, Lizette Alvarez, Natalie Byfield, Tony Guida, Sheryl McCarthy, Richard Esposito, Peter Blauner, Ellis Henican, Patricia Williams, Michael Stone, Cynthia McFadden, Eric Avram, Anna Sims-Phillips, Craig Wolff, and Bill Glaberson.

Others who shared their wisdom included Alan Dershowitz, Barry Scheck, Craig Steven Wilder, Ray Suarez, Saul Kassin, Steven Drizin, Jackie McMickens, Helen Benedict, Gerry Migliore, Robin Steinberg, Sara Cedar-Miller, Elizabeth Barlow Rogers, and Christine Cornell.

Dennis Commedo, Ed Koch, Bill Perkins, Emily Tetzlaff, Aminah Carroll, Kayode Olaiya, Dr. Robert Kurtz, Sister Leontine O'Gorman, and Michael Armstrong revealed their own personal experiences and memories of the Central Park Jogger case, New York City, and the Central Park Five. Matias Reyes granted me an interview at Clinton Correctional Facility.

I am indebted to Jim Dwyer for opening his files and memories to me. He answered my questions when no one else could and remained a thoughtful and knowledgeable source of information about many aspects of the case. I want to thank Francine James and Bob Slade for encouraging this project with contacts and advice, and my dear friend Julie Ehrlich for her expert advice on the law.

Extra-special thanks are due to Jennifer Rudolph Walsh for believing in my proposal and getting it into the right hands, and to Dan Frank, my wonderful editor, who had faith in my book from the beginning and who has remained a patient and thoughtful guide throughout the process. I also want to thank many others at Knopf and Pantheon who answered my endless questions, including Jill Verrillo, Lydia Buechler, Caryn Burtt, and Alissa Kleinman.

Finally, I want to thank my family and friends, who read drafts, gave suggestions, and supported me as I learned how to write a book and worked on this project for more years than I care to admit, especially my husband, Dave; Mom; Dad; Julie; my sisters Lilly, Olivia, and Willa; Sarah Botstein; Ric Burns; and Geoff Ward.

NOTES AND SOURCES

In researching and writing this book, I relied on many sources, most important among them interviews I conducted with many of the individuals who were involved in the case. I also read the complete transcripts of the pretrial hearing and the two criminal trials, and I relied on many other legal documents, in particular the "Affirmation in Response to Motion to Vacate Judgment of Conviction" that was produced by the district attorney's office in the course of their reinvestigation.

I would like to thank those individuals who opened up to me in interviews, including especially the Central Park Five: Antron McCray, Kevin Richardson, Yusef Salaam, Korey Wise, and Raymond Santana, Jr.; some of their family members, including Raymond Santana, Sr.; Gracie Cuffee; and Linda McCray. Jonathan Moore and Michael Tarif Warren, who are among the civil rights lawyers representing the Central Park Five and their families in a civil suit, provided me with abundant information about the case. This book could not have been written without the participation of the following individuals, who gave their time, recollections, and wisdom in interviews: Lizette Alvarez, Michael Armstrong, Eric Avram, Helen Benedict, Jesse Berman, Peter Blauner, Ric Burns, Natalie Byfield, Aminah Carroll, Sara Cedar-Miller, Dennis Commedo, Elliot Cook, Christine Cornell, Alan Dershowitz, Steven Drizin, Jim Dwyer, Richard Esposito, Bill Glaberson, Tony Guida, LynNell Hancock, Ellis Henican, Mickey Joseph, Saul Kassin, Ed Koch, Ron Kuby, Dr. Robert Kurtz, Sheryl McCarthy, Cynthia McFadden, Jackie McMickens, Gerry Migliore, Colin Moore, Sister Leontine O'Gorman, Kayode Olaiya, Bill Perkins, Matias Reyes, Elizabeth Barlow Rogers, Barry Scheck, Anna Sims-Phillips, Richard Siracusa, Robin Steinberg, Michael Stone, Ray Suarez, Tim Sullivan, Emily Tetzlaff, Craig Steven Wilder, Patricia Williams, and Craig Wolff.

I had hoped to also speak with some of the detectives and prosecutors who originally worked on the Central Park Jogger case, but largely due to the pending civil lawsuit, in which many of them are defendants, they were unable to provide interviews. Instead, I represented their thoughts and opinions based on their testimonies at trial and their comments to the media before the civil suit was filed.

I also read hundreds of newspaper articles from the coverage of the Central Park Jogger case and used newspaper accounts to learn more about New York City and its history, especially *The New York Times,* the *New York Post,* the *Daily News,* and *Newsday,* as well as the *Amsterdam News, The City Sun, El Diario/La Prensa, The Wall Street Journal,* and *The Village Voice.* Magazines like *New York, Time, Newsweek, The Nation, People, The New Yorker, U.S. News & World Report,* and *Esquire* were also useful.

A few books were particularly helpful in gaining details about the Central Park Jogger case, including Trisha Meili's inspiring book, *I Am the Central Park Jogger: A Story of Hope and Possibility.* I also referred often to Tim Sullivan's account of the trials in this case, *Unequal Verdicts: The Central Park Jogger.* Though I was able to read the complete trial transcripts, Sullivan's description of the atmosphere and tone of the trial and especially of the behind-the-scenes activity of the lawyers was invaluable. Harlan Levy's book *And the Blood Cried Out: A Prosecutor's Spellbinding Account of DNA's Power to Free or Convict* contains a chapter about the DNA testing in the jogger case as well as a chapter about how DNA helped to convict Reyes for some of his other crimes.

Where specific quotes from newspaper articles, books, or studies were used, they are cited directly in the notes that follow. Other sources and suggestions for further reading can be found in the bibliography.

CHAPTER ONE

Interviews with the Central Park Five, their families, and others who knew them personally helped me to learn about their childhoods and family lives, as did their 50-H hearings (interviews similar to depositions that were taken in the course of the civil suit) and some newspaper and magazine profiles. Information about Trisha Meili came from her own book and from testimony at the trials.

For the story of New York in the 1980s, I relied on many newspaper articles, particularly from *The New York Times,* to give me a sense of what was happening and how residents were experiencing crime and the conditions of the city. I also considered many books that appear in the bibliography, as well as some personal anecdotes from interviewees who lived in New York during those years. The stories of some of the other significant crimes and racialized incidents in New York in the 1980s came from newspaper accounts and several books, in particular *Incident at Howard Beach,* by Charles Hynes and Bob Drury, and George Fletcher's book about the Bernhard Goetz case, *A Crime of Self-Defense. The Park and the People,* by Roy Rosenzweig and Elizabeth Blackmar, is a fantastic history of Central Park, and additional information about the park and crime in the park over the years came from newspaper articles and interviews.

The events of April 19, 1989, were culled from the trial testimonies of many who were in the park that night, as well as from more recent 50-H hearings and interviews. Reyes's actions that night are revealed in the affirmation to the motion to vacate the convictions that was produced by the district attorney's office in the reinvestigation.

7 "WHY NOT COME OVER": Meili, p. 12.

10 HEADLINES THAT INCLUDED: *Daily News,* January 16, 1989; *New York Post,* February 2, 1989; *New York Post,* January 21, 1989; *Daily News,* January 12, 1989; *New York Post,* January 9, 1989; *Daily News,* January 22, 1989.

10 "LADY, LEAVE ME ALONE": Fox Butterfield, "Is Life in New York City Really Getting Worse?" *New York Times,* March 10, 1989.

11 "WORSE CENTERS OF DELINQUENCY": Jacobs, p. 4.

13 "I DON'T SEE HOW": Thomas Moore, "Dead Zones," *U.S. News & World Report,* April 10, 1989, p. 20.

13 "IN THE BARBARIZED CITY": Pete Hamill, "City of the Damned," *Esquire,* December 1990, p. 61.

15 "YOU SEEM TO BE": Richard Stengel, "A Troubled and Troubling Life," *Time,* April 8, 1985, p. 35.

16 HELD BANNERS THAT READ: Otto Friedrich, " 'Not Guilty,' " *Time,* June 29, 1987, p. 10.

16 "IF THE 'STATE OF NATURE' ": "Vigilance to Justice," *Wall Street Journal,* December 21, 1984.

17 "LESS LIKELY TO REACH": McCord and Freeman, p. 173.

17 "BLACKS KILL OTHER BLACKS": Hamill, "City of the Damned," p. 61.

20 "A DIRTY, UNKEMPT": Anna Quindlen, "New York City Park System Stands As a Tattered Remnant of Its Past," *New York Times,* October 13, 1980.

20 "SOME MARTIANS LANDED": Mahler, p. 8.

20 "IT WAS SO QUIET": Rosenzweig and Blackmar, p. 2.

20 "IF YOU SHOULD HAPPEN": Nash, p. 107.

20 "AND I ANSWER": Rosenzweig and Blackmar, p. 473.

21 "CRIME IN CENTRAL PARK": Ibid., p. 474.

CHAPTER TWO

Reconstructing what went on in the interrogation rooms was a challenge. Accounts from those in the rooms often differed, so I relied on places where testimonies agreed and were believable (a subjective judgment, to be sure), and I considered what is now known about the validity of those statements in trying to work out how they came into being. The statements and videotapes themselves provided the basis for quotes taken directly from the confessions.

I learned about the techniques used in interrogations generally from interviews with Saul Kassin, a number of articles about interrogations and false confessions, and the book by Inbau, Reid, Buckley, and Jayne, which is the handbook for police interrogations. I also consulted several significant court decisions that were relevant to the limitations on interrogations. Those articles and cases can be found in the bibliography.

I used trial testimony for details as to how Meili was discovered and treated and what the crime scene looked like. An interview with Dr. Robert Kurtz provided even more detailed information about her condition, as did Meili's book.

Background information on Linda Fairstein and Elizabeth Lederer came from accounts in newspapers and magazines, from Sullivan's book, and from some personal interviews.

56 "MAKES THE OTHER ASPECTS OF A TRIAL": Conti, p. 14.

CHAPTER THREE

Trisha Meili's biographical information comes largely from her autobiography, *I Am The Central Park Jogger.* In addition to the citations below, I read many hundreds of other newspaper and magazine articles as background on the coverage of the case, and Howard Kurtz's *Media Circus* and Ken Auletta's *Backstory* provided excellent information on the media and tabloid competition.

The details about the history of lynching come from the research and writings of Ida B. Wells and the excellent book by Philip Dray, *At the Hands of Persons Unknown.*

68 "A YOUNG WALL STREET INVESTMENT BANKER": "Wolfpack Rapes Jogger." *New York Post,* April 21, 1989.

69 WOLFPACK'S PREY: front-page headline, *Daily News,* April 21, 1989.

69 NIGHTMARE IN CENTRAL PARK: front-page headline, *New York Post,* April 21, 1989.

69 WILDING: front-page headline, *Daily News,* April 22, 1989.

70 "ONE OF TWO BLACK VICTIMS": George James, "Assault Victims Liken Attackers to 'Wolf Pack,' " *New York Times,* December 29, 1987.

71 "I THINK [CALLING THEM A WOLF PACK]": Pete Hamill, *New York Post,* April 25, 1989.

71 "NASTY JOKES, UNAFRAID": Goodman, p. 13.

71 "IT WAS FUN": Mike Pearl, Sonia Reyes, and Karen Phillips, "Rape Suspect: 'It Was Fun,' " *New York Post,* April 23, 1989.

71 "SHE WASN'T NOTHING": *Daily News,* April 23, 1989.

72 "WHEN WILL PEOPLE LEARN": letter from J. Reynolds, *Daily News,* May 2, 1989.

72 "IF THAT WOMAN JOGGING": letter from J. Nicholas, *Daily News,* May 6, 1989.

72 "THIS WAS A SAVAGE": Pete Hamill, "A Savage Disease Called New York," *New York Post,* April 23, 1989.

73 "I'M FOR THE DEATH": WNYW Fox 5, week of April 28 to May 2, 1989.

74 "STORIES OF SEXUAL ASSAULT": Dray, pp. 4–5.

76 "FIRST OUTRAGED WITH DEMONIACAL": Wells-Barnett, *Southern Horrors and Other Writings,* ed. Jacqueline Jones Royster, p. 92.

76 "A SEARCH WAS IMMEDIATELY": Wells-Barnett, *Selected Works of Ida B. Wells-Barnett,* comp. and ed. Trudier Harris, p. 87.

76 "A WHITE MAN": Ibid., p. 87.

77 "MY NAME IS C. J. MILLER": Ibid.

77 "SINCE HIS DEATH": Ibid., p. 90.

77 "THE SIMPLE WORD": Ibid., p. 77.

77 "NOBODY IN THIS SECTION": Wells-Barnett, *Southern Horrors and Other Writings,* ed. Jacqueline Jones Royster, p. 52.

78 "WARNING TO ALL NEGROES": Ibid., p. 125.

78 "WHEN THE DISPATCHES": Ibid., p. 126.

78 "AN EXCUSE TO GET": Dray, p. 63.

78 "WELLS WAS ONE": Ibid., p. 64.

79 "LAZY, THRIFTLESS, INTEMPERATE": Frederickson, p. 260.

79 "A FIEND, A WILD BEAST": Ibid., p. 276.

79 "DURING ALL THE YEARS": Wells-Barnett, *Southern Horrors and Other Writings,* ed. Jacqueline Jones Royster, p. 79.

79 "THE ONLY WAY TO MEET": Ibid., p. 276.

80 "I THINK THAT EVERYBODY": William Murphy, "Park Rape Is Justice Test: Koch," *Newsday,* April 22, 1989.

81 "I DON'T WANT TO UNDERSTAND": Peter Moses, Rocco Parascondola, and Frank Bruni, "Gov Rips City of Shame," *New York Post,* April 24, 1989.

81 "ANYONE WHO COMMITTED THIS RAPE": Frank Bruni and Michael Shain, "Koch Wants All 8 Tried as Adults," *New York Post,* April 23, 1989.

81 "URBAN TERRORISTS": Sam Roberts, "Campaign Matters; Park Rampage and Mayor Race: Fear and Politics," *New York Times,* May 1, 1989.

81 "ANY ATTORNEY WORTH": J. Zamgba Browne, "Attorney Deplores Cops Handling of Rape Arrests," *Amsterdam News,* April 29, 1989.

82 "THE TEENAGE BOYS": Ibid.

82 "HOW CAN A SYSTEM": Ibid.

82 "THEY ARE THE PRODUCT": editorial, "Victims and Criminals in New York City," *El Diario/La Prensa,* April 24, 1989.

82 "THE SAD REALITY": editorial, "New Directions for Our Youth," *El Diario/La Prensa,* April 27, 1989.

83 "THAT ANYONE WOULD": editorial, "It's an Outrage!" *City Sun,* April 26–May 2, 1989.

83 "IF THE CENTRAL PARK": Peter Noel, "Rape & Class: From Scottsboro to Central Park," *City Sun,* May 3–9, 1989.

83 "THE WORST NIGHTMARE": Ibid.

84 "THIS IS HYPOCRITICAL": editorial, "The Central Park Rape Case: Naming Names," *Amsterdam News,* May 13, 1989.

85 "WHAT CAUSED SUCH SAVAGERY?": editorial, "The Jogger and the Wolf Pack," *New York Times,* April 26, 1989.

85 "RACE IS PART": Pete Hamill, "A Savage Disease Called New York."

86 "ONLY MAN SEEMS CAPABLE": Pete Hamill, *New York Post,* April 25, 1989.

86 "EXPECT THESE SO-CALLED": Browne, "Attorney Deplores Handling of Rape Arrests."

87 "A PLACE WHERE THE": Gene Mustain, "2 Worlds Collide: Where Trouble's Called '24-7,' The Kids Grow Up Hard," *Daily News,* April 23, 1989.

87 "HE HAD A CHARMING": Michael T. Kaufman, "Park Suspects: Children of Discipline," *New York Times,* April 26, 1989.

88 "THE APOLOGISTS . . . ARE CHIMING": Abiola Sinclair, "Shocking, Shameful: 'Wilding' . . . Indeed," *Amsterdam News,* April 29, 1989.

88 "ONE SHOULD NOT BRAND": David Seifman, "Koch Calls Them 'Monsters,' " *New York Post,* April 25, 1989.

89 "THE FAMILY HAS TO": Frank Bruni and Michael Shain, "Koch Wants All 8 Tried as Adults," *New York Post,* April 23, 1989.

89 "CHILDREN DO THINGS": "First Lady Points to Parents in Rampage at Park," *New York Post,* April 28, 1989.

89 "WE LIVE IN A PRO-RAPE CULTURE": Joan Morgan, "The Pro-Rape Culture," *Village Voice,* May 9, 1989.

89 "TO BAD-MOUTH": Lisa Kennedy, "Body Double," *Village Voice,* May 9, 1989.

CHAPTER FOUR

The information about the investigation and progress of the prosecution comes largely from the transcripts of the trials and pretrial hearing, and from Tim Sullivan's book, *Unequal Verdicts.* I learned about the science and history of DNA testing from a few sources, in particular Lorne T. Kirby's book *DNA Fingerprinting: An Introduction;* Rudin and Inman's *An Introduction to Forensic DNA Analysis;* and *DNA: Forensic & Legal Applications,* by Kobilinsky, Liotti, and Oeser-Sweat.

Details of Trisha Meili's medical condition and progress in this and later chapters came from the trial testimony of Meili herself and those who treated her, as well as from media coverage of her recovery and from Meili's book, *I Am the Central Park Jogger.*

Willie Bosket's story came from newspaper articles; see in particular *The New York Times,* "Two Decades in Solitary," September 22, 2008.

Details of the various jail facilities and the experiences of the young men came from personal interviews with the Central Park Five and their families, Kayode Olaiya, and some newspaper accounts. Interviews with defense lawyers were also informative.

Dialogue or testimony at the arraignment and pretrial hearing comes directly from the court transcripts or from Tim Sullivan's account of those events.

The details of Reyes's life and his crimes come from the DA's "Affirmation in Response to Motion to Vacate Judgment of Conviction," Reyes's confession tape, an interview Reyes gave for an ABC News program with Cynthia McFadden, Harlan Levy's book *And The Blood Cried Out*, the transcript of Reyes's sentencing, media articles, an interview with Richard Siracusa, Reyes's defense attorney, and an interview with Reyes himself. Levy's book provided the basis for the description of Reyes's interrogation and any dialogue that appears therein.

Joe Sharkey's book *Deadly Greed*, about the Stuart case, provided background on that crime and its aftermath.

94 "IN GENERAL, THE LONGER": Peter Moses and Jane Furse, "Her Docs Find Slim Reason for Optimism," *New York Post*, April 25, 1989.

94 "MILLIONS OF NEW YORKERS": Peter Moses, Jim Nolan, and Timothy McDarrah, "The City Opens Up Its Heart in Prayer," *New York Post*, April 26, 1989.

95 "SHE PRESENTS WITH": Meili, p. 28.

97 "I FEEL LIKE I'VE": Levy, p. 70

104 "MAY NOT BE RECEIVED": New York Criminal Procedure, Article 60, § 60.45.

119 "I DIDN'T TOUCH": Levy, pp. 6–11.

120 "PURE INSINUATION AND SEDUCTION": Ibid., p. 7.

126 "IN THAT RACE": Sullivan, p. 296.

CHAPTER FIVE

As with the pretrial hearing, quotes from the two trials came directly from the court transcripts and written and videotaped statements of the defendants. Tim Sullivan's book *Unequal Verdicts* provided essential behind-the-scenes information, and his book as well as interviews with Sullivan, Patricia Williams, and other journalists gave me insight into the atmosphere of the trials. I also used daily newspaper accounts to get a sense of what went on both inside and outside the courtroom and who was there. Interviews with some of the defense attorneys and the Central Park Five filled out my understanding of what the trials were like.

Details of the murder of Yusuf Hawkins and the protests in Bensonhurst came from coverage in *The New York Times* and from David Krajicek's book *Scooped*.

129 "NIGGERS GO HOME": Krajicek, p. 132.

134 "LITTLE, A TINY-HEADED": Bob Herbert, "Park Rape Scene Is Still Jarring," *Daily News*, June 26, 1990.

136 "THE RESULT [OF BURNS'S CROSS-EXAMINATIONS]": Ronald Sullivan, "Reporter's Notebook; Keeping Emotions Under Control at Jogger Trial," *New York Times*, July 2, 1990.

145 "DESPITE THE DEVASTATING CONSEQUENCES": Mollen Commission Report, 1994.

147 "SEMEN TESTED IN JOGGER CASE": Ronald Sullivan, *New York Times,* July 14, 1990.

147 "DNA PRINTS FAIL": Lizette Alvarez, *Daily News,* July 14, 1990.

147 "WE ARE WAITING TO SEE": Carole Agus, "Salaam's Mom Also Waits for Evidence," *Newsday,* July 18, 1990.

148 "NOTHING CLOSE TO THE WORDS": Jim Dwyer, "Weak Links Strain Chain of Evidence," *Newsday,* July 18, 1990.

149 "WHY WOULD THE JOGGER": Mike McAlary, "Racism Comes in Many Shades," *Daily News,* July 18, 1990.

150 "THE PRESUMPTION OF INNOCENCE": Sam Roberts, "The Nation: The Central Park Jogger; An Old Case in a Different New York," *New York Times,* October 20, 2002.

159 "THE DEVIL HERSELF": Ronald Sullivan, "3 Youths Guilty of Rape and Assault of Jogger," *New York Times,* August 19, 1990.

160 "THE JURY SERVED": James Barron, "Anger Over Verdicts in Jogger Case Is Mixed with Calls for Compassion," *New York Times,* August 20, 1990.

166 "HIS GOAL IS TO": editorial, "Malice at the Jogger Trial," *New York Post,* November 3, 1990.

CHAPTER SIX

Material on the experiences of the Central Park Five since their convictions comes mainly from interviews with them and their families. An interview with Matias Reyes corroborated the story of his encounters with Korey Wise, which also appears in the DA's affirmation to the motion to vacate. Yusef's appeal results are taken directly from the decision and dissent written by Judge Vito Titone in that case.

I learned about the changes that occurred in New York City from interviews and articles, particularly those in *The New York Times.* The crime statistics come from the FBI's Uniform Crime Reports.

The poem Kevin read at his parole hearing is copied from the transcript of that hearing.

Information on and quotations from the district attorney's reinvestigation come directly from the legal document that was produced as a result of that investigation, the "Affirmation in Response to Motion to Vacate Judgment of Conviction." Information on and quotations from the NYPD report are taken from that document. Media coverage of the reinvestigation and vacating of the convictions appeared during 2002 and early 2003, especially in *The New York Times,* the *Daily News,* and the *New York Post.*

196 "I THINK I STOPPED": Susan Saluny, "Convictions and Charges Voided in '89 Central Park Jogger Attack," *New York Times,* December 20, 2002.

197 "IF NANCY RYAN'S": Jim Dwyer and Susan Saluny, "Judge's Plan to Rule Today in Jogger Case Angers Police," *New York Times,* December 19, 2002.

197 "IT'S MY DECISION": Ibid.

199 "WE FOCUSED ON THAT": Jim Dwyer, "One Trial, Two Conclusions; Police and Prosecutors May Never Agree on Who Began Jogger Attack," *New York Times,* February 2, 2003.

200 "DOES NOT RECALL": Dareh Gregorian and Andy Geller, "Jogger Judge Sparks Furor," *New York Post,* December 10, 2002.

200 "IF REYES DID": Barbara Ross and Alice McQuillan, "Say Rapist Tale Full of Problems," *Daily News,* September 27, 2002.

201 "TO VACATE EVERY ONE": Mike Claffey, "Confession Blew Case to Bits: Experts," *Daily News,* December 7, 2002.

201 "THIS LUNATIC CONCOCTS": Andy Geller and Dareh Gregorian, " '89 Jogger Detectives Rip DA for Buying 'Lie,' " *New York Post,* December 7, 2002.

201 "IT'S COMPLETELY OUTRAGEOUS": Barbara Ross and Robert Ingrassia, "Joy and Rage Over Jogger 5," *Daily News,* December 6, 2002.

201 "I THINK THAT REYES": Andy Geller, "Jogger's Prosecutor Stands by Verdicts," *New York Post,* November 25, 2002.

201 "I'VE NEVER BEEN INTERVIEWED": Barbara Ross, "Ex-Prosecutor Reopens Old Rift," *Daily News,* December 2, 2002.

201 "LEGAL EAGLES' RIVALRY": Susan Edelman and Andrea Peyser, *New York Post,* December 8, 2002.

203 "PROBABLY FEELING 'HUMILIATED,' " Ann Coulter, "New York Times Goes Wilding on Central Park Jogger," October 16, 2002, www.wnd.com.

203 "EVERY CRIMINAL IS INNOCENT": Ann Coulter, "Media Support Citizenship Award for Central Park Rapists," December 4, 2002, www.wnd.com.

203 "THE ODDS OF AN": Ibid.

203 "IT IS MORE LIKELY": Ibid.

203 "ANIMALS," "PRIMITIVES," AND "SAVAGES": Coulter, "New York Times Goes Wilding on Central Park Jogger"; Coulter, "Media Support Citizenship Award for Central Park Rapists."

205 "I THINK THAT EVERYBODY": William Murphy, "Park Rape Is Justice Test: Koch," *Newsday,* April 22, 1989.

EPILOGUE

Details about the experiences of the Central Park Five since their exonerations come from interviews with them and their families. Interviews with the plaintiff's attorneys Jonathan Moore and Michael Warren, as well as the complaint itself, provided me with details about the civil suit. Newspaper articles in *The New York Times,* the *Daily News,* and the *New York Post* from April 2010 describe the violent incident in Times Square and Mayor Bloomberg's response.

212 "BAD OLD DAYS": Jamie Schram, Larry Celona, and Murray Weiss, "Times Square Gang Riot Spurs Fear," *New York Post,* April 6, 2010.
212 "GANG MEMBERS": Ibid.

BIBLIOGRAPHY

Auletta, Ken. *The Streets Were Paved with Gold.* New York: Random House, 1979.
———. *Backstory.* New York: Penguin, 2003.
Benedict, Helen. *Virgin or Vamp: How the Press Covers Sex Crimes.* New York: Oxford University Press, 1992.
Bloom, Nicholas Dagen. *Public Housing That Worked: New York in the Twentieth Century.* Philadelphia: University of Pennsylvania Press, 2008.
Bram v. U.S., 168 U.S. 532 (1897).
Brown v. Mississippi, 297 U.S. 278 (1936).
Carter, Dan T. *Scottsboro: A Tragedy of the American South.* Baton Rouge: Louisiana State University Press, 1969.
Chambers v. Florida, 309 U.S. 277 (1940).
Chancer, Lynn. *High-Profile Crimes: When Legal Cases Become Social Causes.* Chicago: University of Chicago Press, 2005.
Coker v. Georgia, 433 U.S. 584 (1977).
Collins, Winfield H. *The Truth About Lynching and the Negro in the South.* New York: Neale Publishing Company, 1918.
Commission to Investigate Allegations of Police Corruption and the Anti-Corruption Procedures of the Police Department, Milton Mollen, chair, *Commission Report.* New York: 1994.
Conti, Richard P. "The Psychology of False Confessions." *The Journal of Credibility Assessment and Witness Psychology* 2 (1999): 14–36.
Cooper, Edith Fairman. *The Emergence of Crack Cocaine Abuse.* New York: Novinka, 2002.
Didion, Joan. "Sentimental Journeys." *The New York Review of Books,* January 17, 1991.
Dray, Phillip. *At the Hands of Persons Unknown: The Lynching of Black America.* New York: Random House, 2002.
Drizin, Steven A., and Richard A. Leo. "The Problem of False Confessions in the Post-DNA World." *North Carolina Law Review* 82 (2004): 891–1007.
Fletcher, George P. *A Crime of Self-Defense: Bernhard Goetz and the Law on Trial.* New York: Free Press, 1988.

Fredrickson, George M. *The Black Image in the White Mind: The Debate on Afro-American Character and Destiny, 1817–1914.* New York: Harper & Row, 1971.

Goodman, James. *Stories of Scottsboro.* New York: Pantheon, 1994.

Higginbotham, A. Leon. *In the Matter of Color: Race and the American Legal Process.* New York: Oxford University Press, 1978.

Hilfiker, David. *Urban Injustice: How Ghettoes Happen.* New York: Seven Stories Press, 2003.

Hynes, Charles J., and Bob Drury. *Incident at Howard Beach: The Case for Murder.* New York: Putnam, 1990.

Inbau, Fred E., John E. Reid, Joseph P. Buckley, and Brian C. Jayne. *Criminal Interrogation and Confessions.* 4th ed. Gaithersberg, Md.: Aspen, 2001.

Jacobs, Jane. *The Life and Death of Great American Cities.* New York: Random House, 1961.

Karmen, Andrew. *New York Murder Mystery: The True Story Behind the Crime Crash of the 1990s.* New York: New York University Press, 2000.

Kassin, Saul M. "On the Psychology of Confessions: Does Innocence Put Innocents at Risk?" *American Psychologist* 60 (2005): 215–28.

Kassin, Saul M., and Christina T. Fong. " 'I'm Innocent!': Effects of Training on Judgments of Truth and Deception in the Interrogation Room." *Law and Human Behavior* 23 (1999): 499–516.

Kassin, Saul M., and Gisli H. Gudjonsson. "True Crimes *False Confessions.*" *Scientific American Mind* 16 (2005): 24–31.

Kassin, Saul M., and Katherine L. Kiechel. "The Social Psychology of False Confessions: Compliance, Internalization, and Confabulation." *Psychological Science* 7 (1996): 125–28.

Kassin, Saul M., and Karlyn McNall. "Police Interrogations and Confessions: Communicating Promises and Threats by Pragmatic Implication." *Law and Human Behavior* 15 (1991): 233–51.

Kassin, Saul M., Christian A. Meissner, and Rebecca J. Norwick. " 'I'd Know a False Confession If I Saw One': A Comparative Study of College Students and Police Investigators." *Law and Human Behavior* 29 (2005): 211–27.

Kassin, Saul M., and Katherine Neumann. "On the Power of Confession Evidence: An Experimental Test of the 'Fundamental Difference' Hypothesis." *Law and Human Behavior* 21 (1997): 469–84.

Kennedy, Randall. *Race, Crime, and the Law.* New York: Pantheon, 1997.

Kirby, Lorne T. *DNA Fingerprinting: An Introduction.* New York: Oxford University Press, 1992.

Kobilinsky, Lawrence, Thomas F. Liotti, and Jamel Oeser-Sweat. *DNA: Forensic & Legal Applications.* Hoboken, N.J.: Wiley, 2005.

Krajicek, David J. *Scooped! Media Miss Real Story on Crime While Chasing Sex, Sleaze, and Celebrities.* New York: Columbia University Press, 1998.

Kurtz, Howard. *Media Circus: The Trouble with America's Newspapers.* New York: Times Books, 1993.

Leo, Richard A. "Inside the Interrogation Room." *The Journal of Criminal Law and Criminology* 86 (1996): 266–303.

Leo, Richard A. "*Miranda's* Revenge: Police Interrogation as a Confidence Game." *Law and Society Review* 30 (1996): 259–88.

Leo, Richard A., and Richard J. Ofshe. "The Consequences of False Confessions: Deprivations of Liberty and Miscarriages of Justice in the Age of Psychological Interrogation." *Journal of Criminal Law and Criminology* 88 (1998): 429–96.

Levy, Harlan. *And The Blood Cried Out: A Prosecutor's Spellbinding Account of DNA's Power to Free or Convict.* New York: Avon, 1996.

London, Herbert. *The Broken Apple.* New Brunswick, N.J.: Transaction, 1989.

Mahler, Jonathan. *Ladies and Gentlemen, The Bronx Is Burning: 1977, Baseball, Politics and the Battle for the Soul of a City.* New York: Picador, 2005.

McCord, Colin, and Harold P. Freeman. "Excess Mortality in Harlem." *New England Journal of Medicine* 322 (1990): 173–77.

McKenna, Thomas, and William Harrington. *Manhattan North Homicide: The True Story of One of New York's Best Homicide Cops.* New York: St. Martin's Press, 1996.

Meili, Trisha. *I Am the Central Park Jogger: A Story of Hope and Possiblity.* New York: Scribner, 2003.

Meissner, Christian A., and Saul M. Kassin. " 'He's Guilty!': Investigator Bias in Judgments of Truth and Deception." *Law and Human Behavior* 26 (2002): 469–80.

Miranda v. Arizona, 384 U.S. 436 (1966).

Mollenkopf, John Hull, and Manuel Castells, eds. *Dual City: Restructuring New York.* New York: Russell Sage Foundation, 1991.

Nash, Ogden. *Everyone But Thee and Me.* Boston: Little, Brown, 1962.

Ofshe, Richard J., and Richard A. Leo. "The Decision to Confess Falsely: Rational Choice and Irrational Action." *Denver University Law Review* 74 (1997): 979–1122.

Pinderhughes, Howard. *Race in the Hood: Conflict and Violence Among Urban Youth.* Minneapolis: University of Minnesota Press, 1997.

Plunz, Richard. *A History of Housing in New York City: Dwelling Type and Social Change in the American Metropolis.* New York: Columbia University Press, 1990.

Rome, Dennis. *Black Demons: The Media's Depiction of the African American Male Criminal Stereotype.* Westport, Conn.: Praeger, 2004.

Rosenzweig, Roy, and Elizabeth Blackmar. *The Park and the People: A History of Central Park.* Ithaca, N.Y.: Cornell University Press, 1992.

Rudin, Norah, and Keith Inman. *An Introduction to Forensic DNA Analysis.* 2d ed. Boca Raton, Fla.: CRC Press, 2002.

Russell, Katheryn K. *The Color of Crime: Racial Hoaxes, White Fear, Black Protectionism, Police Harassment, and Other Macroaggressions.* New York: New York University Press, 1998.

Sanjek, Roger. *The Future of Us All: Race and Neighborhood Politics in New York City.* Ithaca, N.Y.: Cornell University Press, 1998.

Sharkey, Joe. *Deadly Greed: The Riveting True Story of the Stuart Murder Case That Rocked Boston and Shocked the Nation.* New York: Prentice Hall, 1991.

Sleeper, Jim. *The Closest of Strangers: Liberalism and the Politics of Race in New York.* New York: W.W. Norton, 1990.

Suarez, Ray. *The Old Neighborhood: What We Lost in the Great Suburban Migration, 1966–1999.* New York: Free Press, 1999.

Sullivan, Timothy. *Unequal Verdicts: The Central Park Jogger Trials.* New York: Simon and Schuster, 1992.

Vergara, Camilo Jose. *The New American Ghetto.* New Brunswick, N.J.: Rutgers University Press, 1995.

Wells-Barnett, Ida B. *Selected Works of Ida B. Wells-Barnett.* Compiled and edited by Trudier Harris. New York: Oxford University Press, 1991.

———. *Southern Horrors and Other Writings: The Anti-Lynching Campaign of Ida B. Wells, 1892–1900.* Edited by Jacqueline Jones Royster. Boston: Bedford Books, 1997.

Wilson, William Julius. *The Truly Disadvantaged: The Inner City, the Underclass, and Public Policy.* Chicago: University of Chicago Press, 1987.

INDEX

Page numbers beginning with 215 refer to endnotes.

Grateful acknowledgment is made to the following for permission to reprint previously published material: Curtis Brown, Ltd.: "City Greenery" by Ogden Nash, originally published in *Holiday Magazine,* copyright © 1961 by Ogden Nash. Reprinted by permission of Curtis Brown, Ltd. • *El Diario/La Prensa:* Excerpt from "New Directions for Our Youth" from *El Diario/La Prensa,* April 27, 1989. Reprinted by permission of *El Diario/La Prensa.* • NYP Holdings, Inc.: Excerpt from "A Savage Disease Called New York" by Pete Hamill, from the *New York Post,* April 23, 1989. Reprinted by permission of NYP Holdings, Inc., publisher of the *New York Post.* • PARS International Corp.: Excerpt from "The Jogger and the Wolf Pack" from *The New York Times,* April 26, 1989, Editorial Section, Section A, page 26, column 1. Reprinted by permission of PARS International Corp. on behalf of *The New York Times.*